ANTIPATTERNS

ANTIPATTERNS

Identification, Refactoring, and Management

Phillip A. Laplante · Colin J. Neill

Auerbach Publications
Taylor & Francis Group
Boca Raton   New York

Published in 2006 by
CRC Press
Taylor & Francis Group
6000 Broken Sound Parkway NW, Suite 300
Boca Raton, FL 33487-2742

International Standard Book Number-10: 0-8493-2994-9 (Hardcover)
International Standard Book Number-13: 978-0-8493-2994-4 (Hardcover)
Library of Congress Card Number 2005052892

Library of Congress Cataloging-in-Publication Data

Laplante, Phillip A.
   Antipatterns : identification, refactoring, and management / Philip [sic] A. Laplante, Colin J. Neill.
      p. cm.
   Includes bibliographical references and index.
   ISBN 0-8493-2994-9 (alk. paper)
      1. Computer software--Development--Management. 2. Antipatterns (Software engineering) I. Neill, Colin J. II. Title.

QA76.76.D47L385 2005
005.1--dc22   2005052892

Taylor & Francis Group
is the Academic Division of Informa plc.

Visit the Taylor & Francis Web site at
http://www.taylorandfrancis.com

and the CRC Press Web site at
http://www.crcpress.com

Dedication

To our families:

Siwan, Harry, and Kathy Neill;
John and Angela Knipe; and
Nancy, Christopher, and Charlotte Laplante

Contents

Preface

In troubled organizations, a frequent obstacle to success is accurate problem identification. When problems are incorrectly diagnosed by management or by the consultants they hire, then correction of the problem is rarely possible. Conversely, when problems are correctly identified, they can almost always be dealt with appropriately. Unfortunately, organizational inertia frequently clouds the situation or makes it easier to do the wrong thing rather than the right thing. So how can one know what the right thing is if one has the problem wrong? This is where antipatterns can be helpful.

Shortly after the emergence of patterns,[1] practitioners began discussing problem-solution pairs in which the conventional solution does more harm than good, known as "antipatterns." In their groundbreaking work, *Anti-Patterns*, Brown, Malveaux, McCormick, and Mowbray described a taxonomy of problems that can occur in software engineering. They also described solutions or refactorings for these situations. The benefit of providing such a taxonomy is that it assists in the rapid and correct identification of problem situations, provides a playbook for addressing the problems, and provides some relief to the participants who can take consolation in the fact that they are not alone.

Brown et al. organized their antipatterns into three general types: (1) architectural, (2) design, and (3) management. The architectural patterns describe bad practices that lead to unacceptable software architectures (for example, "Kitchen Sink"). The design antipatterns do the same for design (everyone knows about "Design by Committee"). The management antipatterns generally describe dysfunctional behavior of individual managers, or pervasive management practices that inhibit success.

The main contribution of this book is a new catalog of antipatterns that extends and complements that of Brown and colleagues. We cover not only the antipatterns of management — that is, "known" bad practice patterns — but also environmental or cultural antipatterns (where the caustic nature of the atmosphere stifles success), and personality antipatterns or phenotypes (that is, negative personality types). It is our hope that in providing these antipatterns, it will lead the reader to correct problem identification, and hence solution, and a new contribution to the lexicon of business terminology. If nothing else, they should provide stress relief through whimsical sharing of misery.

About Our Approach

Although we are both "academics," we have not taken an academic approach to writing this book. For example, we neither rely heavily on behavioral science research nor do we heavily reference the scientific literature. The reasons for this are threefold.

First, much of the scientific literature provides insight into only very narrow windows of reality. For example, is it reasonable to infer that results obtained by surveying four individuals in a single industry, in unique settings, and under varying conditions, can be applied in every setting? Even the authors of such research caution about making such generalizations. We agree with approaching scholarly research with this healthy skepticism. Therefore, where we do cite scientific findings, we try to place them in context and point out how they might apply and when they might not.

Second, while we are obviously believers in the value of doing research, we also value experience. Indeed, in our own experience, when dealing with human situations (and this book is, after all, about human situations), real-world anecdotes very often provide more information than theory. Thus, our approach to writing this text was to apply our own real-world experiences, our consulting experiences to many companies, and those of the many professionals that we have come to know. We also believe that this approach leads to a more realistic treatment of the concepts we wish to relate.

Finally, reading scientific research is usually boring. We wanted to adopt a lively, engaging, and entertaining style of narrative that would not usually be permitted in a scholarly work. We also want to reach a wide audience of practitioners, not appeal to some small group of academics who control access to important journals. This is a "people" book, and we make no apologies for it.

In deliberately avoiding a scholarly approach to writing this book, we were able to infuse our book with a variety of entertaining "gadgets," which is something we both desperately wanted — hence the rambunctious and sometimes ribald sidebars, cartoons, stories, and even jokes. We both think we are funny people (well, Colin does not think Phil is funny), and our lectures are known for being as entertaining as they are informative (except for Colin's, which are not). Therefore, we wanted the book to convey some of our personality in this regard. In some cases, however, we genuinely want the reader to understand that we are only kidding, and these are the "Wise Alec" comments. We hope that whenever you see this phrase, you will break out in uncontrollable laughter — or at least sigh heavily at our pathetic attempts at humor. We also thought it would be fun to infuse the book with dialogue from our favorite movies and TV shows, as well as tidbits of cultural literacy and history, so that we could both show off our encyclopedic knowledge (actually the fact that we both own encyclopedias).

We also hope you do not mind the choice of names for our antipatterns. We struggled at times with these. We wanted them to be at once visual, iconic, and humorous. We embraced this noble goal not only because we wanted our antipatterns to be fun, but we also wanted you to be able to remember some of them. Of course, we hope we did not go overboard in some of our choices in naming and even humor (except for the sophomoric humor for which we do not apologize).

Book Organization

This book is primarily a catalog of antipatterns that are relevant to management, leadership, and organization in all its forms. As such, it can be used as a desk reference when you feel like your team, department, or company is operating dysfunctionally. Consequently, we have included a simple look-up table in Chapter 1 to help you find the relevant antipattern and its refactorings from the catalog found in Chapters 5 and 6.

Chapters 2, 3, and 4 preceding the catalog provide introductory material to the way humans behave individually and in groups, as well as background on some management theories. These chapters help establish a common framework and vocabulary for the rest of the text. Even if you have formal education in management, it would be helpful to read these chapters.

Chapters 5 and 6 are the heart of the text and provide the catalog of Management and Environmental Antipatterns.

We then provide in Chapter 7 some general advice on dealing with people, whether they are clients, customers, peers, colleagues, supervisors, or subordinates.

Audience

This book is primarily intended for IT and software engineering managers (at all levels) and team members. Therefore, many of our points are illustrated with vignettes from those domains, as well as with others from movies, television, and literature. We contend, however, that the lessons contained herein are broad enough to be adapted to any work environment — indeed, wherever there is group interaction to achieve a goal such as in professional societies, churches, nonprofit organizations, and clubs. We know from some of our reviewers that our antipatterns apply equally well to educational environments, health care, manufacturing, and construction, to name just a few.

Notes on Referencing and Errors

Although we did not adopt the traditional academic approach to citation and footnoting, we have tried to uphold the highest standards for giving credit where credit is due. Each chapter contains a list of related readings, and they should be considered the primary reference for that chapter. Where we utilized direct quotes or non-obvious facts, we provided an appropriate footnote or in-line citation. In particular, some portions of our work appeared in preliminary form in scholarly magazines, and we note that where such is the case.

Despite our best efforts and those of the reviewers and publisher, there are still likely errors to be found, and we want to correct them. Therefore, if you believe that you have found an error — whether it is a referencing issue, factual error, or typographical error — please contact us at pla-plante@psu.edu or cjneill@psu.edu. If we accept your correction, we will acknowledge you for your diligence in future editions of the book.

Disclaimers

We have taken great pains to disguise the identities of any organizations as well as individuals that we mention. In every case, we have changed the names and even elements of the situation to protect the innocent (and guilty). Therefore, any similarity between individuals or companies mentioned herein is purely coincidental.

Note

1. Named problem-solution pairs for architecture, design, management, etc.

Acknowledgments

First and foremost, we would like to thank the many good managers we have worked for and observed. These managers have taught us much of what we present here. But we should not fail to mention also the many bad managers that we have worked for or observed for teaching us about what *not* to do. Many of these managers and others who we have observed are satirized and exemplified in this work, although they do not know it and would not admit to it in any case.

More than 100 seasoned professionals reviewed portions of this text. Several reviewers, however, went further and contributed personal experiences and observations from their professional lives. We would like to acknowledge these individuals:

- Jacqueline Ash
- Russ Cook
- Dan Danovich
- Christine Deckman
- Charlie Hardt
- Ed Hennessey
- John McLoughlin
- Deepak Pandya
- Seth Wambold
- Dan Zima

We would also like to thank our friends and colleagues who reviewed drafts of the book and offered suggestions:

- Tom Costello, Upstreme
- Craig Jacobs, Pennsylvania Institute of Technology
- Peter Kraynak, Info724, LTD

- Nancy Laplante, Neumann College
- Angela Knipe, All Fund Mortgage, Inc.
- Siwan Neill
- Will Robinson, George & Lynch
- Dianne Strunk, Eastern Technology Council
- Chris Traynor, Whipsmart Consulting

Finally, we would like to thank everyone at Auerbach, including our editor John Wyzalek, whose name is difficult to pronounce but it sounds like "Wise Alec." This is surprisingly close to "Smart Alec." So, in addition to providing us with encouragement and guidance, we knew he would like our humor.

About the Authors

Phillip A. Laplante is Associate Professor of Software Engineering and a member of the Graduate Faculty at The Pennsylvania State University. He is also the Chief Technology Officer (CTO) of the Eastern Technology Council, a nonprofit business advocacy group serving the Greater Philadelphia Metropolitan Area. As CTO, he created and directs the CIO Institute, a community of practice of regional CIOs. Before joining Penn State, he was a professor and senior academic administrator at several other colleges and universities.

Prior to his academic career, Dr. Laplante spent nearly eight years as a software engineer and project manager working on avionics (including the Space Shuttle), CAD, and software test systems. He was also Director of Business Development for a boutique software consulting firm. He has authored or edited 22 books and more than 100 papers, articles, and editorials.

Dr. Laplante received his B.S., M.Eng., and Ph.D. degrees in Computer Science, Electrical Engineering, and Computer Science, respectively, from Stevens Institute of Technology and an MBA from the University of Colorado. He is a senior member of the IEEE and a member of numerous professional societies, program committees, and boards. He consults to Fortune 500 companies, the U.S. Department of Defense, and NASA on technical and management issues. He also serves as a CIO/CEO coach.

Colin J. Neill is Associate Professor of Software Engineering and Assistant Division Head, Engineering, at The Pennsylvania State University. Prior to joining Penn State, he worked as a research officer at the University of Wales Swansea, a certified software process assessor and auditor, and as a software engineering consultant for a number of organizations in the United Kingdom and Europe. Notable experiences during this period included working on manufacturing strategies with Rover Cars and enterprise system selection, installation, and enhancement with British Aerospace.

Dr. Neill received his B.Eng. in Electrical and Electronic Engineering, M.Sc. in Communication Systems, and Ph.D. in Software and Systems Engineering from the University of Wales Swansea, United Kingdom. He is a member of the IEE and a senior member of the IEEE and is the author of more than 50 articles and book chapters. Additionally, he serves as a member of several professional societies, conference committees, and boards, and provides consulting services to a number of companies and government agencies. He is a rabid Philadelphia Eagles football fan.

Chapter 1

Patterns and Antipatterns

One of the ways humans solve newly encountered problems is by subconsciously applying a previously successful solution to a similar or related problem. This approach to problem solving is variously known as analogical, allegorical, or case-based reasoning and is a well-known machine-learning technique used in artificial intelligence systems.

In case you were wondering if this really is a common problem-solving technique, think about the last time you were asked to meet a friend somewhere. Did you plot the route you were going to take, take timing measurements of each leg, contact AAA for traffic updates and delays, and then plug all these into a spreadsheet to determine when to leave your house? We suspect not. Instead, without really thinking about it, you reasoned about your previous journeys over that route, or the various legs, factoring in likely traffic conditions for that time of day to arrive at an approximate estimation suitable for the purpose. There was a chance that the estimate might be slightly off, but it was close enough. This is pattern-based problem solving: identifying a similar situation from the past, applying the solution that worked in that situation, modifying it appropriately for the specific context of the new problem. Of course, you might have saved yourself some effort and used MapQuest or Google Maps, but that does not fit the story.

Obviously, the flaw in this approach to problem solving is that the solutions are not calculated; they are borne of experience. In fact, considerable experience and expertise are required before successful patterns are identified, and experience takes time; we must personally experience successes and failures to "bank" enough solutions to make us experts.

And what if you are just starting out in your career or are a newly appointed manager? Where does your experience base come from?

What if, however, we could capture your experiences and those of others — successes and failures — in solving problems? Experts could then share those experiences with each other and, more importantly, with their less-experienced colleagues. While not a foolproof plan (we all know that many people refuse to learn from others' mistakes), at least it provides an opportunity to institutionalize and catalog knowledge so that each successive generation can, if they choose, stand on the shoulders of those who came before, and hopefully progress their chosen disciplines from a solid foundation of expertise.

Well, the goal is a noble one. So how do we achieve it? How do we capture and share personal experience in a form suitable for others, with clarity, rationale, and context such that they can be applied to new problems? That is the genius of Christopher Alexander.

1.1 A Timeless Way of Building

Alexander is an architect (and Professor Emeritus of the University of California, Berkeley) who realized that many medieval cities possessed a certain harmony and elegance and that, indeed, "There is one timeless way of building. It is a thousand years old and the same today as it has ever been. The great traditional buildings of the past, the villages and tents and temples in which man feels at home, have always been made by people who were very close to the center of this way. It is not possible to make great buildings, or great towns, beautiful places, places where you feel yourself, places where you feel alive, except by following this way. And, as you will see, this way will lead anyone who looks for it to buildings which are themselves as ancient in their form, as the trees and hills, and as our faces are" [Alexander1].

In his trilogy of books [Alexander 1, 2, 3], Alexander explores the idea that successful architecture is essentially the application of design patterns that have been around for thousands of years, albeit not recorded. He attempted to record them and to the lay person they certainly feel right. An example is the Four Story Limit pattern:

────────────────▼────────────────

Four-Story Limit

Conflict: There is abundant evidence to show that high buildings make people crazy.

Resolution: In any urban area, no matter how dense, keep the majority of buildings four stories high or less. It is possible that certain buildings should exceed this limit, but they should never be buildings for human habitation.

There is little rationale for high-rise buildings beyond financial gains for landowners and banks. They destroy the landscape, promote crime, and are expensive to build and maintain; so, in the interests of community, society, and aesthetics, we should limit the height of buildings, particularly residential buildings.

[Alexander2]

▲

Of course, this is not a book about architecture and town planning. The point we are making is that a previously undocumented rule or principle has been documented in such a way that future architects can easily identify with and apply it in their work. This, essentially, defines the concept of a pattern.

▼

Pattern Definitions:

"Each pattern describes a problem which occurs over and over again in our environment, and then describes the core of the solution to that problem, in such a way that you can use this solution a million times over, without ever doing it the same way twice."

[Alexander2]

"A named problem/solution pair that can be applied in new contexts, with advice on how to apply it in novel situations."

[Larman]

▲

1.2 Pattern Structure

The most obvious aspect from the Four-Story Limit pattern, and Craig Larman's definition for patterns, is that each pattern has a useful name. It conveys, in a terse and compact manner, the pattern's intent. In fact, the choice of name is very important because the set of patterns on a given topic actually form a vocabulary of communication ... a language, hence Alexander's book title, *A Pattern Language*. These languages allow for groups to communicate broad ideas and complex solutions to problems very effectively. Rather than having to explain intricate details of a problem or the rationale for a solution, groups just use the pattern names they are using and everyone has a clear picture of the work at hand.

The next section is the conflict. This summarizes the problem the pattern addresses. In the full version of the pattern, this summary is followed by more detail explaining the problem, its manifestations, and relevant background or context.

The final section in this pattern language is the solution. This succinctly explains the solution to the stated problem. The important aspect here is that the solution is in general terms, not a specific answer. Patterns describe solutions to recurring problems in a way that each individual solution is different, yet still conformant to the patterns' rationale and intent. For example, Alexander's architectural patterns describe appropriate scale, layout, and use of buildings, parks, and walkways, but the communities designed using them are not identical to one another.

This is just one format for patterns, however, and relative to other pattern languages would be considered a minimalist structure. In addition to the name, conflict (or problem), and resolution (or solution), more expansive formats include sections that describe the consequences of using the pattern, both positive and negative; implementation details that provide more detail in applying the pattern; and the scale or scope of problem the pattern addresses.

1.3 Antipatterns

While it is certainly useful to study the successful ways people solve problems, the old adage that we learn from our mistakes suggests that studying failures might be even more fruitful. This is the concept behind negative patterns, or antipatterns. Whereas patterns describe a recurring problem and its solution, antipatterns describe solutions that have more negative consequences than positive benefits. In effect, they describe dysfunctional approaches to problem solving, followed by the changes that should be made to overcome this dysfunction. That is, antipatterns describe situations that we often find ourselves in, situations that are not healthy for the individual or the organization. We obviously do not set out to create these dysfunctional situations; they occur because of neglect, malice, ignorance, and assorted other reasons. Once in these predicaments, how do we get out and stay out? This is the rationale for antipatterns in general, and our catalog in particular.

The idea of antipatterns emerged soon after that of patterns, but it is unclear who first coined the term. In 1996, Michael Akroyd presented a paper at the Object World West Conference that documented harmful software constructs [Akroyd], and Andrew Koenig published a short article in the *Journal of Object-Oriented Programming* using the term in 1995 [Koenig]. We will happily give credit to both. Credit for promoting the term, however, must go to the authors of the antipatterns book by Brown et al. [Brown]. They expanded the scope of antipatterns to include software project management as well, arriving at a three-pronged taxonomy of antipatterns: architectural, design, and management (Table 1.1).

We have further expanded the scope of antipatterns to include broader management and leadership aspects, as well as introducing another kind of antipattern, the cultural or environmental antipattern. These are dysfunctions that are not attributable to a single person, situation, or practice. Instead, they are due to a series of "solutions" or environmental changes that create a toxic atmosphere — a negative organizational culture.

1.4 Many Eyes

We have not merely sat in a darkened room and created these antipatterns in a vacuum, however. An important aspect of patterns and antipatterns is the "rule-of-three" and we have abided by it. To call a pattern a pattern, it must have been used successfully in practice three times; to call an antipattern an antipattern, it must have been witnessed three times. In most cases, we have personally witnessed each pattern on at least three occasions, in different organizations, in different industries, and often in different countries. In addition, more than 100 IT professionals have validated the antipattern catalog and it has been reviewed by several CEOs, CIOs, CTOs, and assorted other senior executives and managers from a wide range of industries including aerospace, construction, manufacturing, finance, and consultancy. We are confident that every reader will see themselves, their peers, supervisors, subordinates, and companies within the catalog, and hopefully by the end of the book they will be empowered to stride forward as agents of change.

Table 1.1 Management Antipatterns Excerpted from Brown

Blowhard Jamboree	Too many industry pundits influencing technology decisions
Analysis Paralysis	Relentless design and redesign of the system before construction
Viewgraph Engineering	Too much time spent building flashy presentations for customers and management rather than working on the software
Death by Planning	Too much planning, not enough action
Fear of Success	Insecurities and irrational fears emerge near project completion
The Corncob	Any situation involving difficult people
Intellectual Violence	Use of a buzzword or arcane technology to intimidate others
Irrational Management	Habitual indecisiveness and other bad management habits
Smoke and Mirrors	Making overly aggressive use of demonstration systems for sales purposes
Project Mismanagement	Generally, any bad management practice
Throw It over the Wall	Management forces the latest practices or tools on the software staff without buy-in
Fire Drill	Months of monotony followed by a crisis, then more monotony
The Feud	Personality conflicts between managers that directly affect the software team
E-Mail Is Dangerous	Any situation created by an ill-advised e-mail (we have all wished we could have one back)

1.5 Antipattern Structure

As with patterns, antipatterns form languages, so they must have unique and meaningful names. This seems to be the only firm structural requirement, however. Brown et al. adopted a comprehensive format, including:

- Antipattern name and AKA
- Keywords (relating to their antipattern reference model)
- Background

- Anecdotal evidence
- Antipattern solution (general form)
- Symptoms and consequences
- Typical causes
- Refactored solution
- Variations
- Example
- Related solutions

Our antipatterns have a less formal structure, however, one that concentrates on identification of the dysfunctional situation and remedies for all those involved:

- *Name:* a name that conveys the antipattern's meaning.
- *Central Concept:* a short synopsis of the antipattern, enough to make the antipattern identifiable.
- *Dysfunction:* in general terms, the problems with the current practice, possibly with a list of symptoms.
- *Vignette:* the antipattern in a real or prototypical situation, it provides context and richness to the antipattern.
- *Explanation:* expanded explanation of the antipattern, including its causes, consequences, and historical or cultural analogies.
- *Band Aid:* a short-term fix or coping strategy for those in the midst of the antipattern who have neither the time nor influence to refactor it properly.
- *Self-Repair:* the first step for someone perpetuating the antipattern — how you can help yourself improve.
- *Refactoring:* description of the changes that should be made to remedy the situation and their rationale. Sometimes these are under the control of an individual, but often they involve cultural or institutional changes.
- *Observations:* optional section for additional comments or items of note.
- *Identification:* an assessment instrument consisting of a list of questions for diagnosis of the antipattern. It must be stressed that this instrument is for informal evaluation — no validity or reliability testing has been performed. Hopefully, they will resonate with those suffering from the antipattern, and possibly provide humor!

1.6 Management and Environmental Antipatterns

The antipatterns language cataloged in this book is divided into two broad types:

1. *Management.* These are caused by an individual manager or management team ("the management"). These antipatterns address issues in supervisors who lack the talent or temperament to lead a group, department, or organization.
2. *Environmental.* These are caused by a prevailing culture or social model. These antipatterns are the result of misguided corporate strategy or uncontrolled socio-political forces.

1.6.1 Antipattern Locator

Because we have adopted a simplified classification structure for our language, we have identified major foci for each antipattern so that users of the language can quickly identify which antipatterns are at work in their organization. The complete list of antipattern foci is:

- Communications
- Competence
- Courage
- Culture
- Finances
- Honesty
- Leadership
- Personality
- Personnel
- Planning
- Process
- Technology
- Vision

To find the antipatterns affecting you, identify which of the characteristics from the list best captures the type of problems you are experiencing. Trace down from each identified characteristic in Tables 1.2 and 1.3 to find the possible antipatterns that match your situation.

For example, if you believe that your organization suffers from a general lack of courage and honesty, then you may wish to explore the Emperor's New Clothes antipattern. If the problem is due to an individual manager's lack of honesty and competence, then you might wish to explore Fruitless Hoops or Metric Abuse as the antipattern. Knowing ahead of time if the problem is related to a dysfunctional manager or culture allows you to narrow your search to either Table 1.2 (Management Antipatterns) or Table 1.3 (Environmental Antipatterns).

Table 1.2 Management Antipattern Locator

	Communication	Competence	Courage	Culture	Finances	Honesty	Leadership	Personality	Personnel	Planning	Process	Technology	Vision
Absentee Manager	■						■						
All You Have Is A Hammer		■		■									
Cage Match Negotiator	■							■					
Doppelganger								■					
Fruitless Hoops		■				■							
Golden Child									■				
Headless Chicken								■	■				
Leader Not Manager										■	■		
Managerial Cloning								■	■				
Manager Not Leader			■				■						
Metric Abuse		■				■					■	■	
Mr. Nice Guy			■				■	■					
Mushroom Management	■						■	■					
Plate Spinning							■		■		■		
Proletariat Hero				■		■			■				
Rising Upstart								■					
Road To Nowhere											■		■
Spineless Executive		■						■					
Three-Headed Knight							■			■			■
Ultimate Weapon									■	■			
Warm Bodies		■	■			■			■				

Of course, many of the antipatterns have one or more influencing factors in common. For example, from Table 1.3 it can be seen that both the Fairness Doctrine and Pitcairn Island manifest characteristics of dysfunctional cultures and personnel situations. Therefore, you would need

Table 1.3 Environmental Antipattern Locator

	Communication	Competence	Courage	Culture	Finances	Honesty	Leadership	Personality	Personnel	Planning	Process	Technology	Vision
Ant Colony				■					■				
Atlas Shrug				■							■		■
Autonomous Collective				■					■				
Boiling Frog Syndrome				■									
Burning Bag of Dung			■			■							
Buzzword Mania	■	■										■	
Deflated Balloon			■		■								
Divergent Goals	■									■	■		■
Dogmatic About Dysfunction		■		■							■		
Dunkirk Spirit							■			■			■
Emperor's New Clothes			■			■							
Fairness Doctrine				■		■			■				
Fools Rush In		■								■			■
Founderitis				■				■					
French Waiter Syndrome				■					■				
Geek Hazing	■			■									
Institutional Mistrust	■			■		■							
Kiosk City	■												
Mediocracy		■		■		■			■				
One-Eyed King		■				■							
Orange Stand Economics		■			■								
Pitcairn Island		■		■					■				
Potemkin Village				■		■						■	
Process Clash	■			■						■	■		

Table 1.3 Environmental Antipattern Locator (continued)

	Communication	Competence	Courage	Culture	Finances	Honesty	Leadership	Personality	Personnel	Planning	Process	Technology	Vision
Rubik's Cube	■						■		■				
Shoeless Children					■					■		■	
Worshiping the Golden Calf		■				■						■	

to read both of these antipattern descriptions to uniquely identify your predicament.

We suggest, however, that you do not try to locate a specific antipattern by precisely identifying its unique set of influencing factors. Instead, select two or three influencing factors that clearly fit the situation; then read all of the antipatterns that match those factors.

It could also be the case that your predicament involves more than one antipattern, as they tend to exist in swarms. Reading all of the antipatterns that seem to apply will give you the broadest range of solutions, that is, refactorings.

1.7 Consistency and Completeness

The reader may be led to a very obvious question. Is this antipattern catalog complete? That is, does it describe all possible dysfunctional managers and environments? In short, we think not. However, we have spent the better part of two years developing this catalog and we think we have come rather close to completeness. We rejected a number of other candidate antipatterns for a variety of reasons (e.g., was not really an antipattern, did not meet the rule of three, etc.). But it is possible that other unique antipatterns are out there. We will be looking for them.

Finally, a word on consistency. What we mean by this is that some of these antipatterns will look very familiar to you when you read them. You just might know them by another name. For example, one of our reviewers said, "Ah, we knew about that antipattern; we used to call it '30th Street mentality' (for the site of an old office)." It is fine if you do recognize these by another name. We did not invent these dysfunctions — most of these have probably been around since the first human societies. Our mission was to seek to concisely capture and describe these antipatterns so that a new terminology would emerge — one that transcends the local jargon of one company or another. This way, when that reviewer who noted the "30th Street mentality" moves to another company where that term has no meaning, he will be understood because now he can talk about "Institutional Mistrust."

References

[Akroyd]   M. Akroyd, AntiPatterns: Vaccinations against Object Misuse, *Proc. Object World West*, 1996.

[Alexander1]   C. Alexander, M. Silverstein, S. Angel, S. Ishikawa, and D. Abrams, *The Oregon Experiment*, Oxford University Press, 1975.

[Alexander2]   C. Alexander, S. Ishikawa, M. Silverstein, M. Jacobson, I. Fiksdahl-King, and S. Angel. *A Pattern Language: Towns, Buildings, Construction*, Oxford University Press, 1977.

[Alexander3]   C. Alexander, *The Timeless Way of Building*, Oxford University Press, 1979.

[Brown]   W.J. Brown, R.C. Malveau, H.W. McCormick, and T.J. Mowbray, *Anti-Patterns: Refactoring Software, Architectures, and Projects in Crisis*, John Wiley & Sons, 1998.

[Koenig]   A. Koenig, Patterns and Antipatterns, *Journal of Object-Oriented Programming*, 8(1), March–April, 1995.

[Larman]   C. Larman, *Applying UML and Patterns: An Introduction to Object-Oriented Analysis and Design and the Unified Process, 2nd edition,* Prentice Hall, Upper Saddle River, NJ, 2002.

Chapter 2

Human Patterns
and Antipatterns

Before exploring antipatterns in organizations, it is helpful to consider patterns of behavior in people. Neither of us are psychologists or social scientists, but this is not the perspective that we wish to take anyway. Instead, this treatment is based on some theory, a great deal of personal observation, and our own practical experience as consultants, practitioners, and project managers. These observations and accompanying advice should be helpful in their own right; but more importantly, they help establish a language for use in the descriptions of the management and environmental antipatterns.

2.1 Human Patterns

According to the early 20th century work of Carl Jung, all people can be classified along three dimensions: that is, whether they are:

1. Extroverted versus introverted
2. Sensing versus intuitive
3. Thinking versus feeling

People who prefer to direct their energies outwardly in the form of physical or verbal expression are said to be extroverted, while those who direct their energies inwardly are said to be introverted. People who prefer to process information in the form of known facts and familiar terms are said to be sensing types. If they prefer information that is based on implied or unspoken information, they are said to be intuitive. Those who prefer to make decisions objectively on the basis of logic are said to be thinking types. If their decision making is more based on personal values, they are said to be feeling types.

Katherine Briggs and her daughter Isabel Briggs-Myers[1] added a fourth dimension to this system [Briggs], that is, whether an individual is:

■ Judging versus perceiving

People who organize their life in a structured way and make their decisions knowing where they stand are said to be judging. Conversely, if they are flexible and roll with the punches, then they are said to be perceptive.

Now assign the letter E to represent extroverted, I introverted, S sensing, N intuitive, T thinking, F feeling, J judging, and P for perceiving. Then, taking all possible combinations along these four dimensions yields the 16 Myers-Briggs personality types or patterns shown in Table 2.1.

Whether one is born with these personality types, evolves one over time based on life experience, or whether personality is a combination of the two factors is the subject of substantial research. From our perspective, however, let us assume that personality type is a random assignment based on the roll of a 16-sided "die" (see Figure 2.1), although we will not assume that each outcome of the roll is equi-likely.

Two widely used instruments to determine a person's Myers-Briggs type are the Myers-Briggs Type Indicator® questionnaire, published by the Consulting Psychologists Press, and the Keirsey Temperament Sorter, developed by David Keirsey. Of course, neither of these instruments is precise in their assessment. For example, one can self-assess with both instruments and end up as two different types. In fact, one can take the same test on different days and end up with different outcomes.

2.1.1 Myers-Briggs Personality Types

The foregoing observations of the 16 Myers-Briggs types, while not an academic treatment, can assist in identifying the type of a friend or adversary, employee, manager, peer, or significant-other based on observation of their behavior, so that you may adjust your interactions accordingly. These observations also provide a catalog of personality "phenotypes" that might help you to anticipate the behavioral response of a person once you identify their type. Tagging the manager this way

Table 2.1   Myers-Briggs Personality Types and Acronyms

ENFJ	Extroverted, Intuitive, Feeling, Judging
ENFP	Extroverted, Intuitive, Feeling, Perceiving
ENTJ	Extroverted, Intuitive, Thinking, Judging
ENTP	Extroverted, Intuitive, Thinking, Perceiving
ESFJ	Extroverted, Sensing, Feeling, Judging
ESFP	Extroverted, Sensing, Feeling, Perceiving
ESTJ	Extroverted, Sensing, Thinking, Judging
ESTP	Extroverted, Sensing, Thinking, Perceiving
INFJ	Introverted, Intuitive, Feeling, Judging
INFP	Introverted, Intuitive, Feeling, Perceiving
INTJ	Introverted, Intuitive, Thinking, Judging
INTP	Introverted, Intuitive, Thinking, Perceiving
ISFJ	Introverted, Sensing, Feeling, Judging
ISFP	Introverted, Sensing, Feeling, Perceiving
ISTJ	Introverted, Sensing, Thinking, Judging
ISTP	Introverted, Sensing, Thinking, Perceiving

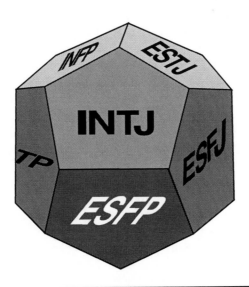

Figure 2.1   Personality types as a 16-sided "die."

can also be helpful in identifying a particular antipattern, as we shall later see.

The ESTPs are action-oriented problem solvers who can deal with big-picture issues. They are fact driven and make good troubleshooters, although they prefer solving large-scale organizational problems to attending to details. Hence, they tend to be somewhat poor in follow-through, although they can juggle many projects at once. Keirsey calls these types "Promoters."

ESTJs are practical and logical and tend to be very businesslike and even impersonal. They prefer to be given facts, not opinions, and will often bluntly state as much — "I don't care what you think, just give me the facts!" ESTJs are detailed oriented, often at the expense of broad strategic planning. They tend to use a small set of well-worn solution strategies and are not terribly innovative in developing new ones. Keirsey calls these types "Supervisors."

ESFJs are action-oriented fact-dealers who, nonetheless, tend to make decisions based on personal values. These are warm people who tend to foster good team relationships and have a strong sense of duty. They struggle with conflict and personal criticism, however. Keirsey calls these types "Providers."

ESFPs tend to be friendly problem solvers who work well with people. They are highly adaptable and somewhat impulsive. Keirsey calls these types "Performers."

ENFPs are creative and insightful thinkers who prefer experimentation to formulas. They are flexible and tend to make value-based decisions, although they sometimes neglect details. They are people oriented. Keirsey calls these types "Champions."

ENFJs are concerned with social and personal stability and dislike conflict and criticism. They prefer dealing with patterns and people in their value-based decision making rather than fact data. Keirsey calls these types "Teachers." [Incidentally, this is Phil, always ready to teach and mentor.]

ENTJ types are logical decision makers who are also controlling personalities. They tend to be impersonal and intolerant of weakness in other people. They are highly task oriented but will consider the long-term ramifications of their decisions. These types are often found in very senior management. Not surprisingly, Keirsey calls these types "Field Marshals." [And for those who know Colin, it will not come as a surprise to hear that this is he, unabashed to tell it like it is, even when it is not!]

ENTPs like dealing with patterns and using logic in their decision making. They are very clever and are engaging conversationalists and debaters. They are "idea people" and also may be change agents within an organization. Keirsey calls these types "Inventors."

INTJs are pattern-oriented strategists who work best when organizing for long-term goals. They tend to be self-deprecating as well as critical of others. Although they are excellent long-range planners, they are also very good with details. Keirsey calls these types "Masterminds."

The INTPs are logical decision makers and problem solvers who seek to find the patterns in things. They are adverse to routines and can be somewhat aloof. They are adaptable and will experiment in order to escape from drudgery. Keirsey calls these types "Architects." Ironically, Christopher Alexander, the "father" of patterns, was an architect by profession. We have no idea whether he is an INTP, however.

INFPs tend to be highly creative but quiet individuals. They are rather adaptable and tend to be warm and insightful. They are comfortable dealing with people and bold ideas. Keirsey calls these types "Healers."

INFJs are emotional dreamers who are empathic and people oriented. They base their decisions on personal values more than logic and they organize their lives and relationships based on these values. They are generally reserved, however, and their concern for others, while present, is often not overtly expressed. Keirsey calls these types "Counselors."

ISTPs are logical, flexible, and have a thirst for knowledge. They are more interested, however, in practical knowledge of things than of people, which often leads them to be rather quiet and seemingly detached. They are good problem solvers, particularly at the macro level, and they can be creative and often impulsive. Keirsey calls these types "Crafters."

ISFPs are comfortable with both facts and people. Although they prefer one-on-one to group interactions, they make excellent team members and avoid confrontation. They are caring and sensitive, and will go out of their way to help people. They are comfortable with facts but are value-based decision makers who can be somewhat rigid. Keirsey calls these types "Composers."

ISFJs are organized and highly perceptive. They are pragmatic and people oriented, and are loyal to those they trust. They tend to be reserved and practical, and they dislike confrontation. Keirsey calls these types "Protectors."

Finally, ISTJs are thoughtful but emotional decision makers who employ logic whenever they can. They are serious and practical people who tend to be quiet and introverted. Keirsey calls these types "Inspectors."

2.1.2 Keirsey Temperament Sorter[2]

The Keirsey temperament sorter, which is based on a test (http://keirsey.com/), provides another perspective on the Myers-Briggs pattern system. We have already seen how Keirsey identifies the base Myers-Briggs

Table 2.2   Keirsey's Descriptive Groupings of the Myers-Briggs Personality Types

Guardians: Supervisor (ESTJ) Inspector (ISTJ) Provider (ESFJ) Protector (ISFJ)	Artisans: Promoter (ESTP) Crafter (ISTP) Performer (ESFP) Composer (ISFP)
Idealists: Teacher (ENFJ) Counselor (INFJ) Champion (ENFP) Healer (INFP)	Rationals: Field Marshal (ENTJ) Mastermind (INTJ) Inventor (ENTP) Architect (INTP)

types. But Keirsey also organizes these types into groups of four, called temperaments, shown in Table 2.2.

Keirsey assigns further characteristics to the groupings and individual types. This more coarse-grained taxonomy often makes it easier to identify an individual's type. For example, while it may be difficult to peg someone as ESTJ or ISFJ, it helps to know that the Guardians, which consist of Supervisor (ESTJ), Inspector (ISTJ), Provider (ESFJ), and Protector (ISFJ) types, are good communicators, planners, and administrators. According to Keirsey, there are quite a few Guardians, at least 40 percent and as many as 45 percent of the population.

Artisans, on the other hand, consisting of the Promoter (ESTP), Crafter (ISTP), Performer (ESFP), and Composer (ISFP) types, are excellent logisticians, highly creative, optimistic, and energetic. There are many Artisans, at least 35 percent and as many as 40 percent of the population.

Idealists, comprising the Teacher (ENFJ), Counselor (INFJ), Champion (ENFP), and Healer (INFP) types, are diplomatic, ethical, and mentoring leaders who are excellent communicators. They are also empathic and sometimes visionary. Idealists represent somewhere between 8 and 10 percent of the population.

Finally, the Rationals, including the Field Marshal (ENTJ), Mastermind (INTJ), Inventor (ENTP), and Architect (INTP) types, are strategic planners, often strong-willed and confident. They are competitive and seek knowledge. Rationals occur infrequently, perhaps as little as 5 to 7 percent of the population.

An amusing sidebar to Keirsey's temperament sorter is a set of famous people organized by the Keirsey system. For example, according to Keirsey, Einstein was a rational (in fact, an Architect–INTP) and Harry Truman a Guardian (in fact, an Inspector–ISTJ). These determinations were apparently made by forensic analysis of the writings and behaviors of the individuals.

Keirsey also provides groupings of Myers-Briggs traits in dyads. For example, "Composers" and "Performers" are together called "Entertainers." These groupings of two help to further identify individuals in the same way that groupings of four do, but we will leave that discovery to interested readers and spare those readers already quite confused. We promise that it gets easier.

2.1.3 Emotional Intelligence

Some behaviorists consider the "emotional intelligence" of individuals as a predictor of their reaction to situations and individuals. Emotional intelligence has been described as "the ability to process emotional information, particularly as it involves the perception, assimilation, understanding, and management of emotion" [Mayer].

Mayer and Cobb suggest that emotional intelligence is a true form of intelligence, which can be defined by such abilities as identifying emotions in faces, music, and stories, and in relating emotions to other stimuli such as taste and color. Emotional intelligence also involves using emotion in reasoning and problem solving such as knowing which emotions are similar and which are opposites.

Emotional intelligence can help identify optimism in individuals and can be used to help them learn to be optimistic. It can also help with knowing when and how to express emotions as well as controlling them, particularly under stress. This empathy is another part of emotional intelligence that can contribute to occupational success.

There are a number of tests that measure emotional intelligence, such as Bar-On's EQ-I, the Multifactor Emotional Intelligence Scale, and the Emotional Competence Inventory, and many others. These can be found quickly through a casual search of the Web.

2.1.4 How to Use Human Patterns

So what is the point of all these bizarre classifications? Why bother to study patterns of human behavior? And why are we bothering with it after proclaiming this book to be non-scholarly and entertaining? First, they can be used to understand what motivates people. Having understood their motivations, it becomes easier to seek win-win solutions or avoid causing problems. Understanding the motivations of each individual also helps a manager in organizing teams. You would not, for example, want to put an obviously introverted, feeling type onto a team of extroverted, thinking types. In fact, some companies use personality tests in their hiring practices to ensure corporate cultural alignment.

There are also some scholarly works that are helpful in this regard. For example, Gorla and Lam studied the implications of traditional Myers-Briggs personality typing to software project team success [Gorla]. They studied a good number of teams, 92 to be exact, but they were all from Hong Kong, so there may be cultural factors that were not taken into account. Their findings are intriguing, however. They suggest that there should be heterogeneity along all four personality dimensions in the most effective teams — managerial cloning is a bad thing.

They go on to suggest that the team leader should be an intuitive (N), feeling (F) type — that is, Keirsey's Idealist group. They further suggest that a judging type is preferred in the team leader (Keirsey's Teacher or Counselor). Systems analysts are preferred to be thinking (T) and sensing (S). Programmers, on the other hand, should be extroverted (E), sensing (S), and judging (J). Finally, for any team member dealing with the outside world (e.g., requirements engineers or customer-service reps), a judging type is preferred. Their findings seem reasonable to us — except almost none of the good developers we know could be described as an extrovert.

Of course, you can also use these personality theories to help understand yourself, which can be helpful in your personal and professional lives. We suggest that you neither spend too much time on introspection nor allow these typings to define your behavior. While Colin tests as a Field Marshal, he really believes he has more compassion than that — although his students probably disagree.

Interestingly, proponents of both Myers-Briggs/Keirsey and Emotional Intelligence seem to imbue their types with mostly positive attributes. Negative types arise only from the lack of positive attributes. It is more likely, however, that one is liable to encounter negative types who defy categorization into any of the usual systems of human patterns. Instead, it is far easier to identify their negative characteristics and cope with them somehow.

2.2 Human Antipatterns and Negative Personality Types

Everyone has to deal with difficult people. In Brown et al.'s *AntiPatterns*, people who cause trouble are called "corncobs." The term "corncob," meaning a general pain in the buttocks, apparently derives from the fact that before the regular use of toilet paper (rolled toilet paper was not introduced until 1890), anything at hand, including the unused parts of shucked corn, were used in the lavatory for personal hygiene. Obviously, anyone who was stuck with what was left after the shucks had been used was in for rough go of it.

In our experience, corncobs probably represent less than 5 percent of the population, but they provide 90 percent of the interpersonal problems in a work environment. Their presence leads to stress for everyone, reduced morale and productivity, and ultimately, a toxic work environment.

Corncobs exist because they have developed certain behaviors, possibly since childhood. Corncobs stick with these behaviors when they elicit the desired response: conciliation, perceived respect, perceived power, material rewards, etc. Because these behaviors are well established, as a manager or team member, you are not likely to "unlearn" them. Instead, you will have to cope with these behaviors.

Here are some general coping strategies. First, do not form an opinion about a person or situation too soon. Often, the suspected corncob is suffering from some other problem. Almost without exception, taking the time to investigate an issue and to think about it calmly is superior to reacting spontaneously or emotionally.

Second, make sure that you listen to all sides of the story when arbitrating any dispute, but particularly those involving difficult people. It is often said that there are three sides to an issue: the sides of the two opponents and the truth, which is somewhere in between. This has been our experience.

Make sure you focus on issues and not people. You can work on this by avoiding the use of accusatory phrases such as telling someone that he is incompetent. Focus, instead, on your feelings about the situation.

Always work to set or clarify expectations. Management failures, parental failures, marital failures, and the like are generally caused by a lack of clear expectations. Set expectations early in the process, and make sure that everyone understands them. Continue to monitor the expectations and refine them if necessary.

Finally, be an optimist about a given situation and the behavior of others. No one chooses to be a failure. Try to give people the benefit of the doubt and work with them. After all, you would want this for yourself.

2.2.1 Confronting Difficult People

Despite your best efforts to avoid dealing with difficult people, sometimes they must be confronted. It is sometimes easier to deal with these difficult people if you can characterize them according to their negative behaviors; that is, to find the human phenotype they fit. One taxonomy for categorizing corncobs, or difficult people, is derived from the work of Robert Bramson, comprising his doctoral dissertation and published in the book, *Coping with Difficult People* [Bramson]. While there are other scholarly taxonomies of difficult people, we like this one. It is a 20-year-old book but people have not changed much since then, and it offers some very practical strategies, which we have used ourselves in dealing with corncobs.

Bramson suggests that difficult people conform to one of seven antipatterns or "phenotypes" (our term, not Bramson's):

1. Hostile Aggressives
2. Indecisives
3. Whiners
4. Negativists
5. Clams
6. Bulldozers
7. Superagreeables

It is a surprising phenomenon, at least in our experience, that most people do not actually know if they fit one of these negative personality phenotypes. Most whiners, for example, would not admit that they are whiners. Usually, it takes someone else to point out the truth to them.

Therefore, it is possible that you, the reader, might fit one of these. We hope not. But one way to find out if you do is to use reflection. As you read the scenarios, be honest with yourself. These are behavioral styles and fitting one of these does not make you an evil person or even a bad person. Everyone is flawed. Work to address your flaws.

2.2.2 Hostile Aggressives

According to Bramson, the Hostile Aggressive phenotype appears in three sub-varieties:

1. Sherman Tanks
2. Snipers
3. Exploders

Each of these types is distinct and easily identifiable. The strategies for dealing with them (their refactoring, that is) are straightforward and usually work but often require a great deal of courage.

2.2.2.1 Sherman Tanks

Bramson's Sherman Tanks are typical bullies; they will pound you into submission because they are openly hostile and aggressive. They know that intimidation works in many situations, largely because many people seek to avoid conflict. For example, we know that more than half of the Myers-Briggs types will seek to avoid confrontations.

Everyone has had to deal with a Sherman Tank; but to illustrate the defense strategy, consider the following sample encounter. It involves Bill and Mike, two peers. Sue is their boss.

------------------------▼------------------------

Bill: Hey Mike! How are you doing?

Mike: Not good. I have a problem … you!

Bill (nervously): What do you mean?

Mike: I understand that you were badmouthing me to Sue.

Bill: No I didn't; we were just talking at lunch…

Mike (louder): BS! Sam overheard your conversation and he told me you were talking about how it was my fault that we delivered late.

Bill: No, I didn't; I was defending you, I was…

Mike: I've worked hard to develop my reputation with Sue and I don't need some pipsqueak like you ruining it!

Bill: But I, but I…

Mike (shouting): YOU HAVE MADE AN ENEMY, BILL, AN ENEMY!

------------------------▲------------------------

The solution to dealing with Sherman Tanks, according to Bramson and our own experience, is to stand up to them — but not in the sense of a nose-to-nose shouting match, which could escalate to a physical confrontation. Instead, state matter-of-factly, calmly, but firmly: "I disagree with you." You can elaborate on your reasons why, but that is not really important. They will try to interrupt you, as they invariably do; do not allow it.

Consider the refactored encounter:

------------------------▼------------------------

Bill: Hey Mike! How are you doing?

Mike: Not good. I have a problem … you!

Bill (nervously): What do you mean?

Mike: I understand that you were badmouthing me to Sue.

Bill: No I didn't; we were just talking at lunch...

Mike (louder): BS! Sam overheard your conversation and he told me...

Bill: Excuse me, Mike, but I was talking. Sam didn't hear correctly. I was defending you to Sue. What I told her was that I thought it was not your fault that we were delayed and that it was because the operating system was constantly crashing on us...

Mike: I didn't realize; um, um, thank you very much for sticking up for me.

━━━━━━━━━━━━━━━━━━▲━━━━━━━━━━━━━━━━━━

What you are demonstrating to the Sherman Tank is that you are not spineless. Remember that Sherman Tanks like to fight. They live for it. But they also like to intimidate. And by showing them that you are not intimidated, they are very likely to back down. In fact, Bramson notes that if you stand up to a Sherman Tank, that it is even possible that you will earn their respect and that in the future, they might even act like they are your friend. Of course, with friends like these, who needs enemas?

2.2.2.2 Snipers

Snipers, as their sobriquet implies, like to hang out in the background and embarrass you through barbs at inopportune moments. They are hecklers, and they derive their enjoyment from embarrassing you, one-upping you if you confront them, and by demonstrating how clever they are. They tend not to confront you one-on-one; but rather, they ambush you in a very public setting when you are unprepared and relatively defenseless. Consider the following prototypical encounter involving Bob, who is giving a presentation to a software development group and Sniper Scott, hanging in the background.

━━━━━━━━━━━━━━━━━━▼━━━━━━━━━━━━━━━━━━

Bob: Ladies and gentlemen, thank you for joining me today for today's information-sharing session. I am delighted to be able to talk to you today about model-driven architectures and their...

Scott: Hey, Bob! Nice slides. Where did you get the clip art from, the Cartoon Network?

(Nervous giggles from the audience)

Bob: As I was saying, model-driven architectures are a relatively new approach to...

Scott: Nice hair, Bob! Is your barber a landscaper?

(Nervous giggles from the audience)

Bob: (flustered now) I um, I um,...

(....and so on...)

━━━━━━━━━━━━━━━━━▲━━━━━━━━━━━━━━━━━

Here is how Bramson suggests you deal with a Sniper. When he makes a sarcastic comment or humorous barb at your expense, stop whatever you are doing, pause, look him in the eye, and call him out; that is, ask him if he intentionally meant to insult you. So, for example, Bob could have responded, "Scott, I took your comment about my hair personally. Did you mean to insult me?" Now two things can happen: (1) the Sniper can immediately apologize for his sarcasm, which will embarrass him and cause him to retreat (at least for a while); Or alternatively (2) the Sniper might say something like, "Oh, I was just joking. Can't you take a joke?" Bob's response to that is something such as, "I don't appreciate a joke at my expense, would you?" This should have the effect, again, of embarrassing the Sniper and causing him to go into hiding, at least for a while.

2.2.2.3 Exploders

Exploders are typically calm and unassuming. But in certain situations, particularly under stress, they shift completely "out of character" and unleash explosive negative behavior — shouting, cursing, insulting, waving of hands, storming about, etc. When you try to address their concern, they will interrupt you, shout you down, and not allow you to get a word in edgewise.

Consider the following sample encounter between Sue, who is manning a help desk, and Tom, someone in the payroll department who is calling in for assistance.

---------------------------▼---------------------------

Sue: Help desk, this is Sue. How may I help you?

Tom: Oh, hi Sue, this is Tom in payroll. I am having trouble with my desktop computer.

Sue: OK, Tom. I just pulled up your hardware and software configuration so I can help you better. What seems to be the problem?

Tom: The problem is that when I try to open up my mail program, the system hangs.

Sue: OK, is your computer on now?

Tom: Yes, it's on now.

Sue: OK, great, now I am going to ask you to do something.

Tom: I just want you to fix it.

Sue: Yes, but first I need you to...

Tom (louder, and sarcastically): You're the help desk person, I'm the accountant. I don't ask you to help me cut your paycheck, so don't ask me to help you fix my problem.

Sue: Yes, but first I have to...

Tom (raising his voice louder): JUST FIX THE PROBLEM...

Sue: I can't until...

Tom (screaming now): JUST GET YOUR BUTT DOWN HERE AND GET MY "(BLEEPING) COMPUTER RUNNING...

(....and so on...)

---------------------------▲---------------------------

Exploders are difficult to deal with because they do not want to listen. The way to handle exploders is as follows. First, do not let them interrupt you. Politely use the same strategy for interruption you used with the Sherman Tank. Second, try to help them understand what is making them unhappy. Let them know that you want to help them, and calmly try to do that. Usually, the Exploder is unhappy with the situation (not you). If the situation is something you can control, then you need to deal with the situation. If the situation is not something you can control, then you have to try to find someone who can help the Exploder. So, here is the refactored encounter.

▼

Sue: Help desk, this is Sue. How may I help you?

Tom: Oh, hi Sue; this is Tom in payroll. I am having trouble with my desktop computer.

Sue: OK Tom; I just pulled up your hardware and software configuration so I can help you better. What seems to be the problem?

Tom: The problem is that when I try to open up my mail program, the system hangs.

Sue: OK, is your computer on now?

Tom: Yes, it's on now.

Sue: OK, great, now I am going to ask you to do something.

Tom: I just want you to fix it.

Sue: Yes, but first I need you to...

Tom (louder, and sarcastically): You're the help desk person, I'm the accountant. I don't ask you to help me cut your paycheck, so don't ask me to help you fix my problem.

Sue: Yes, but first I have to...

Tom (raising his voice louder): JUST FIX THE PROBLEM...

Sue: Excuse me, Tom. But if you won't let me talk, I can't help you. So please just listen for one second. I need you to reboot the computer so we can get you going. So, I want you to simultaneously press the control, alt, and delete keys. Can you do that?...

Tom: Well, yes.

Sue: OK, great. Now I am going to ask you to....

▲

In this instance, Tom complies. If he does not and continues to shout, then it may be necessary to send someone down to his office to take care of the problem.

Exploders are particularly difficult to deal with because this is a behavior that is learned at the earliest age — crying and screaming lead to a bottle or diaper change; and it is an effective strategy. In most cases, the persistent Exploder will get what he wants, one way or another. This coping strategy might seem wholly unsatisfying for the "Explodee," but in all these scenarios it must be remembered that the intent is to reduce stress and find a mutually acceptable solution — not to rehabilitate or "teach them a lesson," regardless of how tempting.

2.2.3 Indecisives

The Indecisive personality cannot make a decision about something that is important. Of course, this is a terrible attribute in any manager. Consider this example encounter with Roger, an employee, and Lisa, his supervisor.

---▼---

Roger: Lisa, you've had the two bids for a couple of weeks now. We're still waiting for you to select a vendor.

Lisa: I need a little more time.

Roger: Yes, but we can't start work on the other components until we know who will be partnering with us on this.

Lisa: I know, but I just need more time. Can't you get started anyway?

Roger: We've done all we can already. We are waiting on you.

Lisa: Just give me a couple of more days.

---▲---

It is not that an Indecisive is a bad person, it is just that she cannot or will not make a decision because something directly or indirectly related to that decision is probably bothering her. You need to find out what is bothering her about the decision, and help her find a win-win solution to the situation. Consider the following refactored dialogue.

▼

Roger: Lisa, you've had the two bids for a couple of weeks now. We're still waiting for you to select a vendor.

Lisa: I need a little more time.

Roger: Yes, but we can't start work on the other components until we know who will be partnering with us on this.

Lisa: I know, but I just need more time. Can't you get started anyway?

Roger: We've done all we can. Look, is there something about the bid or the bidders that is bothering you?

Lisa: I guess, I...

Roger: Did they both come in too high?

Lisa: I am concerned about that. When we add in our development and integration costs, I don't see how we can turn a profit...

(....and so on...)

▲

The idea is to get the Indecisive into a problem-solving mode and help her seek a solution to her dilemma.

2.2.4 Whiners

The Whiners, also known as Complainers, are another phenotype found in just about every organization. They like to complain about everything but offer no solutions because they feel powerless. More profoundly, they like to drag everyone down with them and can set a negative tone for an organization that is difficult to overcome.

Here is an example encounter between Rose and Sam, two peers in a testing group. Their boss is Dave. It will be easy to see which one is the Whiner.

▼

Rose: I heard that Dave wants us to learn JUnit for test case construction on all future projects.

Sam: That sounds like a waste of time.

Rose: I'm sorry you feel that way. But, it's pretty widely used and it looks like it will make our job somewhat easier.

Sam: No it won't. Besides, it will take all the fun out of writing test cases.

Rose: I don't think so. I think it just helps automate their construction and execution. I'm looking forward to learning it.

Sam: This is just another stupid waste of time. Eventually, they are going to outsource us anyway.

─────────────────────▲─────────────────────

It is clear that whatever Rose says, Sam is going to find something about which to complain.

Here is how to deal with Whiners. Do not apologize to them. Actively listen to them and acknowledge their complaints without agreeing with them. Try to engage them in problem solving by asking them to put their complaints in writing with specific details.

So, in the previous encounter, a refactored solution might look like the following:

─────────────────────▼─────────────────────

Rose: I heard that we are going to be asked to learn JUnit for test case construction on all future projects.

Sam: That sounds like a waste of time.

Rose: I hear what you are saying. But, it's pretty widely used and it looks like it will make our job somewhat easier.

Sam: Yeah, maybe easier, but it takes all the fun out of writing test cases.

Rose: I don't think so. I think it just helps automate their construction and execution. I'm looking forward to learning it. I prefer coding to testing anyway, don't you?

Sam: This is just another stupid waste of time. Eventually, they are going to outsource us anyway.

Rose: I think you are going to enjoy learning it, Sam. You always like learning new things. But why don't you send an e-mail to Dave with your concerns.

━━━━━━━━━━━━▲━━━━━━━━━━━━

2.2.5 Negativists

These are your "wet blankets." They complain, usually, because they perceive that they have no power. You probably know someone like this. To illustrate the refactoring, consider the following encounter between Sharon and Tom, two peers.

━━━━━━━━━━━━▼━━━━━━━━━━━━

Tom: Good morning, Sharon.

Sharon: I am sick and tired about the parking here. It took me 20 minutes to find a spot, and it was a mile away in this pouring rain.

Tom: Well, that's what happens if you get here after 8:00.

Sharon: And that's something else that ticks me off. Most of these people who get here even one minute before 8:00 feel like they can leave before 5:00. I'm stuck here until 7:00 sometimes and then I have to walk a mile to that parking spot in the dark.

Tom: Well, you could come in earlier.

Sharon: Haven't you been listening to me these past six months? With one car now, I have to take my husband to work and then get here. Then I have to pick him up afterward.

Tom: Gee, I am sorry I said "good morning" to you. It's only 8:30 and already you have bummed me out.

━━━━━━━━━━━━▲━━━━━━━━━━━━

The way to deal with Negativists is to stay positive and realistic with them. Do not let them drag you down.

Sometimes, a joke can be a powerful mechanism for making an individual realize their own flaws, and the refactoring. Sidebar 2.1 offers a humorous story that can be told to Negativists to show them how they

Sidebar 2.1   Dealing with Complainers

Phil used to like to tell this story to people working for him who complained too much.

The story involves a young woman who decides to join an order of nuns who take a vow of poverty and silence. After a year, the Mother Superior calls in the young nun, Sister Mary, for her annual evaluation. The Mother Superior compliments Sister Mary on her wonderful work over the past year and offers, as a reward, to allow her to speak one sentence. "My room is cold," Sister Mary complains. After reminding her that the order takes a vow of poverty as well as a vow of silence, the Mother Superior sends Sister Mary away. The following year, during her annual review, Sister Mary is again rewarded for outstanding service with two sentences to speak. "My room is still cold. And the food is no good" she says. "Well, we do take that vow of poverty and we do the best we can, but keep up the good work," Mother Superior replies. The following year, again, Sister Mary is rewarded for excellence, this time with three sentences. So she says, "My room is still too cold. The food is still no good. And I quit." "It's just as well," Mother Superior replies, "all you have done since you got here is complain."

The moral of the story, of course, is that people tend to remember your complaints, not the good things you do.

are perceived by others and to remind them that people forget the good that you do when you complain too much.

2.2.6 Clams

Bramson's Clam phenotype describes people who tend to offer little or no reaction in most situations, even to direct questions. Usually, the clam will offer only a blank stare or some meaningless, monosyllabic conversation. They are very difficult to deal with because they offer no feedback with which to gauge the effect of what you say to them and, thus, adjust your approach.

To illustrate a Clam type, consider the following dialogue between Laurie, a software engineer, and Jim, her boss.

------------------------▼------------------------

Jim: Laurie, remember last month when we spoke about the fact that you were showing up late far too often and I told you that this had to stop?

Laurie: <<*blank stare*>>

Jim: I mean, Laurie, this has got to stop; it's becoming impossible to meet our schedule when you aren't here to contribute.

Laurie: Um...

Jim: I don't know what to do with you. This has got to stop.

Laurie: Uh huh.

This is a failed encounter because no information was elicited from Laurie, and no progress was made in changing Laurie's undesirable performance.

As suggested, it is difficult to deal with. The refactoring involves trying to elicit a response from them by asking a specific question such as, "What is your response to my statement?" or "What do you think about the situation?" Then go into a silent, friendly stare of your own, allowing the dead time to force the Clam to respond. If they still do not respond, provide a response, such as, "Well, I'm unhappy with the situation" or "I think what you are doing is terrible." Then state the action you are going to take in response; for example, "So, if you don't come to work on time every day for the next two weeks, then you will be asked to clean out your desk and depart." The actions should be decisive and based on something than can be measured or observed.

For example, in the previous encounter, here is how it might have gone somewhat differently.

Jim: Laurie, remember last month when we spoke about the fact that you were showing up late far too often and I told you that this had to stop?

Laurie: <<*blank stare*>>

Jim: I mean, Laurie, this has got to stop; it's becoming impossible to meet our schedule when you aren't here to contribute. What are you going to do about it?

Laurie: Um...

Jim: <<*long pause*>>

Laurie: Uh, … well I can try harder to come in on time. Maybe I should get a new car.

Jim: Well, Laurie, here is the deal. If you don't come to work on time every day for the next two weeks, then you will be asked to clean out your desk and depart.

━━━━━━━━━━━━━━━━━━━▲━━━━━━━━━━━━━━━━━

Dealing with a Clam is similar if he is your boss or a peer. The main difference is that you cannot give your boss an ultimatum, although you might have some leverage over a peer. With your boss, you can document the encounter in an e-mail summarizing your understanding of the situation. In some cases, you may have to inform your boss that because you cannot get an answer from him, you will need to go to a higher authority. In any case, memorialize any encounter with a Clam in writing.

2.2.7 Bulldozers

Bulldozers are expert know-it-alls who batter their opponents with a presumably superior knowledge of the facts, usually leading to some dire failure scenario. In fact, Bulldozers are a kind of rational negativist who sees the facts only as supporting their worst fears. Here is an example encounter between two peers, Art and a Bulldozer (Karen).

━━━━━━━━━━━━━━━━━━━▼━━━━━━━━━━━━━━━━━

Art: Hey! Did you hear that we are going to be going Open Source for the new Web portal that we are developing for the support group?

Karen: We are doomed to failure. All of the studies show that Open Source platform development, while cost-effective, doesn't have the kind of long-term risk mitigation guarantees that our company needs. We have to go with a commercial suite on that project.

Art: Yeah, but so many people are going in this direction, and it doesn't mean that we are going away from the main commercial vendor.

Karen: Get your facts straight, Art. I just read a study that showed that although the number of defects is lower in some Open Source systems, that this doesn't scale up to enterprise-level applications. Moreover, other studies have shown that the cost of maintaining Open Source systems can exceed commercial products because of the training necessary to bring everyone up to speed and the need to maintain a larger internal development and testing staff.

Art: I, uh, uh, didn't know, but…

Karen: Art, it's fools like you who don't do their fact checking that cost the company millions last year in that failed conversion project for payroll.

Art: Uh, I have to go.

To refactor the Bulldozer, take her analysis to the extreme and show her that her fears are unfounded. So here is the refactored encounter:

Art: Hey! Did you hear that we are going to be going Open Source for the new Web portal that we are developing for the support group?

Karen: We are doomed to failure. All of the studies show that Open Source platform development, while cost-effective, doesn't have the kind of long-term risk mitigation guarantees that our company needs. We have to go with a commercial suite on that project.

Art: Yeah, but so many people are going in this direction, and it doesn't mean that we are going away from the main commercial vendor.

Karen: Get your facts straight, Art. I have read several studies…

Art: OK, so there are some risks in going Open Source. There are risks in using a single-vendor strategy too. What if we were to use a sandbox to develop a proof of concept using Open Source tools? Then we could use some fault injection techniques to see how robust the code is under stress.

Karen: Hmmm. Well, I've read about some companies that have tried that, but that increases their costs, particularly if they decide against going Open Source after all.

Art: Well, that's true. There is some risk in building some throw-away prototypes but that risk is small compared to either going straight away to an Open Source strategy or committing to a single vendor. Based on your research and knowledge of Open Source solutions, do you think you could put together a little proof of concept? Then we could find out just how robust the application might be before we commit real resources to development.

Karen: Yeah. That might be fun, I'd like to try that.

━━━━━━━━━━━━━━━━▲━━━━━━━━━━━━━━━━

Do not try to "out-fact-check" a Bulldozer, because you probably cannot do it. They are well read and are masters at manipulating facts to their advantage. In essence, have them extend their negative scenario so that they provide a solution that mitigates the risks. Often, they will discover that their fears are ridiculous or they will find an acceptable solution to the problem.

2.2.8 Superagreeables

This phenotype dismisses people with patronizing agreeability, but at the end of the day, Superagreeables are just as unhelpful as an Indecisive. To illustrate, consider the following encounter between Barbara, a supervisor, and her subordinate Ravi.

━━━━━━━━━━━━━━━━▼━━━━━━━━━━━━━━━━

Ravi: Barbara, I'd like to attend that embedded systems conference in Salt Lake City next year. Here's my travel request form; can you sign it? I need to get it approved today to make the registration deadline.

Barbara: OK, no problem.

Ravi: So, can you sign it?

Barbara: Let me just check the travel budget. I think there is some money left. Just leave the form with me.

Ravi: OK, I'll stop by later to pick it up.

<<Later that day>>

Ravi: Hi Barbara! I came to pick up my travel form.

Barbara: Oh, can you come back tomorrow? I got side-tracked and didn't have a chance to check the budget.

Ravi: I really need it today to make the registration deadline.

Barbara: No problem. I'll get to it tomorrow.

<<The next day>>

Ravi: Hi Barbara. I came to pick up the form. I called the conference organizers and they told me if I get my registration in today, they will extend the deadline.

Barbara: Oh, I'm sorry. I didn't check the budget yet. Don't worry, I'll get to it...

———————————▲———————————

But Barbara never does, and Ravi never gets to go the conference.

In this case, for example, Ravi should have realized that either there was not enough money in the budget and Barbara did not want to break the bad news to him, or perhaps Ravi has traveled too many times while others have not, and again Barbara did not want to break the bad news. So, when he first submitted the form to her, and she hesitated, he could have said the following:

———————————▼———————————

Ravi: Barbara, are you concerned about the budget? Look, if that's a problem, I'm willing to take less than the usual trip allowance. I really want to go to this conference. If you would just pay the airfare and hotel, I'll cover everything else.

———————————▲———————————

Like the Indecisive, you have to hold Superagreeables accountable. Give them deadlines. Get them to tell you what is really on their mind and preventing them from making the decision. Then try to offer them a win-win solution.

2.2.9 Combination Personalities

It is probably the case that some people, perhaps the more sophisticated "corncobs," exhibit the behavior of more than one of these personalities. When this is the case, some combination of the previously mentioned defensive strategies should be improvised. Sidebar 2.2 provides one humorous illustration of such a personality.

Sidebar 2.2   Combination Negative Personalities

An apocryphal story concerning a former U.S. Secretary of State* illustrates a combination of behaviors characteristic of a Negativist, Sherman Tank, and Bulldozer. The Secretary calls in one of his Senior Assistant Secretaries and requests a report on "The Situation in the Middle East." The Assistant Secretary immediately assigns a group of his top staffers, who go off to work on the project. Two days later, the Assistant Secretary delivers a thick report to the Secretary's assistant. The next day, the report is returned to him with bold letters on the cover — "Not good enough." Disquieted, the Assistant Secretary meets with his staff again. He asks his team to rewrite the report — to double-check all facts, remove all hyperbole, include more data, etc. After two days of burning the midnight oil, the report is again submitted to the Secretary. It is returned the next day with the prominent note — "Still not good enough." Frightened for his job, now the Assistant Secretary cancels all vacations and reassigns staffers from other projects to help with the second major rewrite. After two days, a huge report is produced. This time, however, the Assistant Secretary decides to hand-deliver the report to the Secretary. He gets an appointment and nervously hands the report to the Secretary. The Assistant Secretary confesses, "Mr. Secretary, we have gone over this with a fine-toothed comb, we have slaved over it, and there is nothing more we can do to improve it!" The Secretary replies, "Good! Now I'll read it."

The Secretary's behavior is a combination of intimidation (Sherman Tank), Bulldozer, and Negativist behavior! Refactoring this situation would have been challenging, particularly given the stature of the Secretary. However, the Assistant Secretary should have asked for guidance after the first rejection. This would have forced his boss to either be specific in pointing out the shortcomings of the first version, or admitting he had not read it.

*You might guess who he is, but we will not tell — we do not want to be sued.

Notes

1. Apparently, the indicator is called "Myers-Briggs" rather than "Briggs-Myers" because Isabel Briggs-Myers did not want people to overlook her mother's contributions [Briggs].
2. Much of this is based on materials found at keirsey.com

References

[Bramson] Robert Bramson, *Coping with Difficult People*, Dell Paperbacks, 1988.

[Briggs] The Myers-Briggs Foundation Web site, www.myersbriggs.org, last accessed January 24, 2005.

[Gorla] Narasimhaiah Gorla and Yan Wah Lam, Who Should Work with Whom?: Building Effective Software Project Teams, *Communications of the ACM*, 47(6), 79–82, June 2004.

[Keirsey] David Keirsey, Please Understand Me II: Temperament Character Intelligence, www.keirsey.com.

[Laplante] Phillip A. Laplante, Remember the Human Element in IT Project Management, *IT Professional,* Jan./Feb. 2003, pp. 46–50.

[Mayer] J.D. Mayer and Casey D. Cobb, Educational Policy on Emotional Intelligence: Does It Make Sense?, *Educational Psychology Review*, 12(2), 163–183, 2000.

[McGregor] Douglas McGregor, *The Human Side of Enterprise*, McGraw-Hill, 1960.

Chapter 3

Group Patterns and Antipatterns

While it is interesting to look at the patterns and antipatterns of behavior in individuals, the aggregate behavior of individuals in groups is different altogether. Sometimes, a group of people who individually are nice and easy to work with, clash and never get past being a dysfunctional group. Why might this be? How does this aggregate behavior contribute to an environmentally unsound situation? Does the behavior of groups change over time? As a manager or even "just" a member of a group, how can you help transform a chaotic group of backstabbers into a well-oiled machine? Well, we do not pretend to have all the answers, but let us talk about how people behave in groups in an informal way and talk about some of things that you can do to help move a dysfunctional group in the right direction.

3.1 Tuckman's Theory of Teams

Any discussion of team formation must start with the 1965 work of Bruce Tuckman [Tuckman]. This oft-cited and still relevant work was the first to describe the life cycle of teams from potentially chaotic mobs to well-functioning teams. This was not a "how-to" guide to assist leaders in progressing their team through the stages of development. It did document the evolutionary process, however, thus giving hope that eventually a bunch of raw recruits could be whipped into shape. Additionally, Tuckman described the signs of development as the group moved through the life cycle and this allows managers to diagnose the current state of their team and strategize how best to aid the team's progression.

Tuckman's sequence of group formation is usually referred to by the shorthand sequence of phase names "Forming, Storming, Norming, Performing, Adjourning." The last phase is sometimes changed to "Mourning" to maintain the ryhming pattern. The premise is that a team can dramatically change from one form to the next. This evolution through the phases might be gradual and therefore somewhat imperceptible to the members. Interested readers might want to watch Sidney Lumet's 1957 movie, "12 Angry Men." You can actually see the jury going through Tuckman team formation sequence, and it is also a great film.

3.1.1 Forming

Tuckman's sequence starts at the Formation stage, at the moment that the team members are brought together. All kinds of cultural images are invoked — raw military recruits meeting for the first time, fraternity members during rush period, cast members of a play at tryouts, students on the first day of class, etc. During this period there is the usual eyeing over of individuals, testing of boundaries, perhaps razzing and teasing. Presumably, members begin to carefully explore acceptable group behaviors by testing and observing each other's limits and testing the group leader. Individual members must begin the transformation to member status (or not), and this can be challenging for those who have weak self-images, as well as those who have strong self-identity.

The following behaviors and feelings might be observed or expressed by team members during the Forming phase:

- ■ Behaviors:
  - – Task definition behaviors such as who is going to do what and when
  - – Establishing lists of data to collect
  - – Setting limits and structure for group behavior, deciding to use Robert's Rules of Procedure, informal rules, or no rules, etc.
  - – Abstract discussions of the task at hand and the reason for being (for some members, there will be impatience with these discussions)
  - – Difficulty with identifying some of the relevant problems to be solved (for example, "What are we really being asked to do?" is a common sentiment)

- Feelings:
  - Anticipation
  - Anxiety
  - Attachment to the team
  - Excitement
  - Optimism
  - Pride
  - Suspicion

In the Forming stage, there is much confusion and little work being accomplished. While this is considered "normal," this situation can be a source of great frustration to those team members who are eager to move forward and to the team's immediate leader and his superiors.

------------▼------------

Phil: When I was initiated into my fraternity many years ago, we were assigned a series of rather "interesting" tasks. Later on, I discovered that the purpose of these challenges was to accelerate the pledge class through the Formation sequence. I was told that some of these prank/tasks were similar to those done to rookies on new teams, and even to recruits in the military.

------------▲------------

3.1.2 Storming

At some point, a group recognizes that it needs to begin to evolve into "something" although that "something," that ideal vision of the group, may be different for each member. These discordant visions of what the team should be and do, even in the presence of some stated unified vision, is the cause of great tension, hidden agendas, and anger. The Storming phase is perhaps the most difficult stage for the team because team members begin to realize the road ahead is different and more difficult than they had expected. Some team members become impatient with the slow progress and there is disagreement about next steps. Because team members are trying to rely on personal experience, they resist collaborating with most of the other members.

The following behaviors and feelings might be observed or expressed by team members during the Storming phase:

- Behaviors:
  - Arguing between members over minutiae
  - Differences in outlook on the prospects for success

- Questioning the wisdom of those who composed the team and issued its objectives (e.g., "What genius thought this one up?")
- Resisting improvements suggested by other members
- Resisting tasks assigned
- Setting unrealistic goals
■ Feelings:
- Competitiveness
- Defensiveness
- Disunity
- Jealousy
- Polarization
- Tension

In the environment that creates these feelings, the pressures are such that little time is actually spent on problem solving and goal achievement. With the aid of a good leader, however, a team can progress rapidly through this phase. Without a good leader, the team can languish.

3.1.3 Norming

At some point in the evolution, a majority of the team recognizes that it must escape the storming, although there is not necessarily a tacit recognition that "we are in the storming phase." Characteristically, the team begins to converge on a shared vision, or at least a shared set of tasks. If all goes well, the team may even begin to reach beyond the original scope of the task, setting goals that are more ambitious. Enthusiasm is high and, more importantly, most members begin to set aside their petty differences and agendas, or at least subordinate them. The majority of the team begins to accept the rules of the group and accept the roles assigned to them. A noticeable reduction in tension occurs, although there still may be some flare-ups. Nonetheless, healthy disagreement dominates over nonproductive argument.

The following behaviors and feelings might be observed or expressed by team members during the Norming phase:

■ Behaviors:
- Accepting the existing team membership
- Avoiding conflict
- Expressing a sense of team cohesion, spirit, and goals
- Expressing constructive criticism
- Setting and maintaining team ground rules and boundaries
■ Feelings:
- Camaraderie
- Confidence
- Friendliness

As a result of the normative behavior, the team begins working on the tasks at hand. It is sometimes during this phase that noticeable progress toward completion of the goals should be seen.

3.1.4 Performing

The team has finally settled its relationships and expectations. Team members have discovered and accepted each other's strengths and weaknesses, and have identified their roles. Their efforts are now directed toward diagnosing and solving problems, and choosing and implementing real changes.

The following behaviors and feelings might be observed or expressed by team members during the Performing phase:

- Behaviors:
    - Changing constructively to meet new challenges
    - Demonstrating a better understanding of each other's strengths and weaknesses
    - Preventing or working through group problems
- Feelings:
    - Close attachment to the team

The team is now an effective, cohesive unit. The sign of a performing team is that real work is regularly getting done. At this point, managers should use most of their energies to maintain this state of team being, and to see that it is not upset.

3.1.5 Adjourning

The team debriefs and shares the improved process during this phase. When the team finally completes that last briefing, there is always a bittersweet sense of accomplishment coupled with the reluctance to say good-bye. Many relationships formed within these teams continue long after the team disbands. This phase is sometimes called "Mourning" because it rhymes but, more importantly, because on efficient, well-formed teams there is a genuine sadness when everyone has to move on.

3.1.6 Tuckman's Model Wrap-Up

While the Tuckman model suggests that teams will eventually reach the performing stage, it is dangerous to assume that this will happen naturally and predictably. Without effective leadership, the team can get stuck in

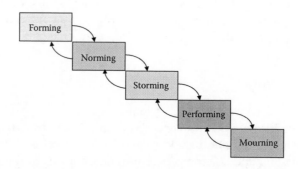

Figure 3.1   Tucker's phases of team formation and devolution.

a sub-optimal phase, or at least be delayed in its progression. At these times, antipatterns abound.

Finally, the model assumes that teams can only progress or stagnate, but is it possible for them to actually regress? (See Figure 3.1.)

We think so. Changes to the external environment, resetting of goals by outside stakeholders, changes in personnel, and other watershed events can cause the team formation to be set back, even to the forming stage. Therefore, leaders should be aware of this possibility.

3.2 Sports Analogies to Teams

Now, we cannot talk about group and team behavior without drawing upon their most obvious form — sports. We are both fanatical sports fans and we recognize that some of our favorite coaches are indeed excellent managers. No one could argue that professional coaches do not wrangle some of the most intense egos and difficult people imaginable. The notion of the team is not consistent across the gamut of sports, however. Each sport draws upon individuals, cooperation, and strategy differently. Consider the role of team play and individual performance in different sports (Table 3.1).

Golf, boxing, swimming, and track, for example, are usually individual sports; and even when "teams" are composed, competition generally occurs on an individual basis. With the exception of relays in track and swimming, and special golf formats like "scramble" (in which the best ball of a group of four is played), team play is really just an aggregation of individual results. This is not dissimilar to a solo consultant or group of consultants working on independent projects. In this kind of the team, the objective is to extract the best possible performance from each

Table 3.1 The Role of Individual and Team Play in Sports

Sport	Team Characteristics	IT Analogy
Golf, boxing, swimming, track	Solo performance Individual results	Independent consultants
Baseball	Team result is mostly aggregated individual performances Some coordination needed	Open Source development
Football	Team result Individuals have specialized responsibilities Specialized teams Highly coordinated	Large-scale software construction
Basketball, soccer, hockey	Team result Interchangeable skills Constant participation	Agile development. Management teams

individual. Interpersonal interaction is less important, although it can become distracting when one person on the team "acts up."

In team sports such as baseball, there is a strong component of individual play (e.g., pitching, fielding, batting) but there is also an element of team play that requires coordination between more than one player (e.g., hit-and-run, double plays, hitting the cut-off man). This is not unlike Open Source software development or testing teams where there is a strong element of individual accomplishment, but some interaction. Here, the cohesiveness of the team is more important than in the previously mentioned sports.

In football, there is a team result but individual tasks are highly specialized and segmented. For example, there are offensive, defensive, and special teams squads, and many players only play on one squad. Within each of these squads there is a great deal of cooperation and coordination, but there is little interaction between squads (it is possible that members of the defensive and offensive squads, for example, never interact during a game). This situation is analogous to large-scale system building where responsibilities are partitioned between requirements engineers, architects, designers, coders, and testers. There might be some limited interaction, but each of these teams works in a highly autonomous way. Breakdowns can occur, however, within each of the squads, as well as at the interaction points between the squads.

Finally, in soccer, basketball, hockey, and similar sports, players have interchangeable skills and play both offense and defense in a more-or-less constant period of activity. Although there is some specialization (e.g., goalies), most players are expected to have similar skills. In information technology (IT), this situation is found in agile development teams, and in teams including managers and staff members who have some shared responsibilities. Problems can arise when individual team members cannot fulfill their responsibilities or when they are disruptive.

Consider the play of a well-coordinated team of "no-name" players compared to the dysfunction of a team with a handful of *prima donna* superstars. The history of all team sports is filled with examples of no-name teams defeating teams that appeared more talented on paper but did not function well as a team. For example, the 1972 undefeated, Super Bowl champion Miami Dolphins had a "no-name" defense. The same no-name defense led the team to win the 1973 Super Bowl.

Throughout this book we use a number of references to sports and sports personalities to illustrate various points. In particular, you will notice quite a few references to football and basketball. Both of us enjoy these sports, and in many ways the group dynamics of IT and software groups are akin to those described for these sports. Most critically, we strongly believe that in the corporate setting, just as in basketball and football, while individual efforts can make a difference, these are no match for an excellent team.

3.3 Evolution to Antipatterns

The transformation of a team through Tuckman's phases — or generally, from a functioning team to a dysfunctional one — does not happen overnight. If this were the case, the watershed event could be identified and potentially reversed. Instead, the evolution of a team from one form to another happens slowly, even imperceptibly, so that one does not know that the transformation is taking place until it is too late. Of course, this happens in two-person relationships too — "We just slowly grew apart, and we just didn't know it until it was too late."

The Boiling Frog Syndrome, described later, helps explain how teams and environments slowly become dysfunctional although most or all of the team members do not want that to happen. On the other hand, slow transformations from a bad situation to a good one can also happen, although living through this kind of epoch takes a great deal of patience.

References

[Tuckman]   Tuckman, B.W., Developmental Sequence in Small Groups, *Psychological Bulletin*, 63, 384–399, 1965.

Chapter 4

Successfully Leading Teams[1]

Chapter 3 described the evolution of teams and group dynamics but made no recommendation for team leadership and management. Leading[2] teams is difficult and there are many reasons why. The presence of difficult people is certainly a factor. The general nature of human relationships is a problem. But aside from these issues, many people are thrust into the manager's role without the proper skills. While these skills can be learned, there is also a personality component to good management. And, in our experience, some managers make it more difficult on themselves by the way they treat other people.

In the IT and computing sector, the challenge of leading successful teams is compounded by the complexity of the end product, the difficulty in measurement, and in the uncertain aspects of software and the software development process itself. Using proper software and IT project management techniques such as careful planning, metrics, reviews, audits, and post mortems can help significantly, but these organizational processes are still insufficient.

In IT, as in many theatres, it is unfortunately the case that we still seek to promote those individuals with the best technical skills to lead the technical teams. But the soft skills needed to lead a team of professionals are vastly different from skills needed to design software, write code, or test systems, for example. Furthermore, simply mastering commercial scheduling and project management tools does not qualify someone as a good project manager.

Our purpose here is not to reproduce a text on project management. However, we would like to introduce some management paradigms and terminology to be used later and to offer some advice that we hope is useful to all team members, regardless of their role or position.

4.1 The Growth of Team Size

Because team leadership is related to personal communications and relations, we can infer that as teams grow, leading them becomes increasingly difficult merely because the number of relationships that must be maintained escalates and each relationship requires attention. Any one of those relationships can deteriorate, and the likelihood of a conflict between any two team members increases if one of them exhibits some of the negative behaviors thus far described.

So how fast does the problem grow? Fast — if n is the number of people in the group, the number of interpersonal interactions is $n \times (n-1)/2$. We can prove it but you are likely not interested in mathematical induction. More importantly, this formula means that if there are two people in the group, then there is one interaction (all interactions are two-way); for a three-person group, there are three possible interactions; and for five people, there are ten interactions (Figure 4.1).

For a soccer team of 11, there are 55 different interactions. Now you know one reason why coaching is so tough. Taking the example further, to up to 100 persons on a team, it is easy to see how quickly the problem of leading that team grows (Figure 4.2).

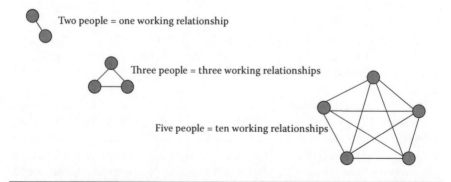

Two people = one working relationship

Three people = three working relationships

Five people = ten working relationships

Figure 4.1 Interpersonal interactions grow as a factor of $n \times (n-1)/2$, where n is the number of persons involved. (From [Laplante].)

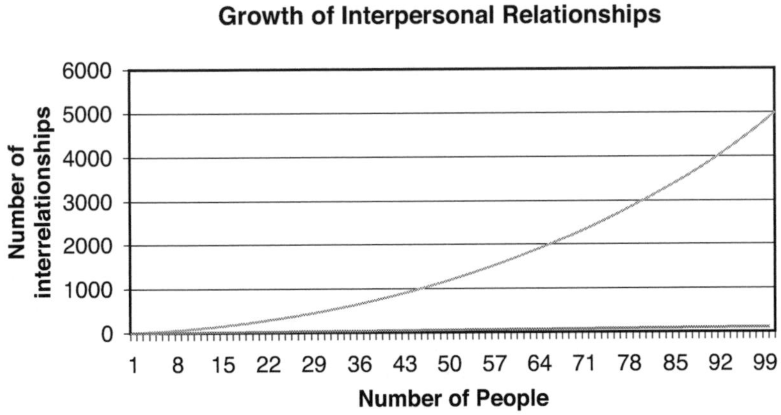

Growth of Interpersonal Relationships

Figure 4.2   Increasing growth of interpersonal relationships as a function of the number of people involved.

So how can software projects that require hundreds of people be successful? Effective managers have the skills needed for team building: negotiating skills, understanding of basic psychology and group dynamics, and good motivational and communications skills, especially listening. Listening skills are so valuable, yet they are often neglected in corporate training programs and academic curricula. Have you ever taken, or even seen, a course in listening? This situation is unfortunate because listening skills can be sharpened through training.

4.2 Micromanagers and *Laissez-Faire* Managers

Most people are familiar with a simple taxonomy of managers along a continuum from those who like to carefully observe and adjust every detail of what their subordinates do, to those who leave the details to others. We typically call the former a micromanager and the latter a *laissez-faire*[3] manager (Figure 4.3).

Figure 4.3   Process management types. Where are you in this continuum?

Those at the micromanager end of the continuum focus on establishing processes and protocols that are "people-proof." That is, they tend to micromanage people through printed directives, manuals of operation, and constant reporting. Presumably, explicit detailed instructions will prevent even the most "incompetent" person from messing up. Much of the military is designed to function this way — "don't think, just follow orders."

Steven Covey, author of *The Seven Habits of Highly Successful People*, says, however, that "we manage things and lead people" [Covey2]. Micromanagers are therefore just that, managers, and not leaders. In our experience, motivating and influencing team members by example and leadership, and not through hierarchical application of authority, is much more effective.

Of course, the problem with viewing people and building organizational structures around micromanagement is that it is impossible to anticipate every eventuality. Consequently, the system breaks down when a script is not available for a particular situation or scenario. The military copes with this in two ways: (1) deep organizational hierarchies of command so that decision makers are available at all levels, making decisions for those below them; and (2) self-organizing and relatively autonomous special forces groups that rely on very highly skilled (often in multiple disciplines), experienced personnel. Some of the high-performing teams in IT organizations probably share some characteristics with the elite military special forces — or at least they like to think so.

At the other end of the continuum in Figure 4.3 is the trusting individual who chooses to leave the details of implementation to others, often preferring friendship to management. There tends to be no written guidelines in these circumstances. Everything is "touchy-feely." Often, this kind of *laissez-faire* management can lead to trouble, such as unreported problems festering too long. Happily, hopefully, most people probably find themselves somewhere in the middle of the continuum.

Of course, a balance of micromanagement and *laissez-faire* practices is needed, depending on the situation. Moreover, different individuals respond to different styles of management, and the good manager is capable of both process-oriented management and people-oriented management when each is required.

This process- versus people-oriented classification system of managers is too simplistic, however. In the classic text *The Human Side of Enterprise*, McGregor proposed two theories in which to view employee motivation, and hence to manage it [McGregor]. He wanted to avoid the use of labels, so he adopted the generic terms "Theory X" and "Theory Y." Later, others added alternate theories of employee motivation, providing a much richer set of management paradigms.

---▼---

Note:

There are other taxonomies of management styles. For example, one classifies management styles along the dimensions of "task focused," "social," "intellectual," and "participative." The Myers-Briggs or Keirsey types can be easily mapped into these four groupings.

In any case, task-focused managers are decision driven. Social executives cultivate the human interactions in the group. Intellectual managers adopt a very analytical and logical style. And participative managers like to consensus-build. All of these styles have advantages and drawbacks.

Managers can have primary and secondary styles, incorporating these as well as behavioral components of all four. We stick to the simple micromanager/not micromanager classifications in this text.

---▲---

4.3 Theory X

Theory X is a variant of micromanagement that is based on a general distrust in human behavior. It is closely related to the hierarchical, command-and-control model used by military organizations and many companies. Theory X holds that top-down authority is necessary because most people inherently dislike work and will avoid it if they can. Hence, managers should coerce, control, direct, and threaten their workers in an effort to get the most out of them.

---▼---

Mr. Fleming: Myron, what are you doing?

Myron: I'm thinking, Mr. Fleming.

Mr. Fleming: You're not paid to think. Get back to work!

---▲---

Theory X further proposes that most people actually prefer to be told what to do rather than have to decide for themselves. One manager we know used to say, "People only do what you audit." This is a classic misinterpretation of Theory X thinking, however. Theory X really suggests that "people only do *what they don't want to do* unless you audit them."

In many cases, employing a Theory X style of management can lead to problems. Most workers wish to be trusted and do not need constant supervision to deliver a great product. They will therefore resent being managed this way.

4.4 Theory Y

McGregor suggested that in contrast to Theory X, Theory Y holds that work is a natural and desirable activity, such that external control and threats are not needed to guide the organization. Instead, individual commitment is a function of how well the task is presented to them. Because, according to the theory, most humans seek responsibility, the level of commitment is proportional to the clarity and desirability of the goals set for the group. Therefore, the task and management processes must be well-structured.

4.5 Theory W

Theory W is a software project management paradigm developed by Boehm and Ross [Boehm1]. It is based on three basic principles: (1) establish a set of win-win preconditions; (2) structure a win-win process; and (3) structure a win-win product.

4.5.1 Establish a Set of Win-Win Preconditions

Win-win preconditions recognize that the best interpersonal relationships are those in which everyone "wins." The alternatives are zero-sum situations where one party must lose for the other to win. While this is often the natural position people take in a negotiation, it favors competition over cooperation and should be discouraged. Here is one way to establish win-win preconditions.

First, recognize that everyone wants to win, so you need to understand what constitutes a winning situation for each individual. That is really the key. Money, power, and recognition represent winning conditions for many people, but there are other, more subtle conditions such as job satisfaction, a feeling of belonging, and moral fulfillment. Above all, you cannot attribute your own winning scenario to another person — theirs may be totally different. So, it is really important to understand the win conditions of your counterpart in the negotiation and the best way to determine them is to ask.

Next, establish reasonable expectations. We cannot emphasize enough the importance of setting reasonable and mutually fulfilling expectations in every aspect of human relations. We are sure you can recall many scenarios in your social, work, and familial relationships in which a promise was broken or an expectation unfulfilled, leading to great strain in the relationship.

Finally, provide an environment that supports the fulfillment of everyone's win conditions. For example, by insuring that people's task assignments match their win conditions. In addition, appropriate financial incentives and communication can head off problems.

4.5.2 Structure a Win-Win Process

Structuring a win-win process means setting up a system that will lead to success. Start by establishing a realistic process plan based on some standard methodology. This methodology can be internal, company-wide, or off-the-shelf. Once you have a plan, it is important to use it to control the project. All too often, managers develop a plan to satisfy the customer and upper management, and then throw it away once it has been approved. Use and maintain the plan throughout the life of the project.

In fact, the activity of planning is an important one throughout a project life cycle. "The plan is nothing, planning is everything" is a quote widely attributed to Dwight Eisenhower and could not be more true. What kind of planning is ongoing? Well, as a project manager, you need to track risks that can lead to win-lose or lose-lose situations, anything from disenfranchised staff to unrealistic customer expectations. Make sure you identify and eliminate these risks as soon as possible.

Keeping people involved and engaged is essential to the win-win process. This ensures that team members feel connected to the project, are emotionally invested in the work, and are open to communication. In addition, a manager should listen to team members; they probably have great ideas.

4.5.3 Structure a Win-Win Product

Structuring a win-win product refers to the process of user requirements elicitation and specification writing. Outside the software engineering context, this principle refers to defining the product the client wants and needs, not just the product the staff wants to build or deliver. Matching the users' and maintainers' win conditions is the key and includes careful expectation setting. As this is not a text on software requirements engineering, we leave it at that.

4.5.4 Win-Win Negotiating

Finally, there is win-win negotiating. Win-win negotiating does not necessarily mean that both parties get exactly what they want. Rather, it means walking away from a negotiation with both parties feeling satisfied. Therefore, understanding all parties' win conditions is essential. This is not always easy, particularly if members choose to hide their win conditions. You can help in this by being forthright with your own win conditions; honesty begets honesty in our experience.

> "One for you, one for me. Two for you, one, two, for me. Three for you. One, two, three, for me...."
>
> **—From an Abbott and Costello routine**

To ensure a successful outcome, you must start with clearly stated, agreed-upon ground rules. These might include where the negotiation takes place, what topics are open for discussion, when the negotiation will conclude, and what to do in case of an impasse.

Next, it is important to start small and work your way up to the big issues. Negotiating some small subset of lesser issues early helps establish a pattern for success. Furthermore, make sure you give a little in the negotiation. If you are obviously intransigent, your antagonist will feel cheated and unfulfilled in the process. Similarly, attempting to "split the difference," while better than settling for the first offer, is often too predictable for both sides to be satisfying. Sometimes, a more thoughtful compromise is necessary.

Finally, be sure to keep negotiating until all parties feel satisfied that the results are fair. In some cases, it may be necessary to postpone some issues rather than always looking for universal satisfaction, but "tabling" issues in this way should not become a habit; it is an obvious stalling tactic that irritates your adversary.

4.6 Theory Z

The last in the alphabetical management paradigms is, appropriately, Theory Z. This was identified by Ouchi, following his observations of Japanese-style management. He reported the theory in his 1981 book, *Theory Z: How American Management Can Meet the Japanese Challenge* [Ouchi]. At its core, Theory Z proposes that workers have a strong bonding to the corporation and happily subordinate their individual identity to that of the company.

> The 1986 comedy "Gung Ho," starring Michael Keaton, highlights the difficulties of American workers in an auto plant adapting to the Theory Z style when their company is acquired by a Japanese one.

The career paths in this model are nonspecific. Most top Japanese managers have worked in all aspects of their business, from the production floor to sales and marketing. This is also true within functional groups. For example, workers will be cross-trained to operate any machine on the assembly floor. Theory Z companies are notoriously slow in giving promotions, and most Japanese CEOs are over 50 years of age. Nevertheless, the cross-functional nature of the workforce is likely central to the success of large multi-sector conglomerates that prevail in Japan, as well as the aptitude Japanese industry shows for agility.

Because the workforce subjugates personal interest to that of the company, explicit control mechanisms typical in Theory X are replaced with implicit controls such as peer and group pressure. The norms of the particular corporate culture also provide additional implicit controls. Japanese companies are famous for their collective decision making and responsibility. This form of management can be found at all levels of a Japanese company, and we see examples appearing in American companies too, particularly with the advent of agile development and eXtreme Programming.

4.7 Principle Centered Leadership

All the management approaches discussed thus far focus on organizational frameworks for management. Conversely, Covey's Principle Centered Leadership [Covey1] focuses on the behavior of the manager as an agent for change.

A key concept in Principle Centered Leadership is that the best managers are actually leaders, and that the only way to effect change in a team or organization is by changing themselves first. This principle, called self-mastery, is embodied in the following recommendations:

- Remember that the only person that you can effectively change is yourself.
- People will respond positively to you if you are forthright, reliable, consistent, and hardworking.
- Maintain a healthy life balance to reduce your stress level.

Additionally, Covey contends that principles are more important than values. Values are society based and can change over time and differ from culture to culture. Principles are more universal, more lasting. True leaders base their decisions on these universal "laws," whereas ineffective managers expend their energies on situation-specific solutions for constantly evolving problems.

4.8 General Advice

Of course, there are many other theories on management style. And we are not suggesting that you literally adopt one style or another. There is no silver bullet for successful leadership of teams. Each leader must adopt a set of rules that fits the organizational culture and their own personality. Regardless of the theory they espouse, however, the following principles usually apply in all situations:

- Lead by example, and communicate often and well.
- Work constantly to monitor and manage your relationship with staff and between staff members.
- Cultural alignment is important — remove those who do not fit the culture. If you do not fit the culture, you should leave, unless you can change it.
- Treat people with respect, manage expectations, be consistent, reward good behavior, and deal with bad behavior swiftly but fairly.
- Have a sense of humor and maintain your self-respect.
- Be an optimist. No one chooses to be a failure. Try to give people the benefit of the doubt and work with them. After all, you would want this for yourself.

When building and maintaining project teams, Boehm offers the following staffing principles [Boehm2], which we like:

- Use better and fewer people.
- Fit the tasks to the skills and motivation of the people available.
- An organization does best in the long run by helping its people to self-actualize (all hail Maslow).
- Select people who will complement and harmonize with one another.
- Keeping a misfit on a team doesn't benefit anyone.

Finally, when managing conflict in teams, Cohen et al. offer advice that focuses on three primary drivers of conflict: (1) processes, (2) people, and (3) organization (Table 4.1) [Cohen].

Table 4.1   Managing Conflict in Teams

	Sources of Conflict	*Managing Conflict*
Processes	Scarce resource of time	Time management: Plan for schedule overruns Manage effect of schedule changes Learn from project experience
	User versus technical requirements	Common goals: Align individual goals with process metrics Value team more than individual success
People	Different strokes	Team building: Train in conflict resolution Sponsor group activities Support informal social contact
Organization	Power and politics	Structure for success: Co-locate teams Integrate functional teams Instill ownership
	Manager's matter	Involved leadership: Create collaborative atmosphere Model effective conflict management

Source: Cynthia Cohen, Stanley Birkin, Monica Garfield, and Harold Webb, Managing Conflict in Software Testing, *Communications of the ACM,* 47(1), 76–81, January 2004.

Dysfunction in processes can occur because of the scarce resource of time and from user versus technical requirement mismatches. Appropriate time management strategies, such as planning for schedule overruns, managing the effects of schedule changes, and simply learning from past experience can mitigate against the first of these. Mismatches in user and technical requirements can be resolved with common goals. Start by explicitly valuing team over individual success and follow up with metrics that measure the contribution to group success for each individual.

People interaction problems arise from the differing ways people work (different strokes for different folks). This problem can be addressed through team-building exercises, such as training team members in conflict resolution, sponsoring group activities, and supporting informal social contact. As we mention again later, we are particularly fond of the FISH philosophy that came out of the Pike's Place Fish Market in Seattle. Having attended many such team-building, motivational sessions, the FISH sessions were by far the most rewarding ... and we are not joking.

Finally, organizational dysfunction arises from power and politics and poor quality managers. Political problems can be addressed by restructuring the organization for success by co-locating teams, integrating functional groups, and instilling project ownership throughout. Collaborative and participative atmospheres can mitigate against poor managers, allowing natural leaders to emerge as necessary. Of course, this is an effective tactic if the bad manager is merely incompetent or out of their depth, but a despotic manager really just has to go.

As one would expect from the preceding discussion, our exploration of management and environmental antipatterns that follows seeks to characterize various configurations of these imbalances along with the appropriate solutions for team members, innocent bystanders, culpable participants, and wayward organizations in an easy-to-reference cookbook form. We challenge you to find yourself, your colleagues, and your organizations...and then refactor relentlessly.

Notes

1. Some of this discussion, particularly sections 4.3 through 4.8, is adapted with permission from Phillip A. Laplante, "Remember the Human Element in IT Project Management," *IT Professional,* Jan./Feb. 2003, pp. 46–50.
2. You will notice we do not say "managing a team." We prefer to say "leading the team" because there is a positive connotation, whereas there can be a negative connotation in the way a team is managed. We describe this later.
3. From the French for "leave it be."

References

[Boehm1] B.W. Boehm and R. Ross, Theory-W Software Project Management Principles and Examples, *IEEE Transactions on Software Engineering,* 15(7), 902–916, July 1989.

[Boehm2] B.W. Boehm, Software Risk Management: Principles and Practices, *IEEE Software,* 8(1), 32–41, January 1991.

[Cohen] Cynthia Cohen, Stanley Birkin, Monica Garfield, and Harold Webb, Managing Conflict in Software Testing, *Communications of the ACM,* 47(1), 76–81, January 2004.

[Covey2] Stephen R. Covey, *The Seven Habits of Highly Effective People*, Fireside Books, 1989.

[Covey1] Stephen R. Covey, *Principle Centered Leadership*, Fireside Books, 1992.

[Laplante] Phillip A. Laplante, Remember the Human Element in IT Project Management, *IT Professional*, Jan./Feb. 2003, pp. 46–50.

[MacDonald] John S. MacDonald, Systems Engineering: Art and Science in an International Context, Keynote speech presented at the 1998 INCOSE Symposium.

[Mayer] Richard J. Mayer, *Conflict Management: The Courage to Confront*, Battelle Press, 1990.

[McGregor] Douglas McGregor, *The Human Side of Enterprise*, McGraw Hill/Irwin, 1960.

[Ouchi] William Ouchi, *Theory Z: How American Management Can Meet the Japanese Challenge*, Avon Books, 1981.

Chapter 5

Management Antipatterns

Management antipatterns are the result of bad managers, management teams, or executives. In some cases, it might just be tolerating or amplifying the debilitating behavior of another team member, such as in Golden Child, Rising Upstart, or Warm Bodies. At other times it is a misguided, incompetent, or even malicious supervisor.

Management antipatterns are different from Bramson's negative personality types. These personality types (or phenotypes, as we call them) describe singular behaviors to specific encounters. Management antipatterns, in contrast, represent patterns of behavior that characterize the individual's management style. Indeed, someone can conform to one of Bramson's personality types and simultaneously exhibit a variety of management antipatterns (for example, an Exploder who is also a Headless Chicken and a Cage Match Negotiator).

Finally, our catalog of management antipatterns expands and complements those of Brown et al. They identified 14 management antipatterns (see Chapter 1), 12 of which are essentially bad management practices (such as E-mail is Dangerous). The remaining two antipatterns, Irrational Manager and Project Mismanagement, are an amalgamation of several, more precise, antipatterns that form the basis of our catalog.

- Absentee Manager
- All You Have Is A Hammer
- Cage Match Negotiator
- Doppelganger
- Fruitless Hoops
- Golden Child
- Headless Chicken
- Leader Not Manager
- Managerial Cloning
- Manager Not Leader
- Metric Abuse
- Mr. Nice Guy
- Mushroom Management
- Plate Spinning
- Proletariat Hero
- Rising Upstart
- Road to Nowhere
- Spineless Executive
- Three-Headed Knight
- Ultimate Weapon
- Warm Bodies

The navigational guide in Chapter 1 will help you diagnose the appropriate antipattern for your particular situation.

And now, on to our management antipatterns.

Name: Absentee Manager

Central Concept

Any manager who engages in avoidance behavior or is invisible for long periods of time — either hiding on premises or away from the office.

Dysfunction

No one wants the constant intrusion of management; it indicates a lack of trust in the workforce, but there are obviously times when management must be visible because they are the primary decision makers. When key managers cannot be found, subordinates are left to make crucial decisions or those decisions are delayed. Either way, the manager's continued absence is hindering, or even damaging the company. Furthermore, it is demoralizing to employees when their boss is not putting in the time. It is one thing to be on the road meeting with customers, vendors, or involved in public relations. It is another thing entirely when the meetings are a cover for personal, or at least nonproductive, dealings. If employees cannot relate the off-work activities of a manager to the requirements of the job, they will resent it. Managers need to understand this. People tire of hearing excuses such as, "Yes, I was playing golf with my brother-in-law, but we might be doing business with him someday."

Before all you telecommuting managers think that we are picking on you, fear not. It is not uncommon today for managers to be physically dislocated from their teams. And it is quite possible to be successful as a manager or leader from afar. But it takes a skilled individual and extra effort to remain connected to the team, accessible, and to maintain a productive and cordial environment. This antipattern, however, is not a knock on telemanagers. It is about those managers who — whether physically co-located with their teams or not — deliberately shirk their duty to stay visible and remain connected to the team.

Vignette

Phil worked at a family-owned software company where the husband and wife owners would disappear, often for days or even weeks at a time, leaving others to make decisions, then undoing those decisions upon their return. To make matters worse, the husband and wife often disagreed and overruled one another's decisions, depending on who happened to be there on a given day. Eventually, the employees would rejoice whenever they arrived at work to discover that neither the husband nor wife's cars were in the parking lot. The apparent lack of work ethic had infected almost the entire company, and it was clearly no longer a productive work environment.

Explanation

The origin of the name of the antipattern is obvious — "you're there, he ain't." But why should this be a problem in this age of telecommuting?

Management by sight or management by walking around is an important management practice. Aside from the fact that much of a manager's job requires direct interaction with the team, customers, peers, etc., it is important that the manager periodically scans the workplace to intercept problems. Moreover, there is something inspirational to the team about seeing the boss working hard. So forget about telecommuting —you might well manage that way, but you really cannot lead effectively that way.

Band Aid

Work around the absent management and, if you feel inclined, fill the vacuum of management and leadership that their absence creates.

Self-Repair

If you are an Absentee Manager — you should be ashamed of yourself. What could be more important than making sure that things are running well back at the office before you go traipsing off to do "business development"?

Refactoring

We have to admit that sometimes an Absentee Manager is a good thing, but only when they already exhibit other management antipatterns that make them ineffective. Perpetuating the situation is still not healthy.

Assuming, however, that the Absentee Manager actually provides value when present, here are some refactorings to increase their visibility and influence:

- Often, Absentee Managers designate a right-hand-man to be their eyes and ears. Find that person and try to work through him.
- Insist on in-person meetings.
- Volunteer the Absent Manager for committees, meetings, and tasks.
- Do not make decisions for Absent Managers — that lets them off the hook.
- Create a situation that forces the Absent Managers to be present or highlights their absence (e.g., birthday celebrations, ad hoc meetings).

Observations

Management absenteeism is frequently found in family-run companies (when the family decides to disappear on a long holiday) or in companies owned by a parent company that does not have a persistent, local management presence.

Cockburn talks about a practice called the "Cone of Silence," in which management cloisters itself away to focus on important items [Cockburn]. There is nothing wrong with this; managerial retreats are useful in isolating managers from their constant distracters. But when the "Cone of Silence" extends for days or even weeks, then it can easily fester into this antipattern.

Identification

The following identification instrument can help determine if your organization has an Absentee Manager. Please respond to the following statements with a "Yes" or "No."

	Yes	No
■ My manager spends more time out of the office than in the office.	—	—
■ When I need to see my manager, I do not go to his office first. I go to his secretary and ask, "Is he in today"?	—	—

	Yes	**No**
■ I resent when my manager is not around because I know it has nothing to do with business or he is deliberately shirking his duties.	—	—
■ My manager is never where he says he is going to be.	—	—

If you responded "Yes" to one or more of these statements, your organization has an Absentee Manager.

References

[Cockburn] Alistair Cockburn, The 'Cone of Silence' and Related Project Management Strategies, Technical Report TR 2003.01, *Humans and Technology*, 2003.

Name: All You Have Is a Hammer

Central Concept

One-dimensional management, where the same techniques are used on all subordinates and in all situations. Sometimes also known as the "One-Trick Pony."

▼

> In the movie "The Brady Bunch Movie" (1995), architect Mike Brady keeps "creating" designs of office buildings, stores, gas stations, etc., but they are all near-replicas of his own home that he had designed.

▲

Dysfunction

Every manager must find his or her own moral compass and follow it diligently; but just as in win-win negotiating, they must understand people's differing win conditions and motivations and tailor their handling accordingly. One of the biggest mistakes you can make is to impose your own values and win conditions on someone else. You might be motivated by money, or title, or whatever… someone else may not be, and assuming that everyone holds the same motivations, anxieties, and needs ensures that most of your subordinates are unhappy and unmotivated.

Vignette

Phil became acquainted with a retired professional football player who played for the NFL's New York Giants from 1984 to 1993, and was coached by the legendary Bill Parcells on two Super Bowl winning teams. Parcells was a notorious "yeller and shouter" on the sidelines and was well known for his overbearing management of quarterback Phil Simms and linebacker Lawrence Taylor. When asked how he dealt with Parcell's heavy handedness, he said, "Oh no, Bill was never harsh with me. At the beginning of the season he sat me down, and told me what he needed from me. That was it. He knew I would deliver without further micromanaging." He went on to indicate that Parcells used different techniques, depending on the needs of the player. This is exactly the opposite of using the "hammer" with each person.

Explanation

This comes from the old saying, "If all you have is a hammer, everything is a nail."

In software engineering circles, it is said that "there is no silver bullet," referring to no single solution or technique that will solve all ills; no methodology, process, model, or technique is appropriate in all situations. Rather, a sophisticated menu of alternatives is needed for each situation, application domain, and environment. Trying to use the same "methodomatic" in all situations is a sure way to send a project into the garbage pile.

The same can be said for leading and managing people. Everyone is different, and it stands to reason that each must be dealt with as such. To do otherwise is a big mistake.

Band Aid

If you are the thumb under your manager's hammer, speak out or get out. If you are the nail for his hammer, however, sit back and learn how *not* to do things.

Self-Repair

Diversify, diversify, diversify. It is not just for investing. It also works for management techniques.

Refactoring

Do not treat people like livestock. Each person is an individual with different needs, different anxieties, and different motivations and goals. The best managers know how to identify these differences and adjust their styles accordingly. Remember that, in reality, if all you have is a hammer, everything is a thumb!

If the manager is not sufficiently self-aware to realize that he needs to work on his perception and empathy, someone else must coach the hammer-wielding manager to adopt a varied management approach. Sometimes, you can inform the manager of what motivates you, and this can lead to a diversification of their tool set. Alternatively, encourage them to:

- Watch more sports — you can learn a lot about management by watching the techniques of different coaches.
- Watch shows such as "The Apprentice," "American Casino," or "American Hot Rod" to learn how *not* to lead and manage.
- Pick up a management book like this one.

Observations

If the situation involves one of software design, then this antipattern is simply Brown et al.'s "Golden Hammer" design antipattern.

Identification

The following identification instrument can help you determine if your organization tends to use one-dimensional management techniques. Please respond to the following statements with a "Yes" or "No."

	Yes	No
■ My manager does not have a "playbook" of solutions for various problems.	—	—
■ Every situation at my place of employment seems to involve a solution looking for a problem.	—	—
■ When I ask my manager how to handle a problem, he just looks at me and shrugs.	—	—
■ My manager gets very confused when faced with new problem situations.	—	—

If you responded "Yes" to one or more of these statements, then all your organization has is a hammer.

Name: Cage Match Negotiator

Central Concept

Any manager who is stubborn beyond reason and employs a "victory at any cost" or "I'm right and you are wrong" approach to management. They often have a coffee mug with the "Rules of Management" across it — Rule #1: The boss is always right. Rule #2: If the boss is wrong, see Rule #1.

Dysfunction

No one can be right all the time; most people are not right even half of the time. So when a manager insists on doing it his way and will not give in during any negotiation, bad things are going to happen. These bad outcomes include erosion in trust, resentment, fear, and feelings of loss for all involved but the "winner."

Vignette

Rod is a software development group manager. Betty is one of his group leaders. Word has come down to Rod that the schedule on one of the deliverables should be accelerated by two weeks. Rod is about to "negotiate" the new schedule with Betty.

Rod: So, we need to complete testing and delivery of that module by March 1st.

Betty: We can do that but the schedule is going to have to slip on the gooey.

Rod: Unacceptable.

Betty: But everyone on my team is already working overtime. Something has to give.

Rod: Nope.

Betty: Can't I release Doug from the Tailspin project for a couple of days to help out?

Rod: Negative on that too.

Betty: But how are we supposed to meet both the new deadline and the GUI deadline with no additional resources or leeway?

Rod: Not my problem. That's your problem.

And so on. Rod isn't going to give an inch. None of Betty's protests are going to persuade him.

Explanation

From the term for a wrestling match or other fight in which two or more persons enter an enclosed ring and only one person may emerge victorious.

The problem here, of course, is that no one can be right all the time. But the Cage Match Negotiator either thinks he is always right, or does not care when he knows he is wrong — but he is the boss. Intransigence is an unattractive quality in a leader and that does not build loyalty in those around the "know-it-all." It is an important tactic in negotiating to give in a little, and the same is true as a manager. If you do not let others win from time to time and soon, no one will want to "play" the game with you. Instead, they will work against and around you.

Band Aid

Surrender easily to the Cage Match Negotiator. You are likely only to waste energy and build frustration battling with them.

Self-Repair

As we discuss in the section on good negotiating, the best negotiators know that it is best to allow your opponent to walk away feeling that he, she, or they got something; otherwise, they will resent the outcome no matter what.

Refactoring

Refactoring Cage Match Negotiators can be very difficult because, like Sherman Tanks phenotype, they like the thrill of battle as much as winning. They refuse to budge except occasionally in the face of incontrovertible logic.

To deal with them, you can use some of the coping strategies discussed in Chapter 2 for dealing with difficult people, especially Sherman Tanks, Bulldozers, and Negativists. For example, in the vignette, Betty could have tried to get Rod into a problem-solving mode (rather than the reactionary "no" mode that he was in). But these are coping strategies, not long-term solutions. Ultimately, these individuals must be removed. Until then, try to focus their stubborn, win-at-all-costs attitude to your benefit.

Finally, sometimes half a loaf is better than no loaf — so be prepared to compromise rather than be stuck at an impasse. It could be that you are being perceived as the immovable one.

Observations

Strength of character and firmness of purpose are admirable, but these should not be mistaken for undue stubbornness. So, there is some measure of art (and a removal of your own personal biases) to discern between valuable firmness and destructive stubbornness.

The 2300-year-old text, *The Art of War* [Tzu], has been used as a basis for management and negotiating principles for many years. One of the basic principles contained therein is that the best-won battles are those that are won without a fight (e.g., through successful negotiation or surrender of the opponent). The best leaders (and martial artists, for that matter) do not look for fights — they look to avoid confrontation. This principle suggests that directly engaging the Cage Match Negotiator is the last thing that you want to do.

Identification

The following identification instrument can help you determine if your manager engages in Cage Match negotiating. Please respond to the following statements with a "Yes" or "No."

	Yes	No
■ There is never any give and take with my boss — it is always "his way or the highway."	___	___
■ My boss never admits when he is wrong.		
■ I know that if my opinion is different from my boss, it is better to just agree with him.	___	___
■ My boss seems to make up his mind before he is even given any facts.	___	___

If you responded "Yes" to one or more of these statements, your manager is a Cage Match Negotiator.

References

[Tzu]   Sun Tzu, *The Art of War,* (R.D. Sawyer translation), Boulder, Westview, 1994.

Name: Doppelganger

Central Concept

A manager or colleague who can be nice and easy to work with one moment, and then vicious and unreasonable the next. A Dr. Jekyll and Mr. Hyde personality that dominates a manager's style.

Dysfunction

While a Doppelganger might otherwise be skilled in his or her job, the split personality leaves colleagues confused and in fear, and can destroy an otherwise happy work environment.

Vignette

A great example of a Doppelganger was captured in an experience report from a graduate student, Larry, who worked for a boutique software company.

One Monday, Larry went to see his boss Jane to get permission to attend a conference. She heartily approved, offered to pay all expenses and to extend a deadline on a project deliverable to allow him to attend.

The following Friday, Larry went in to see Jane to have the paperwork signed. He was met by Jane's "evil twin." "How can you think of only yourself when the project report is overdue," she screamed. Larry tried to defend himself, "But Monday you said it was OK, and you said that the deadline could be extended...." "Shut up Larry! Get out of here and I don't want to hear about this stupid conference again," she raged.

On the following Monday, Larry runs into Jane on the way in. "Oh hi, Larry. I never got the travel authorizations for that conference you wanted to go to. Please get them to me today; I've been holding last week's budget report so I can include those costs." A shocked Larry replies, "Uh, OK...." Unfortunately, the previous Friday afternoon he had cancelled his travel plans for the conference.

Explanation

From the German for "double walker," or evil twin.

Nothing is more difficult to deal with than uncertainty. It would be easier to work with someone who is uniformly mean (because you can structure your responses to him accordingly) than to work with someone whose behavior is unpredictable. With someone who is usually cranky, for example, you can learn what his "hot buttons" are and avoid them. But when someone becomes demonic for unknown reasons, you must always be overly cautious and nonconfrontational.

Band Aid

Hide and pick your moments to go in (ask the secretary when it is safe).

Self-Repair

Doppelgangers do not know that they have dual personalities. They must be told. So, listen to what confidantes are telling you. They might be indirectly trying to tell you that you have a split personality. If you do, you need to be conscious of it and work to join your two halves. If you cannot, you need psychiatric help!

Refactoring

It is possible that the Doppelganger situation is a temporary one brought on by tremendous stress at home or at work. If you can discover the causes of this stress, you might be able to serve as a friend and confidante to the Doppelganger, which increases the likelihood that you will only have to deal with the "good" personality. Other refactorings include:

- Approach the Doppelganger *en masse* rather than individually (strength in numbers).
- Stand up to them using one of the techniques we described for handling the Bulldozer or Exploder personality type. It is possible that by showing some resistance, the negative personality will retreat.
- Promote fellowship and civility in the company and make it more difficult for the evil Doppelganger to emerge. Codes of conduct or civility can help.
- As a worst-case scenario, you can isolate the Doppelganger.
- Throw someone under the bus... if you are evil, you can use the evil half of the Doppelganger to neutralize an unwanted colleague or even boss.

Finally, if your organization is suffering from Institutional Mistrust, Doppelganger behavior emerges as a coping strategy. Fixing the greater trust issues can significantly ease the situation.

Observations

It is quite possible that the Doppelganger personality type is somewhat of a ruse — the manager is using the "good cop, bad cop" technique, using himself as both good and bad cop. But this kind of charade cannot be kept up for long, and one can quickly discover if the individual is a true Doppelganger or simply acting the part to serve a purpose.

Identification

The following identification instrument can help you determine if Ed is a Doppelganger. Please respond to the following statements "Yes" or "No."

	Yes	No
■ Before going to meet with Ed, you ask someone else if is he in a good mood today.	___	___
■ After an encounter with Ed, you wonder what is bothering him today.	___	___
■ You find yourself spending vast amounts of time planning and scripting your meetings with Ed.	___	___
■ You need to use the bathroom before and after you meet with Ed.	___	___

If you responded "Yes" to one or more of these statements, then you are probably dealing with a Doppelganger.

Name: Fruitless Hoops

Central Concept

You are jumping through Fruitless Hoops when managers keep requesting endless data from you before they make a decision. Each time you deliver, they want more and you do not know why.

Dysfunction

There are two significant problems with Fruitless Hoops:

1. Many managers keep requesting more and more data because there is never enough for them to be confident about any decision making or action. This allows the Three-Headed Knight to skate by unnoticed.
2. The time spent by everyone jumping through the Fruitless Hoops is time that could be spent in productive work. Staff who feel that their time is wasted in Fruitless Hoops or endless Plate Spinning will find more interesting things to do and will soon be working toward Divergent Goals.

The main difference between Fruitless Hoops and Plate Spinning is that the former is not really a deliberate delay tactic, while the latter is. For whatever reason, Fruitless Hoops managers are overly analytical and data driven. Perhaps it is because they like the activity of analysis. Or, perhaps quite simply, they are a Thinking type and you are a Feeling type — you "feel" something is the right decision; they need data to justify it.

It is possible that the data-driven manager may not really be looking for real facts. Instead, he has already made up his mind and he is just looking for a set of facts that confirms his position. Others use hoop jumping almost as a coercion technique that can be very frustrating for their staff (recall the apocryphal story of the U.S. Secretary of State in Chapter 2).

Vignette

The following situation involves a software development group led by Larry. Now, Larry is not a bad guy; he just does not always listen to people and when he makes up his mind, it cannot be changed. One day he returns from a seminar on software metrics — it is just an overview and certainly not in-depth enough for him to begin to establish a real metrics program. But all of a sudden he wants to collect metrics. He demands a daily count of function points coded or reworked from each of his developers. Soon, he is asking his team to use some automated tools to compute the cyclomatic complexity of each code module (past and present). Then he is asking his team to track delta lines of code for all projects.

In each case, his team complies. And each time he asks for more. Soon, the team is overwhelmed with the data collection — and yet they have no idea what Larry is doing with it. When one of the senior developers, Barb, steps up to ask what all the data is for, Larry replies, "I'm starting a metrics program; just keep collecting the data." This goes on and on until Barb and some of the other better developers leave in disgust, and those who are left are doing little more than collecting "useless" data.

Explanation

The derivation of the name is suggestive of all kinds of images from a famous "fruity" cereal, to the obstacle course at a dog show in which the trained animals jump through a series of hoops. Whatever the case, the connotation is one of nonproductive (fruitless) effort that could be better spent.

Band Aid

Hide! Let someone else be the data-donkey. Data-driven managers will send you through Fruitless Hoops when they get the chance, so do not give them that chance.

Self-Repair

If you need to collect data, that is great. But you should explain to your staff why it is being collected and what it is going to be used for. Unless you do that, every data request will appear fruitless.

Refactoring

Generally speaking, you should manage your manager by being persistent and requesting precise instructions whenever you are sent away for more data. You should also ask them what it is being used for. This will help you appreciate the task, and you might be able to suggest more appropriate alternative data to your manager. For example, ask questions such as, "What specific data do you need?" "What trends are you looking for?" "Over what period should I gather, and how would you like it presented?"

If you allow the Fruitless Hoops manager to keep getting what he wants, he will exhaust you. But with an honest manager, you will eventually wear him down and he will be satisfied — provided you can support your position with data.

Identification

The following identification instrument can help you determine if your manager is making you jump through Fruitless Hoops. Please respond to the following statements with a "Yes" or "No."

	Yes	No
■ I provide data to my manager and I have no idea what it is used for.	___	___
■ I spend more time collecting data about X than actually doing X (for some necessary activity X).	___	___
■ No one else I know, who is doing the same job I am, collects the kind of data that I do.	___	___
■ I have never satisfied a data request from my manager on the first try — he always wants more, more, more.	___	___

If you responded "Yes" to one or more of these statements, your manager is probably making you jump through Fruitless Hoops.

Name: Golden Child

Central Concept

The Golden Child exists in situations where a manager or a person in a position of leadership provides special responsibility, opportunity, recognition, or reward to a member of their team based on a personal relationship with the individual and contrary to the person's actual performance. While the "Golden Child" is annoying, the true problem lies in the manager.

Dysfunction

Golden Child relationships tend to negatively impact team morale and may cause animosity to develop between team members. A lack of trust can develop between management and the team. Additionally, newer team members find it difficult to become integrated, and many individuals start to feel under-appreciated and underused. The existence of the Golden Child can also disrupt the normal evolution of the team through Tuckman's phases of formation.

The worst kind of Golden Child is one whose efforts no longer contribute to a team's success, but actually hinder it. Not all Golden Children, however, must have a negative impact on the team's productivity; it is an imbalance of reward and performance level that creates a Golden Child relationship.

Vignette

Who has not known a Golden Child? We have seen them in every organization we ever worked in — at times, it has even been us. Of course, in those situations, the credit and candor that came with this status was well-deserved ☺.This is obviously not always the case, however, and even that situation was probably the source of discontent and resentment among our peers. It would be difficult to describe our own situations without considerable bias; so instead, we will use an alternative example.

Chad is a middle-manager at a Fortune 500 company with about 20 direct reports ranging from senior engineers to junior clerical staff. In the course of normal staff turnover, Chad hired a new clerical assistant, Ellie, with responsibilities including customer liaison and sales support. Almost immediately, Chad was treating Ellie like his long-lost daughter and she was soon the effective second-in-command of Chad's department. Every meeting, regardless of the topic, included Ellie and every decision was run by her. Her role was unofficially expanded within a few months to include advising on department strategy, role assignments, and new hires. Very quickly, resentment grew toward both Chad and Ellie. Chad was resented by his senior staff members who were now outside the decision making, while Ellie garnered resentment from her peers who felt she was receiving undue favoritism.

The net result was a rift between Chad and Ellie and the rest of the department. This isolation made Ellie's primary role of liaison very difficult, thus impacting her effectiveness. It also led to Divergent Goals within the department as the recently disenfranchised senior staff rejected the new strategic objectives and ethos coming from their leadership. Ultimately, Chad's leadership eroded as the faith and respect of his team evaporated. When Chad was finally Department Head no longer, Ellie was completely isolated from the rest of the team because of the pent-up resentment.

Explanation

Interestingly, not all Golden Children know they are receiving special treatment, and not all of their managers know they are doing it either. Many of these relationships develop over an extended period of time and usually begin deservingly, only devolving into the antipattern when loyalty and reward cease to be based on tangible performance and instead become simply habit.

Some common examples of Golden Children include:

- Employees who repeatedly receive more recognition than they seem to earn or deserve
- Lower-level managers or team leaders who were promoted on the heels of their manager's promotions but who seriously lack managerial skills
- Lazy team contributors who nonetheless are held in positions of high regard and whose opinions must be appeased during decision-making processes
- Employees who seem to have the ear of management, but use it as a means of shifting blame, avoiding accountability, or getting their way
- Employees who belong to their manager's inner circle, yet do not demonstrate the traits or abilities that purportedly got them there

Band Aid

An effective short-term fix really depends on your disposition.

1. *Ignore it.* If it has little impact on you personally, do not worry about the unfair advancement of others. Viewing your professional life as a competition is a surefire route to disappointment. And eventually, the luster of the Golden Child will wear off — perhaps when they mess up, when a new Golden Child appears, or when the novelty wears off.
2. *Isolate it.* If the incompetents who are benefiting from the cronyism are actually disruptive or damaging, it is sometimes easier to work behind the scenes to get things done.
3. *Complain.* Incompetent managers that get drawn into Golden Child adoption can be managed by you too. Be the squeaky wheel that gets the oil.

Self-Repair

If you are the Golden Child, it probably feels pretty good. But realize that you may be collecting enemies by the special treatment. You might try to help your manager be more inclusive and even point out when you are receiving undeserved favoritism.

If you are a manager with a Golden Child, consider the ramifications of this situation. You are better off without a Golden Child.

Refactoring

When dealing with a Golden Child situation, the awareness of the involved parties must be taken into account. Usually, there are only two parties involved in each Golden Child relationship: (1) a manager and (2) an employee. There are four possible scenarios that can therefore occur:

1. Neither party is aware of the situation.
2. The employee is aware but the manager is not.
3. The manager is aware but the employee is not.
4. Both parties are aware.

In cases where neither party is cognizant of the relationship, a simple meeting with the manager may be sufficient. The situation should be gently brought to the manager's attention. This can most likely be accomplished by stating honest observations and concerns.

If only one of the individuals is aware of the relationship, it is most likely going to be the employee and not the manager. This is because the employee will probably have had to exert some effort to keep the manager in the dark, usually along the lines of inflating their accomplishments, misappropriating credit, and informing the manager of other employees' performances. In this case, again, a conversation with the manager may be enough to rectify the situation.

If it is the manager, however, who is knowledgeable of the relationship, it may be more difficult to rectify the situation. There is a possibility that when called on it, the manager will cease and desist, but that eventuality is certainly not guaranteed.

The worst situation for attempting to break up a Golden Child relationship is the case where both parties are aware of the relationship. In such a scenario, it can be extremely difficult to improve the situation; any action taken may actually make things worse.

As a rule, it is probably best in all of these scenarios to try and be as aware as possible of the relationships that exist between any of the involved parties. The best approach for rectifying the situation is communication. That communication can certainly be directly with the manager or the Golden Child, but it could also extend to additional parties within the organization such as other managers and human resource representatives. It is, of course, a good idea to be respectful of the individuals spoken to and spoken about. It is also important to be aware of the fact that taking action involves the risk that the situation could worsen.

Identification

The following identification instrument can help you determine if you or someone you know is a Rising Upstart. Please respond to the following statements with a "Yes" or "No" concerning hypothetical Golden Child, Ellie.

	Yes	**No**
■ I do not know why, but Ellie seems to be included in every decision, even in areas that do not affect her.	——	——
■ Ellie and the boss seem to be tied at the waist.	——	——
■ I do not know when Ellie actually gets her real duties done — she seems to be involved in everything but her job, and with the boss' encouragement.	——	——
■ Ellie has been acting like she is the boss lately — she even has started ordering people around who do not report to her.	——	——

If you responded "Yes" to one or more of these statements, Ellie is likely a Golden Child.

Name: Headless Chicken[1]

Central Concept

A very confused manager who lacks focus, has no plan, and never follows through with anything.

Dysfunction

Confused behavior; trying this idea and that; running from one problem to another, without focus. Those observing the Headless Chicken performance are themselves confused and demoralized.

Vignette

In Phil's early days of academic administration, he worked under a Headless Chicken. The college was struggling in all aspects, from attracting students to retaining faculty, and the Headless Chicken was panicking, worried for his job. Every week started with a four-hour executive meeting where Department Heads would gather with the Headless Chicken to try and come up with a strategy for recovery...every week. You cannot strategize every week; that is tactical management. What tactics came out of these meetings? Well, each week brought a new degree program idea, a suite of new responsibility for the Department Heads, the faculty, and the staff. Staff members were reassigned to new groups one week, then moved again the next. Advisory panels were constituted from local company executives, then faculty members were pulled together for creative brainstorming sessions, then student groups were asked what they wanted and needed. Each group would present a raft of suggestions, but within weeks all were discarded as the Headless Chicken relentlessly moved from idea to idea.

In case you were wondering, it did not work out too well for the Headless Chicken; he was soon "reassigned." It was the motivating factor that propelled Phil into senior administration, however; so at least one good thing came from it. As we have said repeatedly, leaders emerge naturally when times are tough and that happened here.

Explanation

When butchering a chicken, sometimes the headless body can continue to move, and even run for minutes after decapitation. We have never witnessed this event — thankfully.

The problem with the Headless Chicken is that he has no apparent plan (see Road to Nowhere). This perceived lack of planning prevents him from gaining the full support of his team, and retards his ability to help that team through its normal formation sequence. Because you cannot follow someone if he does not know where he is going, those observing the Headless Chicken's performance are themselves confused and demoralized.

Band Aid

Stay out of the Chicken's way or try to keep up with him (or her).

Self-Repair

Listen to those around you. Stop and think about what you are doing. Cost-justify each decision you make.

Refactoring

Somehow the Headless Chickens must be made to realize that they are headless. Maybe a close confidante can tell them. Maybe they can be made to realize it on their own. You can also try to document the sequence of the haphazard decisions to show how ridiculous it appears. But if the Headless Chicken does not come to his senses, the organization (that manager, anyway) is doomed and the only other solution is to find a way for upper management to put the chicken out of his misery, or for you to flee.

It may be that the Headless Chicken is simply a very badly organized person, in which case you might be able to mentor him by:

■ Providing information to him in a better, more organized form
■ Being more clear in your communications with him
■ Trying to anticipate his confusion and head it off
■ Praising and thanking him when he exhibits behaviors that are not true to form
■ Trying to give him more time and information when you need him to make a decision

Other general refactorings for the Headless Chicken include:

■ Provide the manager with a plan — he might be grateful for it.
■ Try to engage the manager in a planning process.
■ Seek and force feedback from the manager.

Identification

The following identification instrument can help you determine if your manager is a Headless Chicken. Please respond to the following statements with a "Yes" or "No."

	Yes	No
■ I come to work each day asking myself, "What now?"	___	___
■ If I were to document a sequence of decisions that my manager made, it would look ridiculous.	___	___
■ My company's "strategy" is like no other, and I don't mean that as a compliment.	___	___
■ I wish I understood what my manager wants to do.	___	___

If you responded "Yes" to one or more of these statements, then your manager is a Headless Chicken.

Name: Leader Not Manager

Central Concept

Manager Not Leader stresses the importance of effective leadership by supervisors, managers, and executives; but being a great leader does not necessarily mean being a great manager. This antipattern illustrates the problem of having vision but no plan.

Dysfunction

An absence of effective management manifests itself in:

- Poorly considered, myopic plans
- Unrealistic budgets
- Staffing problems (bad hires, unsatisfactory schedules)
- Unfocused workers
- Missed targets and deadlines
- General firefighting and chaos

Vignette

Because many workers resent administration and those who work in it, they rarely give credit to great managers. Indeed, they rarely even notice them. Consequently, it is also rare for people to notice poor administration unless it is accompanied by a lack of leadership or an abundance of aggression, derision, control, or suppression. These problems are the source of most of the other antipatterns, however. This antipattern is concerned with the well-intentioned, perhaps even inspirational leader who, through either a lack of aptitude, training, or concern, struggles with the daily administration required in teams or on projects.

Perhaps the most famous example of a Leader Not Manager was Sir Winston Churchill. His leadership throughout World War II was critical to the Allied success, but his lack of planning and preparation was the source of many mistakes, including the Allied invasion of Norway in 1940. He was also considered a lamentable Prime Minister in peacetime following the war and is thought by many to be responsible for the collapse of the British Empire.

While not as inspirational and transformational as Churchill, one Department Head we have known equally epitomized the Leader Not Manager. Martin was a charismatic, funny guy who was universally respected and liked by his staff and peers. He oozed positivism and charm but matched it with:

- *Tardiness* — he was always late for appointments and meetings.
- *Budget incompetence* — his department spent its annual budget a little over nine months into the fiscal year.
- *Missed targets* — the department suffered the largest backlog of work in the organization, but also missed the most delivery deadlines.

Essentially, Martin was incapable of planning his own day and this extended into his department. Without a plan, the staff never focused on a particular task or project and instead worked on anything that interested them at the time. Martin's enthusiasm for innovation and creativity prevented him from intervening, so he never leveraged his considerable influence. He did not last.

Explanation

Inspiring leadership is very important, but so are the day-to-day operations of an organization, project, or team and to do them effectively requires

Table 5.1 Geisler's Illustration of Leadership versus Management Competencies

According to...	A Manager...	A Leader...
Warren Bennis	Promotes efficiency	Promotes effectiveness
	Is a good soldier	Is his or her own person
	Imitates	Originates
	Accepts the status quo	Challenges
	Does things right	Does the right things
John Kotter	Copes with complexity	Copes with change
	Plans and budgets	Sets a direction
	Organizes and staffs	Aligns people
	Controls and problem-solves	Motivates people

management acumen that even great leaders can lack. Some might view these tasks as drudgery, but while leaders inspire, managers organize, plan, supervise, and advise.

Jill Geisler condensed the observations of two of the most prominent leadership scholars, as shown in Table 5.1 [Geisler].

She goes on to remark that these characterizations would make being a manager, and not a leader, sound almost derogatory...that the term "manager" is almost pejorative. This is not true at all. We certainly hope that our leaders are managers, just as we hope our managers are leaders. But leadership does not subsume management, it complements it. Management is concerned with:

■ Work schedules
■ Internal and external communication
■ Procuring tools and technology
■ Hiring
■ Training
■ Evaluating
■ Holding people accountable
■ Developing systems

It should be emphasized that while many management and administrative tasks are not exactly exhilarating, it is a grave disservice to, as Rost put it, "denigrate management to ennoble leadership" [Rost].

Band Aid

Divide and conquer. Give the management tasks to someone else, leaving the leader to focus on broader issues. This is actually a great opportunity to mentor a junior- or middle-manager.

Self-Repair

Get an administrative assistant who can help with schedules and budgets.

Refactoring

Effective leaders are in short supply so discarding them is usually not an option — far better to rehabilitate them. It can be as simple as encouraging professional development in the areas of budgeting, organizational management, and planning. These are taught in business schools but many emergent leaders are not business majors or MBAs; they are promoted from their professional areas into management positions.

Of course, not everyone is detail-oriented and task-focused; so despite training, some will not be able to plan, budget, or schedule. In these situations, the band aid might be the only option. For those few leaders who refuse to modify their habits — the ones who actually like chaos because it obfuscates their personal objectives and activities — it might be time for them to move on.

Identification

The following identification instrument can help you determine if Doug is a leader but not a manager. Please respond to the following statements with a "Yes" or "No."

	Yes	No
■ Doug has a clear vision of his goals but he frustrates me with his disorganization.	___	___
■ Although I will do anything for Doug, I am tired of our group's failures.	___	___
■ Doug is well liked but he is not well respected.	___	___
■ Doug's group is consistently outperformed by others, even those whose managers are despised.	___	___

If you responded "Yes" to one or more of these statements, then Doug is probably a leader but not a manager.

References

[Geisler]   J. Geisler, Are You a Manager, Leader, or Both?, *Poynter Online*, The Poynter Institute, available at http://www.poynter.org/column.asp?id=34&aid=62579.

[Rost]   J.C. Rost, *Leadership for the Twenty-First Century,* Praeger, 1991.

Name: Manager Not Leader

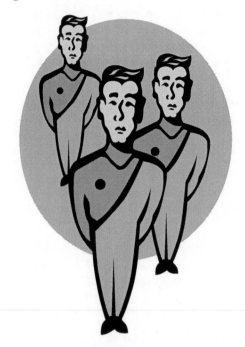

"Managers are people who do things right, while leaders are people who do the right thing."

**—Warren Bennis,
"On Becoming a Leader" [Bennis]**

Central Concept

The manager who is proficient at administrative and managerial duties but lacks leadership ability.

Dysfunction

When things are going well, the leadership shortcomings of those in charge are diminished and the organization can function satisfactorily. In tough times, however, it takes a leader to rally the troops, maintain morale, and ultimately make the difficult decisions. When the managerial staff lacks leadership, the natural leaders in the group will become apparent. This can be a significant hindrance to the manager and can cause conflict, dissension, and possibly even insurrection.

Of course, a coup d'etat is an extreme reaction against poor leadership, and spectacular failure of an organization is unlikely. A lack of leadership can result in a number of negative consequences, however:

- Meandering strategy; tactical rather than strategic focus.
- Low morale in the workforce, reduced productivity.
- In-fighting with and between departments. The forming of cliques and silos.
- Lost competitive advantage and market share.

Vignette

This antipattern can occur at many levels within an organization and, in fact, is unfortunately too prevalent. Managerial positions are coveted by power-hungry individuals with little leadership potential, but considerable drive and ruthless endeavor. In one small department of a medium-sized enterprise, we know that both the department head and his senior associate were Managers Not Leaders, as was the chief executive.

Too many times, the senior associate would complain how his assistants were never working hard enough. Whenever they were not in direct line of sight, they would become distracted, instant messaging their friends, making personal telephone calls or off to the coffee machine was his claim. "I will give them tasks to do, but I do not know if they ever get them done," was a common refrain as he bemoaned the reporting structure to the department head, who nodded in agreement. "If they do not report to me, how can I control them," he continued. "Well, they are all lazy down there, and they do not respect their superiors," replied the department head as he nodded further.

Both failed to recognize that if they were really leaders, their subordinates would be followers. They had no personal leverage with the staff to ensure that work got done; they had failed to motivate their staff and to instill personal satisfaction and reward for completing tasks. In fact, their first and last resort was direct oversight, command, and control.

This type of Manager Not Leader can be found in abundance on reality television shows. Boyd Coddington, the owner of the hotrod builders featured in *American Hotrod* on The Discovery Channel, constantly berates and subjugates his employees while proclaiming he maintains a positive working atmosphere.

Ninya Perna, the Hotel Operations Manager from American Casino on the same channel, is often portrayed in an even worse light. In one episode, Perna is berated by her supervisor, the late Michael Tata, because the arrival schedules and plans for some "high rollers" arriving at the hotel that day were not up to standard. She called her junior managers to a meeting and hauled them over the carpet for getting it wrong and told them she expected better. When there was another problem with the next day's plan, the gloves really came off. Perna practically keel-hauled her junior managers with relentless, crude, and derogatory abuse and she did this in front of the Vice President so that she could demonstrate her own passion and fire. The tongue-lashing culminated in Perna telling her staff that because they were incapable of performing their duties in a five-day week, she was extending it to a six-day working week and anyone who did not turn up on the sixth day was effectively resigning!

————————————▼————————————

Perna: I called another mandatory meeting with my managers because of all the errors that were made last evening in light of the packet.

Tata: Ninya had a meeting with you guys and it was a very serious meeting. It's gotten to the point where she needs my help, so she's come to me.

Perna: They get paid a certain amount of money to do a job that they are here to do, and they don't do it. I'm not gonna tolerate any more ignorance. This morning we distributed a packet with a sight-inspection sheet that no one could read.

Sue: It couldn't get any darker. I went to every copier, and that's just how it printed out.

Perna: You print it off of your computer, or you type it out. I expect Justin, as a senior member of this management team, to help us solve the problem, but once again, he is sitting there, saying nothing and not offering any solutions. Seriously, Michael made a big recommendation today.

Tata: I told Ninya, "At this point, if I were you, I would put everyone on a six-day work week."

Justin: Absolutely not. There's no way.

Perna: Well, too bad.

Justin: I'm working ten-, twelve-hour days. There's no way I'm gonna do a six-day week.

Perna: Then you need to find alternative employment because it's not an option for any of you. You will all work six days. What do I need to do in this operation to make it run? Why don't you three understand that this is affecting this operation, and it is no longer acceptable? This lack of urgency is no longer acceptable; and if all of you need to put in your resignation, fill it out right now and resign your position. I am sick of it. Done, finished, over. I had a meeting yesterday and discussed these issues. Why do I have to discuss them again today? What is your rebuttal? Seriously, this is ridiculous. I'm being confronted by the vice president as to why this operation doesn't run. It is no longer going be tolerated. And you will work six days a week, or all of you put in your resignations right now. I will work your shift, I will work your shift, and I will work your shift, because then I will at least be accountable for what happens around here.

Justin: I think you guys are being very unreasonable. We work very hard for you. We work ten hours a day.

Perna: Don't be insubordinate. If you're not here on Sunday...

Justin: There's no way. I work way too hard.

Perna: Thank you to the senior manager of this operation for making an [bleep] of yourself.

Justin: I'm the [bleep]?

━━━━━━━━━━━━━━━━▲━━━━━━━━━━━━━━━━

Explanation

We could not ask for a more obvious demonstration of Manager Not Leader than Captain Bligh, the overthrown captain of the HMS Bounty. Bligh has been described as someone of "poor leadership, uneven temper, insensitive, humorless, abusive, and prone to nag worse than a fishwife" but also as an "excellent navigator, brilliant cartographer, superior seaman, brave in the face of danger, and follows his orders to a fault." While Fletcher Christian was perhaps not the most enigmatic leader either, his empathy for his fellow crew members, and his vision for a better life, demonstrated sufficient leadership potential for him to lead the mutiny and overthrow Bligh's command. Christian and his fellow mutineers eventually settled on Pitcairn Island and we will see how that turned out a little later.

We talk a lot about poor management or lack of leadership as though we are describing the same thing; but while they are very related and we always hope for bosses and decision makers to have considerable ability in both, they are not the same. Effective management is the efficient use of resources to effectively execute a plan. The larger the plan, the greater the scope and responsibility of the manager ... hence middle-managers. There are no middle-leaders, however. Leadership is a much less tangible, yet far more obvious attribute. Some of us lead, some follow, and that is how it should be. Can someone be an effective manager without being an inspiring leader? Absolutely. Equally, someone not managing can be an effective leader — indeed, leaders emerge regardless of their rank in an organization.

John Gardner examined the concept of leadership and determined that there are a number of functions and attributes of leadership, as shown in Table 5.2 [Gardner].

Table 5.2   Functions and Attributes of Leadership

Leadership Functions	Leadership Attributes
Envisioning goals	Action oriented
Motivating others towards those goals	Adaptable
Managing the process for reaching those goals	Assertive
	Courageous
Affirming and regenerating group values	Decisive
Achieving unity	Eager to accept responsibility
Creating an atmosphere of trust	Empathetic
Explaining and teaching	Great people skills
Serving as a symbol of the group's identity	Motivator
Representing the group's interests to external entities	Physically fit
	Self-confident
Adapting the organization to the changing world	Task competent
	Trustworthy

Band Aid

Generally, although certainly not ideal, being supervised or managed by a Manager Not Leader will not be the downfall of an organization, department, or team, so fear not. It is unlikely that as an individual you can change the situation unless you are a natural leader, in which case your influence will eventually come to the fore anyway.

Self-Repair

Adopt a leader. If you cannot become one, you will need to find one: a friend with natural leadership ability that shares your philosophy and beliefs.

Refactoring

Despite common perceptions, leadership is not a simile for control, responsibility, power, or official authority. One does not become a leader merely because one has direct reports or a chain of command; the potential must be innate. Leadership, as the functions and attributes listed in Table 5.2 indicate, is about motivation, vision, unity, and trust, so these must be the focus of any refactorings.

- Organizations must work to identify the natural leaders within, and this can be difficult in the absence of a catastrophe. Why? Because explosive events force the leaders to emerge, but slow-burn decay such as in the Boiling Frog Syndrome does not. Seek out individuals who their peers, superiors, and subordinates trust; turn to for help and to rely on.
- Emergent leaders still need to be trained. While naturally disposed to motivate and unify, naïve leaders must learn how to articulate their vision, be steadfast in the face of cynicism, and to focus on long-range strategic issues rather than tactical minutiae.
- Be wary of self-promoters. Leadership is a desirable characteristic, so it is not uncommon for would-be despots to present themselves as natural leaders. Remember that actions speak louder than words. Work to empower the genuine leaders, not the charlatan.

Identification

The following identification instrument can help you determine if you are dealing with a manager and not a leader. Please respond to the following statements with a "Yes" or "No."

	Yes	No
■ I cannot make an important decision in the absence of my boss.	___	___
■ When I need advice, I do not really want my boss' opinion.	___	___
■ I often worry that whatever I do will be second-guessed by my boss.	___	___
■ I really do not know what my boss wants from one day to the next.	___	___

If you responded "Yes" to one or more of these statements, you are probably dealing with a manager and not a leader.

References

[Gardner]   J.W. Gardner, *On Leadership*, Free Press, 1989.
[Bennis]   Warren Bennis, *On Becoming a Leader*, Perseus Books Group, 1994.

Name: Managerial Cloning

Central Concept

Middle managers tend to act like their bosses over time.

Dysfunction

Whether the transformation to be like the manager is a deliberate one or happens accidentally is unclear, and may differ based upon the situation in any case. Regardless, managerial cloning has a chilling effect on creativity as it can lead to groupthink and it amplifies negative personality characteristics and bad management practices.

Vignette

In Manager Not Leader, the lack of leadership skills exhibited by Ninya Perna from The Discovery Channel's *American Casino* are highlighted; but in fairness to Perna, she did learn from another Theory X manager, Vice President of Hotel Operations, Michael Tata. He would often use sarcasm and condescension in his dealings with her and his other subordinates. In fact, he went so far as to use an intended reward mechanism as a punishment and symbol of incompetence. The casino rewards good performance with ceremonial "Championship Chips," but Tata would "reward" these to his subordinates in a grotesque display of feigned congratulations whenever they made a mistake. We cannot think of a worse way to contort a positive into a negative, and it is no surprise that Perna displays the same spiteful traits. The following excerpt from the show illustrates the point.

─────────────────── ▼ ───────────────────

Tata ridiculing Perna with sarcasm over leaving the hotel to let her dogs out and one of her managers messing up.

Perna: Marcel? How could he have screwed up?

Tata: You tell me. He reports directly to you. It is your responsibility to train your staff about how we escort a VIP here.

Perna Well, I will talk to him as soon as I get back.

Tata: While you're letting your dogs out? Take your time. Nothing else is going on here. Don't worry about it. Make sure they have water, too.

Perna dreads her meeting with Tata. Tata then uses a reward mechanism as a ridiculing punishment.

Perna: Michael has called me in for a meeting that I'm definitely dreading. But I've taken care of it; so if he lays into me, I'm not gonna take it.

Tata: Regarding the situation with our VIP guest, what have you done since I spoke to you about it?

Perna: You asked me to prepare an acknowledgment form.

Tata: I asked you to prepare an acknowledgment form.

Perna: Oh, guess what? I prepared one.

Tata: You know who I would start with?

Perna: My managers and Marcel.

Tata: Thank you.

Perna: I've already talked to him as well and he made a judgment call, and I congratulate him on a judgment call. It just happened to be the wrong kind. There you go. I encourage them. They're empowered.

Tata: That usually makes things go a lot smoother. Keep up the good work. Good job. Empowerment is different from stupidity.

Perna: He actually took on the initiative of taking care of her other inquiries.

Tata: Oh, he sent a newspaper. Where he goes, to my alma mater, I'm quite scared of the type of people they're producing out of the university because they taught me a little bit more than sending a newspaper to a room as a huge achievement. Hey, Marcel? Ninya brought to my attention that you went above and beyond by sending a newspaper to a guest, so I just wanted to give you a Championship Chip. Thank you for going out of your way. Keep up the good work and tell the professors at UNLV that I'm very proud of them.

Perna tries to speak up for her junior but Tata again is unprofessional in his handling (using Dr. Evil speech).

Perna: However, …

Tata: Nails on the chalkboard. Shh!

Perna: Very good. Anything else?

Tata: No, I'm done with you.

Perna: Can I go and walk my dogs?

Tata: You can do whatever you want with your dogs. Have them put to sleep [laughs].

————————————▲————————————

Explanation

Bosses (the stupid ones anyway) will hire subordinates who have identical perspectives on the world, exhibit the same habits, etc. It is as if they are cloning themselves, flaws and all.

---▼---

Wise Alec!

There is an old joke about a young man who cannot find a girlfriend who can please his mother. Finally, he meets a young lady who acts just like his mother, has the same background, and even looks and sounds like her. His mother loved the girl!

His father hated her.

---▲---

Consider an organization where the hiring process is set up to encourage this kind of practice. Perhaps personality testing is used and only those who conform to a certain profile are hired. In other cases, only those who graduated from a certain university are hired and no others.

Everyone goes through the same management training as well; and if the training regimen is narrow and rigid, then all of the staffers are going to start acting the same. Some companies seek this kind of uniformity. And it might make sense in the fast food or service industries where franchises are expected to be managed identically. However, Managerial Cloning can lead to a stifling atmosphere.

Band Aid

You can confront a clone directly: "Why don't you speak your own mind and not just echo 'Bob'?"

Self-Repair

Middle managers: resist the temptation of engaging in this practice.

Refactoring

The following refactorings can be used to combat Managerial Cloning:

- Chase out the clones. That is, resist the sycophants at every turn — so long as you do not commit insubordination.
- Try to get involved in the hiring process. This way, you can resist the hiring of clones.

- Point out what is going on, as some managers might not see what is happening.
- In speaking with the manager, point out the flaws in the clones — you would think that managers would reject criticism of their clones, but strangely, they usually fail to see the similarities in their clones.

Observations

This antipattern reminds us of the factoid that dogs tend to look like their owners, and spouses tend to look like each other. For what it is worth, Phil (author) has a GoldenDoodle!

Identification

The following identification instrument can help determine if your organization has a tendency toward Managerial Cloning. Please respond to the following statements with a "Yes" or "No."

	Yes	No
∎ Whenever my boss disagrees with someone too much, they slowly lose influence with him, but those that mindlessly agree with him will advance.	—	—
∎ I know people in my group who pretend to agree with the boss and behave against their better judgment simply because "that is the way he wants me to act."	—	—
∎ I notice that whenever we hire someone new, my boss seems to look at specific features that emulate him rather than on the candidate's relevant experience.	—	—

If you responded "Yes" to one or more of these statements, your manager may engage in Managerial Cloning.

Name: Metric Abuse

Central Concept

The misuse of metrics, either through incompetence or with deliberate malice. Reported by Dekkers and McQuaid [Dekkers].

Dysfunction

At the core of many process improvement efforts is the introduction of a measurement program. In fact, sometimes the measurement program is the process improvement. That is to say, some people misunderstand the role measurement plays in management and misconstrue its mere presence as an improvement. This is not a correct assumption. When the data used in the metric is incorrect or the metric is measuring the wrong thing, the decisions made based upon them are likely the wrong ones and will do more harm than good.

▼

Perhaps a series of observations reveal that software written by developers wearing yellow shirts has significantly less defects in their code — should companies start requiring a dress code of yellow shirts?

▲

Of course, the significant problems that can arise from Metric Abuse depend on the root of the problem: incompetence or malice:

- Incompetence: failure to understand the difference between causality and correlation; misinterpreting indirect measures; underestimating the effect of a measurement program.
- Malice: selecting metrics that support or decry a particular position based on a personal agenda.

Vignette

In software development, the misuse of metrics is very well known. The prominent methodologist Tom DeMarco even had to revisit his own comments on software metrics following the lamentable attempts at early measurement programs. His original contention was that metrics were central to controlled development ("You can't control what you can't measure") but he subsequently revised his position to highlight the pitfalls of bad metrics. "At its best, the use of software metrics can inform and guide developers, and help organizations to improve. At its worst, it can do actual harm" [DeMarco]. Our favorite metric misuse in the software industry is still the source lines of code (SLOC) as a measure of productivity. Developers do not need further explanation of how corrupt this assumption is; but for those nontechnical readers, lines of code is the number of lines of text in the program code. It is a flawed measure because it does not even refer to the number of executable statements (because there can be any number of these per line of code) and fails to account for increasingly more powerful languages, code libraries, or frameworks (collections of pre-written code).

There are many other, equally horrendous software engineering metric miscues, but our personal favorite example of Metric Abuse comes from the electronics manufacturing industry.

While gathering data on machine utilization on the shop floor at a European electronics producer, it was clear that something must have changed that day because queues were suddenly forming at the inspector's workstation and this had not happened previously. The inspector was part of quality assurance and was expected to randomly inspect up to 10 percent of the circuit boards as they left production on their way to the testing workshop. On this day, however, every board was being visually inspected before going for testing. The explanation was that the new metric for the shop floor was "percentage of test passes" and that the target was 85 percent of the boards passing test. The shop floor manager's solution was to inspect every board before it reached the test phase so that obviously faulty boards would not get to testing and therefore lower the metric. It sounds sensible, until you look at the throughput of each process: inspection versus testing. Visual inspection is a human-intensive task that only two people were trained to do and each inspection takes seven to twelve minutes. Testing, on the other hand, is automated and takes less than one minute per board, and ten boards can be tested at a time. The difference is considerable, and particularly significant when multiplied by the many hundreds of circuit boards produced each day.

The problems are clear in this example. The metric was intended to measure the quality of the production processes and therefore increase the yield. The shop floor manager saw, however, that the easiest way to reach the benchmark was to catch the faulty boards before they were part of the metric. This injected significant delay into the process without increasing yield, so that it was actually counterproductive.

Explanation

Tom DeMarco wrote about "metric madness" once he realized how corporations were adopting mindless measurement programs without regard to measurement theory and in the absence of any thoughtful plans. He was referring to the software industry but the problem is far more widespread than just software development, as the vignette above demonstrates. Modern technology has allowed the gathering and processing of increasing amounts of raw data. At the same time, advanced enterprisewide IT systems have provided previously impossible accessibility to this detailed "information" regarding the state of an organization.

A decade ago, C-level executives would only have access to this data as part of weekly or monthly reports from management staff. Now they can view almost any aspect of the organization directly via the enterprise system or indirectly through a business intelligence engine. As the organization moves from management-by-feel to management-by-fact, it is critical that the "facts" used in decision making are accurate and meaningful; when they are not, it is a case of Metric Abuse.

Band Aid

Unless you feel like educating the misinformed, your best recourse is to abide by the metrics, however ridiculous, and try to find the best way to meet the metric while still performing your job — just like the shop floor manager.

Self-Repair

Stop using the faulty metric.

Refactoring

The first thing to do is stop! In many cases, measuring nothing is better than measuring the wrong thing. When data is available, people use it in decision making, regardless of its accuracy.

Once the decks have been cleared, Dekkers and McQuaid suggest a number of necessary steps for the introduction of a meaningful measurement program [Dekkers]:

1. *Define measurement objectives and plans* — perhaps by applying the goal-question-metric (GQM) paradigm.
2. *Make measurement part of the process* — do not treat it like another project that might get its budget cut, or that you hope to complete one day.
3. *Gain a thorough understanding of measurement* — be sure you understand direct and indirect metrics; causality versus correlation; and, most importantly, that metrics must be interpreted and acted upon.
4. *Focus on cultural issues* — a measurement program will affect the organization's culture; expect it and plan for it.
5. *Create a safe environment to collect and report true data* — remember that without a good rationale, people will be suspicious of new metrics, fearful of a time-and-motion study in sheep's clothing.
6. *Cultivate a predisposition to change* — the metrics will reveal deficiencies and inefficiencies, so be ready to make improvements.
7. *Develop a complementary suite of measures* — responding to an individual metric in isolation can have negative side effects. A suite of metrics lowers this risk.

Sidebar 5.1   What is GQM?

GQM is a simple framework for determining appropriate metrics for an organization. First state the goals, what the organization is trying to achieve. Next, derive from each goal the questions that must be answered to determine if they are being met. Finally, decide what must be measured in order to be able to answer the questions.

If you believe that you are being metric mismanaged, then you can try to instigate the above process by questioning management regarding why the metrics are being collected, how they are being used, and whether there is any justification for such use. You can also offer to provide corrective understanding of the metrics with opportunities of alternate metrics and appropriate use or more appropriate uses of the existing metrics.

Identification

The following identification instrument can help you determine if your organization suffers from Metric Abuse. Please respond to the following statements with a "Yes" or "No."

	Yes	No
■ We collect metrics, but I do not know how they are used or how to use them.	—	—
■ I cannot describe the causal relationship between the metrics we are collecting and the actual use of those metrics.	—	—
■ I can think of another metric that is more appropriate to measure what we want but we are not using it for some reason.	—	—
■ I did not know anyone was collecting metrics!	—	—

If you responded "Yes" to one or more of these statements, your organization has a tendency to misuse metrics.

References

[Dekkers] C.A. Dekkers and P.A. McQuaid, The Dangers of Using Software Metrics to Mismanage, *IT Professional*, 4(2), 24–30, March 2002.

[DeMarco] T. DeMarco, *Why Does Software Cost So Much?*, Dorset House Publishing, New York, 1995.

Name: Mr. Nice Guy

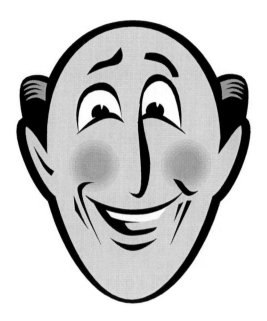

Central Concept

A manager who focuses on being everyone's friend, ends up disappointing everyone and failing in his duties.

Dysfunction

When managers are more concerned with maintaining friendships, not causing unhappiness, and avoiding controversial decisions, they fail to do their job. You cannot lead without having to deal with some form of controversy or negative situation or without having to deliver bad news. Therefore, the nice guy manager does not get the job done. Furthermore, to maintain this posture, he must create Fairness Doctrines so that he can say, "It is the same for everyone," when posed with a situation of failing to perform.

Mr. Nice Guys frustrate everyone. Observers eventually realize that the nice guy is avoiding essential tasks and decisions because they are onerous. He may be delegating these tasks to others — forcing those without the authority (or compensation, for that matter) to do the tough jobs. Those being asked to do the dirty work resent it. Those on the receiving end resent it too because they feel that they are being disrespected by a manager who does not have the guts to deliver the bad news himself. Indeed, Nice-Guy managers are very likely to be branded as cowards, and in fact, an argument can be made that Mr. Nice Guy is just a Spineless Executive. The main difference, however, is that the Spineless Executive chooses not to do what is right because he is afraid to do it. Mr. Nice Guy, on the other hand, chooses not to do what is right because he does not want to hurt anyone.

Nice guys actually tend to have few close friends at work. Instead, "everyone" is their friend so there is no chance to form close relationships.

Vignette

Greg is a nice guy and wants to be perceived as such by his staff of five developers. But when Jean starts to slack off on her deliverables, the project schedule begins to suffer. The other four developers try to indirectly inform Greg that Jean is slacking. But they quickly realize that Greg knows this…. "Jean's just having a rough time these days at home, give her some time, and she'll turn around."

But after a couple of months, Jean does not turn around. In fact, her performance worsens and now she is openly hostile to any criticism from her colleagues.

Finally, two of the more senior developers, Sue and Nancy, confront Greg about the situation. "Greg, she is dragging us down. She is nasty. You have got to do something about it." Greg responds, "But she really is such a nice person. She was just having a bad day. You guys, please just try to work with her. I will talk to her."

Greg does talk to Jean but is indirect in his approach and makes no real criticisms of her work. Therefore, Jean's behavior does not change. Sue, Nancy, and the other two developers begin to resent Greg's masking of Jean's shortcomings and his unwarranted defense of her. Greg will eventually lose the support of his team.

▼

Google's corporate motto is "Don't be evil." This does not mean to be naively too nice. It means doing the right thing without unduly hurting others. Sometimes, doing the right thing, however, means doing necessary harm.

▲

Explanation

The origin of the name is self-evident, but why it should be an antipattern might not be. Not every nice guy is a bad manager, and not every good manager is a nice guy. But being a nice guy all the time as a deliberate management strategy is nearly certain to lead to failure.

Band Aid

Who does not want to work for a nice guy? Enjoy the situation and understand that it is the squeaky wheel that gets the grease — so get squeaky. You have to accept that less-deserving wheels will also get grease at times, however.

Self-Repair

Detach yourself from the personalities involved in the tough situation and focus on the facts.

If you do not have the stomach to do the right thing and get tough on those who deserve it, then maybe you should not be a manager.

Refactoring

The manager has to learn, or be taught, how to make tough decisions that sometimes impact people negatively. No more "Mr. Nice Guy." To help in this transformation:

■ Provide moral support to Mr. Nice Guy and help him see the benefit of being tough.
■ Force him to make decisions with aggressive and ruthless questioning.
■ In a sense, make him feel guilty when he does not do what he is supposed to do. He wants to make everyone happy. Let him know that when he does not do the right thing, he is making you unhappy. This makes it a choice for him; and if you are the more valuable asset, you will prevail.

Identification

The following identification instrument can help determine if your hypothetical manager, Greg, is Mr. Nice Guy. Please respond to the following statements with a "Yes" or "No."

	Yes	No
■ Greg often uses elaborate behaviors to avoid necessary confrontations.	—	—
■ Greg always uses an intermediary to deliver the bad news.	—	—
■ Although Greg tries to be nice to everyone, few actually like him.	—	—
■ People take advantage of Greg.		
■ People disrespect Greg behind his back although he is polite and respectful to everyone else.	—	—

If you responded "Yes" to one or more of these statements, Greg is probably Mr. Nice Guy.

Name: Mushroom Management

Central Concept

A situation in which management fails to communicate effectively with staff. Essentially, information is deliberately withheld to keep everyone "fat, dumb, and happy."

Dysfunction

When members of the team do not really understand the big picture, the effects can be significant. It is somewhat insulting to assume that someone working on the front lines does not have a need to understand the bigger picture. Moreover, those who are working directly with customers, for example, might have excellent ideas that may have sweeping impact on the company. So, Mushroom Management can lead to low employee morale, turnover, missed opportunities, and general failure.

Vignette

The insidious aspect of Mushroom Management is that it is symptomatic of deeper trust issues; but even overlooking this, the effects of keeping people in the dark can be severe.

At an architectural metal-working plant, we were trying to track down the causes of bottlenecks in tool production. One of the key processes in making tools is an annealing step, or something similar, that involves heating the tools in a large kiln. Walking around the shop–floor, it was quickly obvious that this kiln was the bottleneck because the racks at the kiln door were full of tools ready for heating, and it was not running. The operator explained, with great pride, how the kiln operated and how much it cost to run — many thousands of dollars per heat. Given the high cost of running the kiln, the operator always ensured he had a full load before starting it; he did not want the company to lose money by running it for a small batch of tools when he could wait a week or two and run it full. When we relayed this to the chief production engineer, he was flabbergasted. "I'm waiting on a batch of stamps so we can finish the architraves," he exclaimed. No, we did not know what they were either, but he explained that they were past their due date and were worth hundreds of thousands of dollars to the company. "Does Jim (the operator) know that?" we asked. "Of course not, what does he need to know that for?" he replied. Unfortunately, Jim found out that day, in no uncertain terms, what he should do the next time these stamps arrived in the queue, but it clearly was not his fault; he thought he was doing the company a favor.

This exact problem is not at all uncommon it appears, because the same situation was found in an electronics company with the flow-solder machine that solders the underside of printed circuit boards. The operator delayed running it until it was full because it took a long time to set up. He did not realize he was delaying up to a $1 million worth of product getting delivered ... and no one thought to share this fact with him.

Explanation

The name is derived from the fact that mushrooms thrive in darkness and dim light, but will die in the sunshine. As the old saying goes, "keep them in the dark, feed them dung, watch them grow... and then cut off their heads when you are done with them."

There is something very "Theory X" about deliberately depriving people of information that is not confidential. Why would you not want to have your employees fully educated about your business unless you do not trust them, or you think they are too stupid to understand it?

In Bob Lucky's wonderful collection of essays, *Lucky Strikes Again*, he describes a classic situation of Mushroom Management in a chapter entitled "The Bean Counters" [Lucky]. Here is the setup. The metaphor of a ship in search of a precious resource, beans, is used. The engineers who toil away in the hold of the ship are the mushrooms. The omnipotent managers are running the ship, although they are utterly clueless (see Road to Nowhere).

"The engineers have now been relegated to the engine room below deck, where there is no sunlight or any notion about where the great ship is headed. Still, they take great pride in the gleaming new engines, which they continually improve and polish. 'Does the captain know the potential capabilities of our wonderful new engines?' asks one of the faceless engineers. An equally faceless companion looks up from her engine-software 'How could he?' says the software designer with resignation. 'He has never been down here.' [...] Unfortunately the captain is too busy to meet with the engineers. He has a full calendar of appointments with various people who specialize in predicting bean crops. The humble engineers are not surprised; they had expected as much. None among them had ever met the captain, though they had often seen his picture in the popular magazine *Beaness Week*."

The sentiment expressed in this excerpt is precisely the kind that many software engineers and IT professionals feel in those companies in which software is not an end product.

Band Aid

Live with it. If you are not being given a great deal of information, chances are you are not being asked to make decisions. This can be a good thing for some people.

Self-Repair

Do not be a mushroom farmer. Use open-book management and share as much information with your staff as possible.

Refactoring

Those eager to perpetuate Mushroom Management will find excuses for not revealing information, strategy, and data. Some simple strategies to employ include:

- Take ownership of problems that allow you to demand more transparency.
- Seek out information on your own. It is out there. You just have to work harder to find it and you may have to put together the pieces. Between you and the other mushrooms, you might be able to see most of the larger picture.
- Advocate for conversion to a culture of open-book management.

Observations

This antipattern is identical to Mushroom Management found in Brown et al. [Brown].

The "opposite" of Mushroom Management is open-book management where all but the most confidential information (including finances) is shared with all employees.

Identification

The following identification instrument can help you determine if your organization or manager uses Mushroom Management. Please respond to the following statements with a "Yes" or "No."

	Yes	No
■ At least once a week I ask myself "Why am I doing this?" with respect to some major task.	___	___
■ I only work on "tasks." I am unsure of how my work fits into the bigger picture.	___	___
■ I have no idea what everyone else around me is doing.	___	___
■ My colleagues and I talk about being mushroom managed all the time.	___	___

If you responded "Yes" to one or more of these statements, your organization or manager probably uses Mushroom Management.

References

[Brown] W.J. Brown, R.C. Malveau, H.W. McCormick, and T.J. Mowbray, *Antipatterns: Refactoring Software, Architectures, and Projects in Crisis,* John Wiley & Sons, 1998.

[Lucky] Robert W. Lucky, *Lucky Strikes Again,* IEEE Press, Piscataway, NJ, 1992, pp. 151–153.

Name: Plate Spinning

Central Concept

An insincere manager can distract his critics from the real problems by dispatching employees on a series of meaningless and time-consuming tasks.

Dysfunction

The Plate Spinning manager leaves a wake of frustrated and disgruntled employees. Time is wasted and projects are late as workers are constantly engaged in busywork.

Vignette

John is the manager of a software development group consisting of five developers. These five developers are assigned individually or in groups of two or three to support various small projects throughout the company — each of which should last no more than one to four months.

John is worried that his five developers are getting too "cozy" and that they are beginning to realize that he does not really qualify for his job. He also does very little but make their work assignments — including assigning them much of his own job responsibilities.

To keep them off balance, therefore, he regularly shuffles the project teams to break continuity. He also switches them from one project to another. He uses the justification that "Sue's expertise in Java is needed on project X now" or "Ed's better at documentation" but he is really only self-interested. He also makes up small tasks related to past projects (like post-documentation). But to Ed and Sue and the other three members of John's staff, they see an endless stream of Plate Spinning activities.

▼

A Wise Alec from Phil

When my niece was six years old, I used to tease her in the following way:

I'd say, "Honey, there's a piece of tape stuck to your shoe," and then point vaguely at her feet. She'd look at one shoe, and I'd say, "no, the other one." Then I'd say, "No Honey, in the back." Then "on the side." Then I'd say, "No, it's the other shoe." I could keep this going on for a few minutes before she caught on. This is the essence of plate spinning.

▲

Explanation

The Ed Sullivan variety show used to feature different magicians and jugglers, along with more traditional comic and singing acts. One type of performer used to specialize in spinning plates atop a series of flexible sticks. The trick involved moving from one plate stick to another and imparting spin on the plate as it spun down to a wobble. If the spinner was fast and skillful enough, he could keep dozens of plates spinning.

A likely reason why your manager might engage you in Plate Spinning is the case where the manager does not have enough for you to do. Rather than leaving you idle where you can "get into trouble," he engages you in busywork. This is insulting to you and is a perpetration of company fraud on the part of the manager.

Some managers use this technique to keep their staff (and detractors) off balance. Perhaps they are trying to hide something. It could be that they are trying to cause you to fail for some reason. Or there could be fear that there will be some sort of mutiny against him; and by assigning a never-ending sequence of repeatable tasks, their detractors do not have time to organize against them. Really, it is a disturbed manager who engages in this sort of behavior.

Band Aid

Do not spin your own plates. That is, do not ask for more work than you can handle. To avoid being given busywork:

- Be task-oriented. That is, focus on one project or task at a time rather than on noncontiguous activities.
- Try to look busy so that the Plate Spinner does not find work for you. When Phil worked as a warehouseman, a senior guy saw him idling about, waiting for the next delivery. He said, "Grab a clipboard and pen and start walking around. If you look busy, no one will bother you."

Self-Repair

Do not make people plate spin. You are wasting valuable human resources. If this is some kind of deception, then you need to be psychoanalyzed. If you are simply trying to keep your staff busy to keep them out of trouble, then revisit your staffing needs.

Refactoring

In the case where you are being engaged in Plate Spinning because your boss believes he is protecting your job, you need to confront him about the situation. Is there some way that your job can be reconfigured so that you are busy, but doing useful work? In the case that your manager is Plate Spinning you for more nefarious reasons, the following refactorings can help:

- Demand rational management — ask to look at the overall work distribution (are you the only Plate Spinner because you say "Yes").
- Do a cross-the-board job analysis.
- If this is a situation of Deflated Balloon, point out that downsizing will alleviate the problem. Just try not to be one of the casualties by establishing your value to the company.
- Learn to be a better Plate Spinner — that is, satisfy what management needs and then find time to do the real work.

Identification

The following identification instrument can help determine if you are being forced to play the game of Spin the Plate. Please respond to the following statements with a "Yes" or "No."

	Yes	No
■ Much of the work that I do keeps me busy, but it does not seem to contribute anything to the company's goals.	___	___
■ I never seem to be able to finish projects before I get asked to do another, meaningless task.	___	___
■ I have multiple projects in play, but my manager has no plan to complete any one of them.	___	___
■ I have this dread of being asked to take on yet another project.	___	___
■ My manager seems to be insensitive to the fact that I am overworked, yet he seems underworked.	___	___

If you responded "Yes" to one or more of these statements, you are probably engaging in Plate Spinning.

Name: Proletariat Hero

Central Concept

The "everyman" worker is held up as the ideal, when in reality, he is a prop being used to mask inadequacies of management. A form of labor discipline as a means of "motivating" staff that gives an excuse for management to raise output expectations ... get more with less.

Dysfunction

The basic, and we obviously believe flawed, assumption at work in the plight of the Proletariat Hero is that people are lazy; that is, Theory X prevails as an explanation for people's motivation. Managers who believe this then utilize some form of labor discipline that coerces workers to become more efficient. This is one of the pillars of Taylorism; people will work at the slowest rate that is not punished. It treats workers as unthinking cogs in a machine and is a mindset solely interested in efficiency. Paradoxically, removing individuality and creativity from work can often reduce productivity as people become bored and inefficient.

While much of the understanding of mass production that came from Frederick Taylor's Scientific Management is valid, there are two specific flaws that invalidate it:

1. That there is "one best way" for everyone to perform every task
2. That the workforce is motivated by fear, and will not react against standardized work practices that treat them like automatons

So, while there are often some short-term improvements in productivity following the proclamation of a Proletariat Hero, these gains are soon lost as workers struggle against unrealistic work goals. Resentment builds against management, and sometimes even against the Heroes themselves.

Vignette

Clearly, the assumption that people are automatons that can be worked relentlessly without consideration for their emotional well-being is wrong. It is unlikely, then, that such aggressive measures are employed in modern corporate America, but some of the ideas do still persist. The employee-of-the-month practiced at fast-food restaurants, for example, is an example of Proletariat Heroes being praised for their exceptional output. Sales targets and commission-based compensation can also be considered a form of labor discipline because it punishes those who fail to meet, often unrealistic, goals and creates a competitive self-interest that destroys morale and encourages Mediocrity.

Worst of all, the general ideas of Taylorism and Theory X motivation, that workers are lazy unless driven hard, and that resource utilization is a primary goal of an organization are still readily found. Too many managers still consider an idle resource a waste before understanding if there is useful work for that resource to do at that time, or even if useful work at that time could actually cost more in the end. If you yourself are questioning this, the refactorings below will help.

Explanation

The exploitation of the Proletariat was best captured by George Orwell in *Animal Farm*, his allegorical novel of Stalinism. In it he wrote about Boxer and Clover, the ever-loyal draft horses, representing the ill-educated and unskilled proletariat. They are manipulated by the persuasive arguments of the ruling pigs to do increasingly more work on the farm in the name of the animal revolution, but are ultimately taken for granted and fail to reap the benefits of the Revolution that was meant to be for them and their fellow working class.

The stoic Clydesdales were a direct analogy to Aleksei Stakhanov, after whom the Stakhanovite movement was named. He was a miner who became a celebrity in the Soviet Union in 1935 as part of a movement that was intended to increase worker productivity and demonstrate the superiority of socialist economic systems. He was acclaimed to have mined over 100 tons of coal in a six-hour shift, five to ten times the norm. For this feat he was heralded as the "model Soviet worker" that all other workers should strive to emulate. In reality, his achievements were exaggerated for propaganda purposes by adding the production of his co-workers to his own total so that those artificially high targets could be set for all workers. The movement lasted only a year because it soon became obvious, even to Stalin, that the hoped-for gains were short-lived and worker resentment grew ... even with the threat of labor camps or death hanging over them. This mechanistic view of workers is not unique to the Soviet Union, however. China experimented with the same propagandist approaches, and they are both merely manifestations of Taylor's scientific management that was first employed at Bethlehem Steel in Pennsylvania.

Band Aid

Reject unattainable targets whenever you can. Overcoming the odds in Dunkirk Spirit fashion will only strengthen your supervisor's belief in them. As a wise colleague once said, "In my annual review, I only state targets I've already attained," and this is a great coping tactic whenever you are required to set your own goals.

Self-Repair

Treat those who work for you fairly. Do not single out anyone publicly for undeserved praise or punishment. Recognize that people may be motivated by different things, but everyone wants to succeed without coercion.

Refactoring

At its core, the problem at work in the Proletariat Hero is the misconception that people can be treated like machines, and that treating them like that will yield benefits. Instead, harness and encourage the creativity, innovation, and individuality within the workforce. When people feel that their opinions and ideas are valued, they take pride in their work and are motivated to succeed both personally and collectively. Remember what your mother told you: "You catch more flies with honey than with vinegar."

The supplemental problem that must also be addressed is the belief that utilization is akin to throughput. In his book *The Goal* [Goldratt], Eli Goldratt explains the failure in this assumption. While we always seek maximum utilization of resources, we must recognize that it is the throughput of the bottlenecks in any critical path that must be optimized; increasing utilization in other processes just builds WIP or inventory and therefore costs money...better to leave that process idle.

This can be a difficult concept to apply in practice because, intuitively, letting a resource that costs money do nothing is ridiculous; but in reality, the resource cost is fixed, the only variable is the cost of the inventory, and if increasing the utilization of a resource does not increase overall throughput, we are increasing costs and not producing revenues.

Identification

The following identification instrument can help determine if your organization promotes Proletariat Heroes. Please respond to the following statements with a "Yes" or "No."

	Yes	No
■ There seems to be a handful of people in my organization who always win awards — and some are undeserving.	___	___
■ No matter what I do, I am always made to feel like someone in my company is outperforming me.	___	___
■ Every time I reach the goal, it seems that the goalposts have been moved farther away.	___	___
■ I am always made to feel as if I am not working hard enough, no matter how hard I work.	___	___

If you responded "Yes" to one or more of these statements, your organization promotes Proletariat Heroes.

References

[Orwell]   G. Orwell, *Animal Farm*, Harcourt, Brace and Company, New York, 1946.
[Goldratt]   E. Goldratt and J. Cox, *The Goal: A Process of Ongoing Improvement*, North River Press; 2nd ed., 1992.

Name: Rising Upstart

Central Concept

Rising Upstarts are superstars that cannot wait their time and want to forego the requisite time to learn, mature, and find their place. This can sometimes be through ignorance, they do not know what they do not know; and sometimes it is through impatience, they know what others do not know. The Rising Upstart presents a real challenge to all but the most proficient managers.

Dysfunction

Uncontrolled Rising Upstarts can cause an imbalance in an organization, a situation that can be difficult to manage. A happy equilibrium must be found that allows the cream to rise to the top in step with their talents (artificially holding them down will force these valuable assets to leave) but not too quickly that they prematurely crash and burn or they offend the still effective old guard.

Vignette

Everyone has encountered a Rising Upstart ... at least everyone who has met either of us (although Phil is now a little old for "rising," and a little conservative for "upstart"). We admit that we are both type A personalities with the requisite ego, arrogance, determination, and will. This can make us difficult to manage at times. We see solutions clearly, arrive at strategies quickly, and expect the same of everyone around us. Because the pace of change is rarely that fast, we can become frustrated and temperamental. On these occasions, Phil tends to explode a little (although he prefers to call it "venting") and Colin tends to become resentful. Fortunately, we are both sufficiently self-aware that we can manage these situations, and we work in an environment where we self-direct most of the time and can take the helm when necessary.

Other Rising Upstarts are not so fortunate, however. One case in particular concerned a very driven individual working at an international aerospace company as a junior software engineer. He was described by his peers and supervisors as an extremely motivated and bright guy, a quick study. Right from the get-go, despite his lack of technical knowledge and his complete lack of experience, he sought more and more responsibility within his team, then project, then group.

He had only been with the company a year when he literally demanded a promotion because he had spent long enough being "just a programmer." His manager promoted him, giving him more responsibilities. Very quickly it was obvious to his teammates that the workload and expectation were too much for him as he became increasingly irritable as his work-hours kept increasing. Undaunted, he soon demanded further recognition and promotion, and again his demands were met. More responsibilities led to more hours and more stress, but also an increasing burden on his lack of experience. He had to work long hours just trying to understand the task at hand and to attain the skills necessary to complete his work. This left him no time to hone his interpersonal and leadership skills so that he was left to the last resort of exploding and chastising his subordinates.

The sad conclusion, at least for now, is that this obviously talented and industrious person now suffers regular panic attacks at work and home, and finds even the thought of going into work in the mornings a challenge. Amazingly, and regrettably, his ambition is still not diminished; he is his own worst enemy. Hopefully at some point, a manager will finally realize that they must protect him from himself and let him develop his career at a sustainable pace.

Explanation

Rising Upstarts are often the lifeblood of an organization. They can be the most productive and exceptional of employees, but they bring with them special challenges for their supervisors and peers. When harnessed properly, the accomplishments they can bring to an organization can be transforming; but despite their own protestations, they require close management.

Some are full to the brim with leadership potential and vision and cannot wait to stride to the front; others are astounding talents within their fields and thirst for bigger and better challenges; while still others have huge untapped potential hidden behind a veneer of fear or self-criticism. Each type requires careful management to:

- Protect the organization from their unfettered hubris
- Protect the Upstart from self-fueled burnout
- Avoid rancor and hostility from the old guard and peers
- Leverage their remarkable potential

The first stage for the manager is to identify these Upstarts, recognize their potential, and work with them on a plan to develop their careers carefully. Beyond that general advice, specific approaches must be taken, depending on the individual's particular characteristics.

Band Aid

Humoring them often works. Sometimes, their ideas will be useful, at other times they do not understand the ramifications of their ideas. After all, they lack experience and are often not afforded the broad perspective that would allow them that foresight. You might be inclined to push back at these times, to try and show them up for their hubris. Do not do this. It will only stir their spirit greater, and they have more energy for such battles than you do.

If you do not have time for that, fill their time and exhaust their energies with Plate Spinning.

Self-Repair

Be patient. It is not what you want to hear, because you feel you can save the world; but remember the story of the wise bull standing at the top of the hill looking down at the herd with his young friend!

Refactoring

The best strategy is effective mentoring. Good mentors will gain the trust and confidence of the Rising Upstart so that they can teach, advise, and even admonish when appropriate. In particular, mentors should help the Rising Upstart work on his people skills. Unfortunately, mentoring is not always possible, as it requires mentors who are competent enough to gain the respect of the Upstart. In the absence of mentors, we can turn to other disciplines more accustomed to dealing with superstars — sports.

Phil Jackson is renowned for his ability to manage superstars, having coached Michael Jordan, Scottie Pippen, Shaquille O'Neal, Kobe Bryant, and Dennis Rodman. He recognized that he had to make personal connections with each player. While this is common sense, Jackson's genius is to appreciate that the nature of that relationship must be different for each individual. He realized that O'Neal needed discipline based upon his upbringing with a military father, but that Rodman needed space, time, and freedom based on his extravagant lifestyle and rejection of social norms.

Tom Duening and Jack Ivancevich also identified the need for individualized treatment of Einsteins, as they call them. They identified six types, each with their own refactoring [Duening]:

1. *Arrogant:* the frequent praise and reward has gone to their head and now they believe they are better than everyone else. Do not be intimidated by them; in fact, try to overlook their arrogance. If their complaining becomes too disruptive, have a quiet word, but do not humor them; they expect their suggestions to be acted upon.
2. *Know-It-All:* similar to Arrogants, but usually operate behind the scenes so sometimes more insidious. Do not challenge them directly; use indirect management, a delegate perhaps, to keep track of them.
3. *Impatient:* need constant challenges, otherwise they become bored and everyone knows what idle hands turn to!
4. *Eccentric:* obsessive people who relish their differences whether it is their Star Trek trivia or their workaholism. Provided they are not disruptive, humor their eccentricities.
5. *Disorganized:* the epitome of the super-geek. Relatively harmless, provided they are left to their own devices and not asked to take on managerial tasks.
6. *Withdrawn:* the bookworm who has always felt alienated and needs to be coaxed into releasing his potential. They often crave recognition, so offer them the opportunity to publish their work.

Another possible refactoring is to institutionalize Rising Upstarts, even encourage them. Many companies have fast tracks to management in which "Rising Upstarts" (these companies do not call them that) are identified by their supervisors and placed in established programs to help these superstars advance quickly to managerial positions. Many of the fast-track programs do emphasize people skills as well as the usual corporate culture training, financial skills, planning skills, etc. Another advantage of this kind of refactoring is that it will almost certainly prevent a company from becoming a Mediocracy because excellence is recognized and rewarded. However, this kind of fast-track program does produce an intensely competitive environment with all of the downsides therein — jealousy, sabotage, distrust, etc.

Identification

The following identification instrument can help you determine if you or someone you know is a Rising Upstart. Please respond to the following statements with a "Yes" or "No" concerning hypothetical Rising Upstart, Lester.

	Yes	No
■ Lester is often given tasks that are far above his job authorization by his boss when his boss cannot do them.	—	—
■ Despite the fact that he is the busiest guy in the department, Lester always seems to get the toughest and most important jobs.	—	—
■ Lester sometimes gets frustrated that he does not have the authority to do all things he would like to do.	—	—
■ If I did not know any better, I would say that Lester was actually at a higher staff level than he really is.	—	—

If you responded "Yes" to one or more of these statements, then Lester is likely a Rising Upstart.

References

[Duening]   T. Duening and J. Ivancevich, Managing Einsteins: Leading High Tech Workers in the Digital Age, McGraw-Hill, 2002.

Name: Road to Nowhere

Central Concept

The lack of a plan causes confusion and a crisis of leadership.

"The plan is nothing, planning is everything."

—Dwight D. Eisenhower

Dysfunction

Without a plan, how can you organize to achieve your goals? How can you properly partition the work that must be done and track its progress? How do you get buy-in from your superiors, subordinates, and peers for the direction in which you are taking them? Furthermore, if you somehow manage to meet your goals, even by luck, how will you be able to repeat that success, learn from mistakes, and extract best processes? It is exceptionally difficult to make even the simplest of tactical decisions when a broader plan is not in place — it is like walking in the dark with your hand outstretched.

Even those managers who prefer *ad hoc* techniques and, through their hard work and luck, sometimes manage to be successful, the dissatisfaction and frustration of everyone else that has to work "blind" is palpable. Moreover, how are you going to learn from someone who does not even know why he succeeds himself?

Vignette

Ralph is the project manager for a software product. He has a team of three software engineers: Art, Jane, and Debbie. Consider their three perspectives of a typical work week:

1. *Art's story.* On Monday morning, Ralph called me into the office and gave me a software specification for a GUI component that I had to design for later coding in Java. He gave me until Friday to do it. I managed to finish on time. Monday morning he called me into his office, thanked me for designing the GUI, and then told me I would be writing code for some business logic component in Java and he handed me a design. He gave me until Wednesday to do it. On Wednesday, he checked in with me and I told him I was done. He then handed me a design spec and some MySQL source code to test. I had no idea what the hell I was doing.

2. *Jane's story.* On Monday morning, Ralph called me into his office and gave me a software specification for a database and he wanted me to produce a database schema for later coding in MySQL. He gave me until Friday to do it. I managed to finish on time. Monday morning he called me into his office, thanked me for designing the database, and then told me I would be writing code for some GUI component in Java and he handed me a design. He gave me until Wednesday to do it. On Wednesday, he checked in with me and I told him I was done. He then handed me a design spec and some Java source code for a business logic component I had to test. I had no idea what the hell I was doing.

3. *Debbi's story.* On Monday morning, Ralph called me into his office and gave me a software specification for some business logic component and he wanted me to produce a design for later coding in Java. He gave me until Friday to do it. I managed to finish on time. Monday morning he called me into his office, thanked me for designing the business logic, and then told me I would be writing code for some database component in MySQL and he handed me a schema. He gave me until Wednesday to do it. On Wednesday, he checked in with me and I told him I was done. He then handed me a design spec and some Java source code for a GUI component I had to test. I had no idea what the hell I was doing.

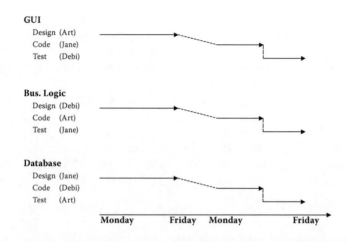

Figure 5.1   Ralph's plan.

To Art, Jane, and Debbi, Ralph is a crazed lunatic without a plan. But what if Ralph really has a plan, and it can be illustrated simplistically with the Gantt Chart shown in Figure 5.1?

The simplified Gantt Chart depicts the exact sequence of events just described. Now it makes sense! Of course, Gantt Charting is not planning, but it is a visual artifact that suggests that planning was done.

But what if Ralph never had such a plan and the sequence of events described by the three team members happened as Ralph "managed" the project on-the-fly? The result is a team that is totally confused and demoralized. If only Ralph had his plan ahead of time and communicated it to his engineers, everything would have been fine. Either way, this is a manager who needs some help with planning.

Explanation

As a manager and leader, you have to have a plan for, as the old saying goes, "when you don't know where you are going, all roads will take you there." Without a plan, work is undirected and without rationale. Outcomes are unpredictable, risk escalates, and chaos soon reigns.

In Bob Lucky's wonderful collection of essays, *Lucky Strikes Again*, he writes about the dangers of pursuing money without a plan [Lucky]. He uses the metaphor of a ship in search of a valuable commodity, beans.

> "In the days of old the crew of the ship would gather around the captain to listen to tales of the great land beyond — the joys and benefits that would ultimately compensate for the

hardships of the long voyage. The echoes of those wondrous tales still resonate about us, but those who tell them no longer abound. Now, should a passenger or crew member ask the captain about the final destination of the voyage, the same answer reverberates from boat to boat. 'Wherever there are beans,' intones the chorus of new captains. 'But where shall we steer?,' asks the crew, pleading for a motivating vision. 'Toward the beans,' comes the predictable wisdom from above."

Band Aid

Enjoy the ride. Continue to work without a plan by being task-oriented only. This is no way to gain job satisfaction, however; and without a plan it is very difficult to work successfully on more than one project at a time.

Self-Repair

Do you have a plan, or are you just winging it? You must have a plan. Then monitor and change the plan as necessary.

Refactoring

There are a number of techniques that can assist with project planning. Gantt Charts, Program Evaluation and Review Technique (PERT), and the Critical Path Method (CPM) all provide familiar visual artifacts that can help capture and communicate a plan. While they are useful tools in the project manager's arsenal, they must not, however, be considered a substitute for a comprehensive plan or the planning activity itself.

The best managers clearly develop and articulate a plan, get buy-in for the plan, then see to it that it is executed, providing resources and encouragement and adapting the plan when necessary. How you communicate this reality to a plan-less manager is the tricky part. But some form of intervention is needed or the situation will end in a death march.

Some first steps to take include:

- Use project *post mortems* to learn from projects — even from those that did not have a plan in the first place.
- Create an environment that rewards planning.
- Teach people how to plan and learn from mistakes and successes.
- Instigate capability assessments or process reviews such as ISO 9000 or CMMI that enforce a regimen of planning.

Identification

The following identification instrument can help you determine whether or not your organization has a plan. Please respond to the following statements with a "Yes" or "No."

	Yes	No
■ My organization does not have any stated goals.		
■ My organization does not have a published plan to meet its goals.	——	——
■ My organization does not engage in any planning activities.	——	——
■ I never have a sense of how my work is contributing to the overall achievement of our goals.	——	——
■ My manager changes direction inexplicably.	——	——

If you responded "Yes" to one or more of these statements, your organization is probably on the road to nowhere.

References

[Lucky]   Robert W. Lucky, *Lucky Strikes Again*, IEEE Press, Piscataway, NJ, 1992, pp. 151–153.

Name: Spineless Executive

Central Concept

Any manager who does not have the courage to undertake a necessary confrontation or deal with a challenging situation. Instead, he avoids the confrontation or situation altogether or asks you to deliver the bad news for him.

> "When danger turned its ugly head, he bravely turned his tail and fled."

> **—The Ballad of Sir Robin,**
> **Monty Python and the Holy Grail**

Dysfunction

Generally, the negative effects of Spineless Executives are felt at the personal level, rather than organizational, although persistent spineless behavior can filter to customers, stakeholders, and consumer confidence, depending on the situation. At the personal level, the staff who are fed to the wolves become very discouraged and can turn subversive ... working against the executive, and therefore the organization, out of spite.

Vignette

In a discussion with Louise, a Project Manager for a bespoke system development company, we heard the following tale of woe. The company was one of several similar point-providers subcontracted to deliver different components for the same system. The overall project was run by a large information services provider that had performed the original vision exploration and planning before farming out the work to the subcontractors. The overall project was very behind schedule and numerous memos had sailed around requesting increased productivity and efficiency, but, as far as Louise could tell, the original estimates were so woefully inaccurate and optimistic that the original plan had no chance of success. As the project fell further and further behind, the penalties for the solution provider were becoming ominous and they needed to act. They hired a consultancy well known for troubleshooting and reigning in wayward projects. The lead consultant soon decided that a shakedown was needed. He called the senior executives of all the subcontractors to a meeting to read them the riot act, crack some skulls, and every other cliché for Theory X management you could muster.

None of the executives from any of the subcontractors was pleased to be attending this meeting as they all knew their fate, and to Louise's chagrin, her CEO decided not to go and instead sent a trusty sergeant... Louise. Lo and behold, the meeting was everything everybody expected — a real tongue-lashing at the hands of this no-nonsense (and no-sense) consultant. For over an hour, he went around the table attacking the attendees for their lack of performance, control, professionalism, and anything else he cared to comment on in blaming them for not meeting the specified targets. This was clearly not appropriate and unlikely effective, but particularly for the poor project manager. She had no say in her company's strategy and no influence in the organizational matters at issue, yet she took the verbal beating due her CEO. The upshot for that relationship was a complete erosion of trust and respect.

As an aside, it turns out that all the executives in attendance were pretty spineless because they all collapsed under the barrage and accepted both the accusations and the remedies leveled at them...except Louise. She stood up to the consultant, telling him that despite the acquiescence of all the other executives, they all knew that the project schedule was still not feasible and that she was not prepared to be spoken to in such a manner. With that, she stood up and walked out.

Explanation

Courage is an important characteristic in leaders. They are accountable and responsible for their team or department and this sometimes means taking the heat for their subordinates when things go wrong. Unfortunately, many managers are too worried about their own career or pride that strong advocacy or assertive leadership is beyond them. We should not, however, satisfy ourselves that such people can be easily overthrown or confronted. Many people who lack courage to face the music are still quite capable of admonishing and disciplining their subordinates. Their lack of courage in some situations is borne of their pride, the same pride that props them up in the face of dissention.

The Spineless Executive is slightly different from Bramson's Superagreeables and Indecisives. As described in Chapter 1, these types avoid making decisions because they have other reasons why they do not want to make the decisions that are hidden from you. The Spineless Executive, on the other hand, is basically a coward. His reason for not making the decision is because he is afraid to deliver bad news, to "break someone's heart," or is afraid of the angry backlash from the recipient of the bad news.

▼

Wise Alec!

Lazy, dull, or cowardly individuals will show amazing energy, genius, and courage to protect their right to continue to be lazy, dull, and cowardly.

▲

Band Aid

Use kid gloves. You do not want them to suddenly grow a spine with you. As mentioned above, the lack of courage can be situational; they might lack courage in situations they do not control, but in others they can be ruthless.

Self-Repair

Accountability is a part of leadership. If you cannot take it, get out.

Refactoring

If you were asked to deliver the bad news for the coward, sometimes the refactoring is as simple as asking questions. Perhaps you were sent to the lion's den because they trust you to represent the organization well, or perhaps they see this as a perfect trial by fire, to test your mettle in the face of adversity. Also remember that senior managers must pick their battles and use their time effectively. Not personally attending a meeting that yields nothing but rancor might actually be wisdom, not weakness.

In other cases it may be that the manager is not doing the right thing because there are some hidden reasons, in which case you should use some of the techniques we discussed for the Indecisive or Superagreeable personality type.

Of course, if there is a pattern of behavior forming where individuals are consistently avoiding contentious situations, alternative refactorings are necessary. Perhaps the most drastic is to bring the issue to a higher level of management — you probably do not risk retribution from the manager because you have established that he is unwilling to take harsh action. Another possibility is to undertake some kind of intervention — a group of leading and respected members of the team need to confront the manager about his inability to make decisions and insist on those decisions being made.

Identification

The following identification instrument can help you determine if your boss is a Spineless Executive. Please respond to the following statements with a "Yes" or "No."

	Yes	No
▪ I tend to not bring problems to my manager's attention because I know he will not do anything about them.	—	—
▪ I never learn about anything important from my manager — I always hear it from someone else.	—	—
▪ My manager spends too much time trying to make people like him.	—	—
▪ My manager is virtually incapable of making a decision when it really counts.	—	—

If you responded "Yes" to one or more of these statements, your manager is a Spineless Executive.

Name: Three-Headed Knight

Central Concept

The indecisive manager. This manager is consistent with Bramson's Indecisive phenotype.

Dysfunction

Indecision kills. The inability to make a decision means things happen to you, rather than you making things happen. This reactive, rather than proactive mode means you are permanently on the back-foot. In this stance, it is very difficult to:

- ▪ Motivate subordinates
- ▪ Garner confidence from superiors
- ▪ Plan ahead

This leads to:

- ▪ Missed opportunities
- ▪ Constant firefighting
- ▪ Frustration and eventually disillusionment with your leadership

Vignette

One day, your manager is full of support for the idea you expressed so eloquently; the next day, his words, or more often his actions, tell a contradictory story. The problem is not that he lies to you, or dismisses you with feigned support, but that his own internal conflicts are battling it out for supremacy and balanced equilibrium is elusive.

We described a scenario involving the indecisive manager in Section 2.2.3. The Three-Headed Knight type manager is a pathological case of someone who regularly engages in indecisive behavior.

Explanation

The vacillating manager comes in many forms. Some are paralyzed and are unable to make any decisions through fear of the consequence (we call this Fear Uncertainty Doubt); others consistently make decisions one day and reverse them the next (the Trolley and Pole); and then others seem like the Three-Headed Knight from Monty Python's *The Holy Grail* — they can't decide on any course of action as they battle internal conflict.

Brave Sir Robin encounters the three-headed knight and tries to pass. Each head of the knight wants to do a different thing ... including lopping off Robin's head. In the end, their arguing allows Robin to escape.

——————————▼——————————

All heads: Halt! Who art thou?

Minstrel: He is brave Sir Robin, brave Sir Robin, who—

Robin: Shut up! Um, n-- n-- n-- nobody, really. I'm j-- j-- j-- ju-- just, um — just passing through.

All heads: What do you want?

Minstrel: To fight and—

Robin: Shut up! Um, oo, a-- nothing. Nothing, really. I, uh-- j-- j-- just-- just to, um-- just to p-- pass through, good sir knight.

All heads: I'm afraid not!

Robin: Ah. W-- well, actually I-- I am a knight of the round table.

All heads: You're a knight of the round table?

Sidebar 5.2 The Trolley and Pole

In control systems the inverted pendulum, or trolley and pole, is a classic problem in trying to control unstable systems. The pole is hinged at one end onto a trolley that runs on straight tracks. The goal is to keep the pole from falling over by moving the trolley along the track in response to the motion of the pole (see Figure 5.2).

Some solutions involve minute movements of the trolley so that the pole stays almost still in an upright position, but purists hold this solution in disregard ... they prefer solutions to the tougher problem of controlling the swaying pole.

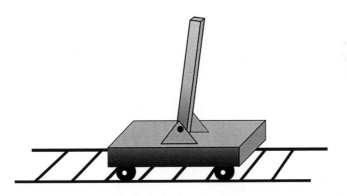

Figure 5.2 A simplified diagram of the Trolley and Pole Control problem.

Robin: I am.

Left head: In that case, I shall have to kill you.

Middle head: Shall I?

Right head: Oh, I don't think so.

Middle head: Well, what do I think?

Left head: I think kill him.

Right head: Oh, let's be nice to him.

Left head: Oh, shut up.

Robin: Perhaps I could—

Left head: And you. Oh, quick! Get the sword out. I want to cut his head off!

Right head: Oh, cut your own head off!

Middle head: Yes, do us all a favor!

Left head: What?

Right head: Yapping on all the time.

Middle head: You're lucky. You're not next to him.

Left head: What do you mean?

Middle head: You snore!

Left head: Oh, I don't. Anyway, you've got bad breath.

Middle head: Well, it's only because you don't brush my teeth.

Right head: Oh, stop bitching and let's go have tea.

Left head: Oh, all right. All right. All right. We'll kill him first and then have tea and biscuits.

Middle head: Yes.

Right head: Oh, not biscuits.

Left head: All right. All right, not biscuits, but let's kill him anyway.

All heads: Right!

Middle head: He buggered off.

Right head: So he has. He's scarpered.

━━━━━━━━━━━━━━▲━━━━━━━━━━━━━━

Band Aid

Take control yourself. Indecisive people want others to take the risk of making decisions, so be that risk taker.

Self-Repair

Use simple game theory to help your decision making. This does not deal with your courage issues in making tough decisions, but at least it provides a framework for arriving at decisions.

Table 5.3 Simple Decision Table

Choice	Best Outcome	Worst Outcome
Fill vacant position	A superstar is hired Improved software quality Satisfies contractual obligations	Another jerk is hired
Leave position vacant	Save money Avoid some hassles	Cannot meet contractual obligations Software quality low

Refactoring

In general, the strategies that we described for the Indecisive phenotype in Section 2.2.3 can be used to cope with the indecisive behavior of the Three-Headed Knight on a situation-by-situation basis. To forestall such behavior, the refactorings must deal with the root causes of indecision.

There are many causes of indecision, so there are a number of refactorings:

- For fearful managers concerned about the consequences of their decisions, use game theory. In the simplest form of game theory, the best and worst possible outcomes for the two choices being weighed, are identified. In most cases, this makes the right decision obvious. For example, consider the situation in which a vacant software testing position needs to be filled. The manager is reluctant to fill the position because the previous software tester was a jerk and incompetent, and he is not a big believer in software testing anyway. A simple decision table (Table 5.3) can help the manager see the possible outcome. For the worst outcome column, you can extend it to include a refactoring for that. You can use a further probabilistic analysis, but assigning probabilities to these outcomes is guesswork at best, and the act of completing the table should be enough to convince the rational (though three-headed) manager of the right decision.
- The Trolley and Pole is often working toward a hidden agenda or is personally conflicted by Divergent Goals. They can make a decision one day when confronted with supporting evidence, but lack a strategic direction that helps guide decisions, and the next day, contrary evidence makes them change tack. Hidden agendas are insidious and there is no helpful refactoring unless they are

uncovered. Tactical rather than strategic management can be overcome, however. The first stage to strategic management is identifying core goals and values. Evidence pertinent to those goals then becomes the primary decision driver.

■ The Three-Headed Knight is also internally conflicted, but not as calculating as a Trolley and Pole. They are confused by the trade-offs that must be made in business, so game theory can also help them, but really they are not ready for leadership. As in most indecisive managers, courage is absent; and without the Wizard of Oz, we are not sure where you can get courage for the leader.

Identification

The following identification instrument can help you determine if your manager has more than one head (is indecisive). Please respond to the following statements with a "Yes" or "No."

	Yes	No
■ I know that whenever my manager renders a "final" decision, it may not be final.	___	___
■ My manager's decisions always seem irrational.	___	___
■ Everyone knows that when my manager makes a decision, there is always a way to change that decision through subterfuge, complaining, or nagging.	___	___
■ Other managers do not respect my manager because of his perceived inability to make a decision.	___	___

If you responded "Yes" to one or more of these statements, then your manager is probably a Multi-Headed Knight.

References

Monty Python and the Holy Grail, 1975.

Name: Ultimate Weapon

Central Concept

Phenoms can be relied upon so much by their peers or organization that they become the conduit for all things.

Dysfunction

Ultimate Weapons can do great things, but often they know how great they are and their arrogance and self-righteousness can be just as great. If these individuals are not managed effectively, the harm they cause can overshadow their achievements.

- Despite their talents, even a superstar cannot win on their own all the time.
- The Ultimate Weapon's teammates can feel second-rate and forgotten.
- The organization is setting itself up for a Kiosk City by allowing critical knowledge to reside only in their Weapon's head.
- Weapons often eschew standardized processes and practices.

Vignette

Individuals with great talent are the keystones to successful organizations and are highly sought after; but as with Rising Upstarts, they require careful management. There are many cases of individual heroics in software development where, in the depths of dismay, a wizened veteran emerges from his cubicle with a cunning work-around or fix. Indeed, these uber-geeks even have their own nerdy competitions such as the "obfuscated C competition" where gifted programmers can compete in writing the most convoluted programs for simple problems such as HelloWorld. There is, of course, nothing wrong with this, provided the obfuscated style does not work itself into production code. The problems arise in how these talents are employed. This is a well-known problem in the software industry and has been written about by many. McConnell called them programming heroes who "take on challenging assignments and write mountains of code. They work vast amounts of overtime. They become indispensable to their projects. Success, it seems, rests squarely on their shoulders" but "for every programming hero ... there are other pathological programming disasters who just don't know how to work well with others. They refuse to participate in technical reviews. They refuse to follow standards established by the team. The sum total of their actions is to prevent other team members from making potentially valuable contributions. A significant number of programming heroes don't turn out to be heroes at all; they turn out to be prima donna programming ball hogs" [McConnell].

Managers can become so seduced by the prodigious talent of these individuals that they involve them in everything. They become so important to their project, team, or even company that without them success seems impossible. This was the case at a small software house in the United Kingdom run by a close friend of ours. Now it must be said that their Ultimate Weapon was quite astoundingly good and is now one of the very top Linux developers, so it is somewhat understandable how integral he was to the company, but even more reason to institutionalize his knowledge of their products, systems, and processes and to encourage him to mentor and coach the rest of the team. Here again, the company was lucky in that he was roundly respected by all his colleagues and readily helped anyone. He even mentored college students at his alma mater, so he was naturally disposed to disseminating his knowledge and to helping make those around him better. We have seen many examples where this is not the case, however.

Kathy, a middle-manager at an enterprise system producer, had joined the company five years prior and quickly became a go-to gal for several executives. She was widely respected for her technical abilities, but also for her work ethic, energy, and focus. In fact, if it was not for her age (she was a career-changer), she would be considered a Rising Upstart. Before long, Kathy's status as the go-to gal had her fully integrated into all her department's product lines to the extent that she was now the only person with enough knowledge to make any decision. She had effectively engineered her supervisor and most of her colleagues out from their products. She was now the confluence through which every plan, change request, design decision, marketing blurb, and tool choice flowed ... and she knew it. Soon her demands started, her cooperation ebbed, and the company had a problem on its hands.

Explanation

Randall Cunningham, who played quarterback for 17 years in the National Football League, mostly for the Philadelphia Eagles, was known as the Ultimate Weapon because he could freelance and improvise a gain in yardage or a score when plays broke down and despite a mediocre supporting cast. Michael Vick is a modern incarnation of this, where his phenomenal athletic abilities can overcome a bad team.

While a team solely relies on an individual, it will not win. In football, the latest dynasty, the New England Patriots, epitomize this concept. While they have some undoubtedly good players, they win with discipline, technique, and coaching rather than phenomenal individual play-making. Corporate America must also be that way. Reliance on a few great individuals is a needlessly high-risk proposition, the rewards of which can be accomplished with effective leadership and management.

Band Aid

If you are in a team with an Ultimate Weapon, you are either:

- Bored that you get to do nothing significant, in which case take control of your own destiny and seek responsibilities; or
- Happy to sit back and let them be the champion, in which case this is not an antipattern to you.

Self-Repair

If you are the Ultimate Weapon, learn how to "pass the ball" like Michael Jordan did. Help your teammates be better by first respecting them and then later mentoring them.

Refactoring

The key is to diversify. You would not want all your savings invested in a single stock, regardless of its past performance or potential; the risk is too high. The same applies in the workplace. This makes for a careful balancing act because Ultimate Weapons can be so valuable and you do not want to risk losing the good ones because you did not challenge them enough, but you must allow other team members to contribute. The first step is to build trust between the superstars and the role players. Even at crunch time, Michael Jordan trusted his teammates to make the winning play when he could not. For interested, or skeptical, readers: John Paxson against Phoenix in 1993 and Steve Kerr against Utah in 1997.

The second step is to assess the Weapon's potential outside their technical brilliance. Are they organized and detail-oriented enough to be effective managers? Are they perceptive and empathetic enough to be leaders? Are they natural communicators who can talk to customers and clients? Where they show aptitude and interest, use them, while delegating away some of their technical tasks ... in other words, mentor them.

Finally, you just have to accept that there are prima donnas out there that can do great things but do not play well with others. You must weigh how valuable they are against the harm they can cause, but always remember that "Individual heroics can contribute to project success, but teamwork generally contributes more than individual accomplishment" [McConnell].

Identification

The following identification instrument can help you determine if Jeff is an Ultimate Weapon. Please respond to the following statements with a "Yes" or "No."

	Yes	No
■ All project assignments start off with Jeff's duties.	___	___
■ No project excludes Jeff.	___	___
■ You have to remind the group leader that others on the team need assignments too.	___	___
■ You and your friend ask yourselves, "What am I, chopped liver?"	___	___

If you responded "Yes" to one or more of these statements, then Jeff may be an Ultimate Weapon.

References

[McConnell] S. McConnell, After the Gold Rush: Creating a True Profession of Software Engineering (Best Practices), Microsoft Press, 1999.

Name: Warm Bodies

Central Concept

A management situation in which a worker who barely meets the minimum expectations of the job and is thusly shunted from project to project, or team to team. The defective individual is called a "Warm Body" although the true problem lies in the manager. This antipattern is the opposite of Rising Upstart, with respect to skills and potential.

Dysfunction

There are two primary dysfunctions with Warm Bodies.

The first focuses on the practice of moving workers on to late-running projects to help get them back on schedule. This is a flawed resource-leveling approach because it fails to account for time spent on the learning curve. New team members are therefore unproductive as they learn the ropes; but even worse, they also need assistance from the existing team members (thus reducing the productivity of the latter), and the work they do get done is often so error-riddled that it needs repair, thus reducing productivity even further.

The second dysfunction occurs when the Warm Bodies are shunted around from department to department because nobody wants them. Certainly, everyone has the right to earn a living, but holding on to these perennial poor performers handicaps each department that they pass through. These kinds of liabilities cannot be afforded in the competitive business environment, not just because they can potentially harm the organization, but also because all cylinders must be firing to be successful.

Vignette

Warm Bodies are unfortunately everywhere, and far more prevalent than Rising Upstarts regrettably. It is fortunate, then, that the superstars are so much more productive than the average (up to 20 times as productive in the software industry apparently). Nevertheless, the impact of a transient Warm Body can be significant.

One depressed software developer recounted the tale of a Warm Body colleague by the name of Eric. The root of the problem was that Eric should never have been hired as a software developer. He was a nice guy and quite good with people, but the truth was he had few technical skills and was hired at a time when anyone who could spell HTML could get a developer position. For a few years, the good times rolled and Eric flew under the radar, his lack of productivity not an issue while the software industry filled its pockets. As the IT recession hit, however, Eric's life changed. His lack of production was now an issue and, realizing that programming was not his forte, he was moved to customer liaison. This should have suited his people skills because he was now providing user support, but this often called for him to work alone, which he did not like to do.

Once the complaints started arriving regarding the absent technical support, Eric was moved again, this time to a junior management position leading a small development team. The thinking was that while he was technically deficient, he should be able to manage other developers. Again he failed. Despite good working relations, Eric had neither leadership potential nor management acumen. A series of poor decisions and a lack of planning soon had his team in a tailspin that required last-ditch heroics and a good deal of Dunkirk Spirit to complete the deliverables.

At this point you would expect that Eric would be on the chopping block, but the tale of woe continued through several other appointments, culminating with Eric as a project manager with 30 direct reports below him (mediocracy at its best!). In less than five years, he had been shunted six times as the organization tried to find a fit for his skill set and personality, all the while demoralizing his colleagues, driving away his subordinates, and failing to meet any targets. And he is still there!

Explanation

In the software development world, Warm Bodies refer to those individuals who tend to be thrown at late projects under the Taylorist assumption that increasing the resources will increase productivity [Brown]. Brooks reported decades ago, however, that this assumption was flawed and that adding people to a late project in fact only makes it later [Brooks]. The best analogy Brooks makes is to pregnancy. It does not matter how many mothers you throw at it, it will still take nine months. Because there can be no breakdown of the tasks involved, and therefore no parallelism, the extra woman-power has no effect.

Obviously, software construction can be decomposed into more discrete tasks than pregnancy, but the general principle is still valid. If a developer is working on a device driver, it will not get completed in a fifth of the time if you give him four buddies to help out. In fact, delays will result as he is forced to spend precious time explaining what he was doing, why he was doing it, and how it fits into the bigger picture. Consequently, utilizing Warm Bodies as a productivity driver is a complete fallacy.

Band Aid

Pass the buck. The simplest fix is to do what everyone else did and send the Warm Body on to the next department, project, or team. Unfortunately, this is exactly how they stick around, so we are really reluctant to promote this tactic.

Self-Repair

Do not be a Warm Body yourself. If you are not successful at what you are doing, then reeducate yourself. If you find that after several different positions in the same industry that things still are not working out, then consider changing careers. After all, you and your employer both deserve to be happy with your work.

Refactoring

The obvious refactoring is to terminate the Warm Bodies, although encouraging them to resign on the basis that they need to "find something they enjoy" is a more tactful approach. Be aware, however, that there are a great many more Warm Bodies than there are Rising Upstarts, and Upstarts resent having to take on the day-to-day trivia that could be handled by role players.

Another strategy is to use education and training to tune the skills of the Warm Body to fit their assigned roles, rather than shopping them around to find a role that fits their skill. This approach is potentially more costly in the short run, but cost-effective in the long run.

Consequently, the best management approach is to identify the Warm Bodies and work with them to find their roles in the organization. This is different from passing them off to the next job function, or the next team — that is the band aid. Evaluate their potential to determine their best fit and help them develop that potential. If they balk at the role you determine, or at the notion that they are indeed a role player, then help them "find something they enjoy."

Identification

The following identification instrument can help you determine if hypothetical person John is a Warm Body. Please respond to the following statements with a "Yes" or "No."

	Yes	No
■ John is inexplicably assigned to a new role in the organization every few months.	——	——
■ John is never quite happy in any of the many assignments that he has had.	——	——
■ John is always the last person to be assigned when work assignments are made.	——	——
■ John's skill set does not seem to be well matched with any role in the organization.	——	——
■ Everybody likes John — but no one can figure out what he actually does.	——	——

If you responded "Yes" to one or more of these statements, then John is probably a Warm Body.

References

[Brown]   W.H. Brown, R.C. Malveau, H.W. McCormick, and T.J. Mowbray, *Antipatterns: Refactoring Software Architectures, and Projects in Crisis*, John Wiley & Sons, 1998.

[Brooks]   F. Brooks, *The Mythical Man-Month*, Addison-Wesley, 1995.

Note

This antipattern is based on an earlier work, "Mal Managerium: A Field Guide" by Phillip Laplante, ©ACM, 2005. *Queue*, Vol. 3, No. 4, May 2005, pp. 64 ff, http://doi.acm.org/0.1145/1066051.1066076.

Chapter 6

Environmental Antipatterns

Cultural or environmental antipatterns are those that are not attributable to a single person, incident, or practice. Instead, these are antipatterns due to a series of poorly thought-out strategies or environmental changes that create a toxic atmosphere, a negative organizational culture. Environmental antipatterns in our catalog include:

- Ant Colony
- Atlas Shrug
- Autonomous Collective
- Boiling Frog Syndrome
- Burning Bag of Dung
- Buzzword Mania
- Deflated Balloon
- Divergent Goals
- Dogmatic About Dysfunction
- Dunkirk Spirit
- Emperor's New Clothes
- Fairness Doctrine
- Fools Rush In
- Founderitis
- French Waiter Syndrome
- Geek Hazing

- Institutional Mistrust
- Kiosk City
- Mediocracy
- One-Eyed King
- Orange Stand Economics
- Pitcairn Island
- Potemkin Village
- Process Clash
- Rubik's Cube
- Shoeless Children
- Worshipping the Golden Calf

Let us look at these environmental antipatterns.

Name: Ant Colony

Central Concept

On the surface, a model society where everyone understands, and is content with, their role, and success of the society is paramount. Beneath the surface, discontent within the society is policed aggressively.

> "Attention all employees. The beatings will continue until morale improves."

Dysfunction

While the issue of a deceptive exterior is ethically troubling, the fact that reality is masked from outside perspectives is not a particular problem. Indeed, we would struggle to find a single organization that is not this way. The primary problems in a police state, such as that of an Ant Colony, can be summarized as follows:

- Such a state favors the stick over the carrot and crushes morale.
- Low morale leads to low productivity, increased absenteeism, and staff retention and recruitment problems.
- Suppression and oppression are the root causes of rebellion and revolution. In the workplace, this means strike action, work-to-rule, and subversive work practices.

- Surviving the police brutality becomes a rite of passage and thus a self-fulfilling prophecy.
- Negativism pervades the organization, and major overhaul becomes the only savior.

Vignette

The Ant Colony is often the reality behind the veneer of an Autonomous Collective, and a prime example of this is in the higher education system. Unlike in industry settings, the U.S. higher education system retains the concept of tenure...a job for life, in simple terms. In most universities, there is a probationary period of between five and seven years during which time those working toward tenure, known as tenure-track faculty, work to show proficiency and accomplishment in teaching, research, and service to the university and their profession. At the end of this probationary period, the tenure-track faculty are judged by numerous levels of university administration and committees of tenured faculty. This judgment can award or deny tenure, and denial usually requires that faculty member to seek alternative employment.

So where is the Ant Colony? Well, the reality of the tenure system in some universities is that for five years or so, tenure-track professors walk on eggshells, frightened to contradict or argue with any tenured faculty member out of fear of recrimination on "judgment day." Whether this is a rational fear or merely a groundless phobia is rather irrelevant because the fear exists, and many tenured faculty relish the apparent power they wield.

Outside observers understand the publish-or-perish maxim that faculty live by, but generally are not aware of the closeted proceedings involved in tenure review. There is no due process, no sharing of information and judgment, and no oversight. In such a system, the fear that a poisonous individual or clique could decide based on personal feelings rather than tangible evidence is very real. Consequently, tenure-track faculty members are often reluctant to engage in public debate or argument, or indeed, offer anything but the most couched of responses to any question.

Explanation

"On the surface, beehives and ant nests seem to be model societies, with each individual striving for the common good. But maintaining this social order sometimes calls for brutal tactics."

—Whitfield

Who would not want to work within an Ant Colony? It seems like such a positive example of community and cooperation. We recall images of hundreds of ants bridging gaps with their bodies to allow others to cross and find food for the colony. Is this not the very essence of a healthy society where everyone gives their all, plays their role as best they can, and, consequently, enjoys the spoils of the collective labor? Well, yes. Superficially. But looking at it more closely, researchers have found that some are more equal than others (not that surprising, as we know there is a queen after all) and also that not all the other citizens are happy with this situation. The workers do not work without "encouragement," for example. So what are we to think? Even nature, without the trappings of ambition, greed, and sloth (save the mammal of the same name!) cannot find a utopian society where citizens will give gladly of everything they have to help the collective good.

Clearly, the Ant Colony is closely related to the Autonomous Collective. Both have the outward appearance of utopian societies where every citizen feels personal reward in the collective success. In the case of the Ant Colony, this appearance is merely that — an appearance. Under the surface we see that not everyone is interested in the greater good, particularly when that greater good conflicts with personal advancement. The rub is that many in the organization are really self-sacrificing, working under the illusion that everyone else is too...these people, in the human context, are being abused and manipulated, which is unfair, and could end up disenfranchised at best, and murderous at worst ("going postal," for example).

Band Aid

The soldier ants in the colony brutalize the ineffective and inefficient workers. Provided you do your job well, you should not be a target; so keep your head down and don't sweat it.

Self-Repair

Try to remember that even the most stubborn mule needs <u>both</u> the carrot and the stick. If it is respect you are seeking, you will find more with encouragement and trust than you will with fear and loathing.

Refactoring

It is unusual for the Ant Colony to be an institutionalized culture; it is usually just a few powerful individuals that keep martial law. In this case, these individuals must be the focus of the refactoring. They are bullies and must be dealt with as such. Look to Bramson's coping strategies for Bulldozers, Sherman Tanks, Exploders, and Snipers.

Identification

The following identification instrument can help determine if your organization is an Ant Colony. Please respond to the following statements with a "Yes" or "No."

	Yes	No
■ I fear retribution if I voice my opinion when it differs from the majority.	___	___
■ There seems to be only one way, "the company's way" of doing things.	___	___
■ Whenever I try to question the status quo with my friends, I am shushed to silence.	___	___
■ There are a few "moles" among my colleagues who seem to exist only to ferret out pockets of resistance and report it to the authorities.	___	___

If you responded "Yes" to one or more of these statements, your organization is an Ant Colony.

References

[Whitfield]   John Whitfield, The Police State, *Nature*, 146, 784–792, April 25, 2002.

Name: Atlas Shrug

Central Concept

Organizations that have had too much recent success lose energy and focus, thereby failing to make additional achievements.

Dysfunction

A company cannot survive on past glories. It must proactively seek improvements and innovations; otherwise, it will lose essential agility and competitive advantage.

Vignette

Let us consider a fictional software company called Atlas Software, which came into being during the heyday of the dot.com era. Atlas Software's flagship product was an enterprise solution based on a client/server architecture. The client application was based on Visual Basic and the server was implemented with a relational database. The company sailed through the dot.com era and survived the subsequent bust because it had a captive client base with substantial revenues for ongoing software customization, maintenance, and incremental improvements, as well as professional services related to the product. The clients were captive because the cost of changing to a competing solution was very high.

Unfortunately, over the years, Atlas ignored the emerging technologies of object-oriented design, multi-tier architecture, and Web-based applications, and are thus in no position to take advantage of the upcoming wave in Web Services integration and Service-Oriented Architectures. It seems clear that soon the company's flagship product will be antiquated with respect to the competition, and the lost opportunity of not switching to a competing product with its advanced features will soon outweigh the cost of switching. Atlas Software is clearly coasting on past successes, and its future is in jeopardy.

This is fictional, of course, but take a look at IBM's history, or Psion, Commodore, or Atari, or recall the panic that ripped through the bricks-and-mortar companies when online retailers turned up in the dot.bomb era. Complacency kills!

Explanation

Imagine a giant, successful company symbolically shrugging its shoulders in disinterest. This is also a passing reference to the highly controversial and complex novel *Atlas Shrugged*, in which along with many of the other ideas of Ayn Rand's philosophy, objectivism is a call to arms to overcome complacency against the existing order.

Companies that fail to innovate and rest on past successes are quickly beaten down by unforgiving customers and the competition. Moreover, the corporate "muscles" needed to introduce, vet, and execute new ideas and products become weak when not constantly exercised.

Band Aid

How bold are you? You can choose to:

- Go along with the crowd — it is the easy way out.
- Wait for others to lead and innovate in the organization.
- Be a cheerleader for others to lead the way out of the slump.
- Or take ownership yourself — unleash your creative spirit and lead the charge.

Self-Repair

Lead the charge. If you are a leader or member of a group that has fallen into complacency, you can start the transformation with yourself. Change the way you work somehow. Innovate. Do whatever it takes to break the *status quo*.

Refactoring

There are a number of steps to take. First, fight complacency. In the 1980s, one company's motto was "we're number one, and it's not too late to change." This is the kind of attitude that leads to long-term success.

In their must-read text on organizational excellence, *Built to Last*, Collins and Porras identified a number of characteristics that distinguished visionary companies from those that were simply very good [Collins]. The two that apply here are:

1. "Good Enough is Never Good Enough," which is consistent with the previous refactoring and contrary to the somewhat worrying trend in software engineering.
2. "Big Hairy Audacious Goals" (or BHAGs). Setting such goals all the time, swinging for the fences as it were, prevents a company from becoming lazy.

Stir things up. Sometimes, causing a little chaos can lead to a burst of creativity and break an organization out of its malaise. At the 3M company, which is famous for product innovation, one of their mantras has been "thou shall not kill a new product idea (no matter how crazy it seems)" [Collins]. If inspiration is not coming from within, then look without; hire an outside visionary to inject new ideas and new ways of thinking.

Finally, the company can spin off a new company that is in a better position to take risks and protect the parent company.

Observations

This antipattern is the organizational equivalent to an individual "resting (sitting) on their laurels." This phrase originates from the use of a crown of laurels as a symbol of victory and significant accomplishment during Greek and Roman times.

Identification

The following identification instrument can help you determine if your organization is an Atlas Shrug. Please respond to the following statements with a "Yes" or "No."

	Yes	No
■ My company still dwells on successes that have been overshadowed by recent failure.	___	___
■ It feels like my organization has no sense of urgency to try new things — even though the world seems to be changing around it.	___	___
■ No one in my organization is encouraged to take risks — in fact, they are discouraged.	___	___

If you responded "Yes" to one or more of these statements, your organization is a bored giant.

References

[Collins]   James C. Collins and Jerry I. Porras, *Built to Last: Successful Habits of Visionary Companies*, Harper Collins, 1994.
[Rand]   Ayn Rand, *Atlas Shrugged*, 1957.

Name: Autonomous Collective

Central Concept

The myth of equality and uniformity of employees within organizations can lead to inaction, decay, and downfall.

Dysfunction

The basic concept of autonomy and self-governance is a very appealing one in many situations. Indeed, academic institutions are a prime example of working versions of such organizations. Unfortunately, however, in any organization there are many tasks, decisions, and administrative detail that must be performed, made, and considered in the effective running of an organization, and this requires a set of skills not found in everyone. Everyone cannot know the whole picture and everyone cannot be involved in every decision — not if we want decisions to ever be made.

Vignette

There are some real examples of an autonomous collective in the IT industry, or at least some of the trappings of such, even if there is a wealth of hierarchical organization too. A great example we witnessed recently was, in fact, a reaction against the malaise of Mediocracy that permeated the company. Upper-management had identified this and generally lacked confidence in the middle managers responsible for day-to-day project operations. Their solution was to introduce peer–review, which can be best described as Survivor-esque (from the popular CBS reality show); the employees receiving the worst peer evaluations were terminated. Of course, empowering the self-interested competitive individuals like this only exacerbated the Mediocracy further and they would have known this had they read that antipattern!

Other examples arise in collective ownership, exhibited in open source development and agile methods such as eXtreme Programming. They sound good in principle but they hide or obfuscate those that lead and they minimize the value of effective management, something technical people are wont to do unfortunately.

In the academic setting where "shared governance" is viewed as an inalienable right, the net effect is often paralysis. The faculty demand input on every aspect of university operations and they accomplish this with a profusion of senates, councils, committees, and sub-committees that examine, reexamine, report, discuss, and vote on everything and anything. Now, much of this busywork is related, and sometimes even critical, to the university's function — curricula, for example — but many other aspects probably best left to accountants, attorneys, or other accomplished administrative and managerial staff are also deliberated.

Explanation

The name comes from the scene in *Monty Python and the Holy Grail*, when King Arthur comes across peasants in a field.

─────────────▼─────────────

King Arthur: How do you do, good lady? I am King Arthur, king of the Britons. Whose castle is that?

Woman: King of the who?

King Arthur: The Britons.

Woman: Who are the Britons?

King Arthur: Well, we all are. We are all Britons, and I am your King.

Woman: I didn't know we had a King. I thought we were an autonomous collective.

Dennis: You're fooling yourself. We're living in a dictatorship: a self-perpetuating autocracy in which the working classes...

King Arthur: Please! Please, good people. I am in haste. Who lives in that castle?

Woman: No one lives there.

King Arthur: Then who is your lord?

Woman: We don't have a lord.

Dennis: I told you. We're an anarcho-syndicalist commune. We take it in turns to act as a sort of executive officer for the week,...

King Arthur: Yes.

Dennis: ...but all the decisions of that officer have to be ratified at a special bi-weekly meeting...

King Arthur: Yes, I see.

Dennis: ...by a simple majority in the case of purely internal affairs,...

King Arthur: Be quiet!

Dennis: ...but by a two-thirds majority in the case of more major--

King Arthur: Be quiet! I order you to be quiet!

Woman: Order, eh? Who does he think he is? Heh.

King Arthur: I am your King!

Woman: Well, I didn't vote for you.

──────────────▲──────────────

Band Aid

The short-term fix depends on your predisposition. There is a leadership vacuum in autonomous collectives that you could attempt to fill yourself if you believe you are up to the task, and leadership becomes you. Otherwise, you can either:

- Focus your energies on your own responsibilities and avoid the tedium of collective decision making; or

■ Relish in the banter, interplay, and debate of such ceremonies —
we know many people who live for such occasions and seem very
happy.

Self-Repair

By definition, you cannot have an Autonomous Collective if you are a
real leader. Do not abrogate your power to others.

Refactoring

The Autonomous Collective is the Marxist dream, but history teaches us
that the utopia Marx had envisioned does not come to fruition. We are
not all equal, and it is folly to contrive it. Indeed, for organizations to run
effectively, someone must lead and others must follow.

To turn things around:

■ Demand decisiveness and accountability of your leaders.
■ Encourage transparency of information whenever possible but also
accept that some things are not for your eyes.
■ Trust in the abilities of others — Autonomous Collectives often
exist because workers do not trust their leaders to do the right thing.

Identification

The following identification instrument can help you determine if your
organization is an Autonomous Collective. Please respond to the following
statements with a "Yes" or "No."

	Yes	No
■ In my organization, no decision seems final — each is subject to endless second-guessing by various groups.	—	—
■ In my organization when something needs to be done, we have to decide which committee (not person) to bring the decision to.	—	—
■ No one seems to have enough authority in my organization to get his or her job done.	—	—
■ I feel like where I work there are too many committees.*	—	—

* Committees are not necessarily bad. But they often do not work the way they were
intended to.

If you responded "Yes" to one or more of these statements, your organization is probably an Autonomous Collective.

References

Monty Python and the Holy Grail, 1975.

Name: Boiling Frog Syndrome[1]

Central Concept

Gradual negative changes in the work environment are too subtle to be noticed, until it is too late.

Dysfunction

Slow, negative changes in workload, work culture, or expectations will be tolerated, even embraced, until the next set of challenges is presented. Then the cycle of acclimation repeats. That is, until individuals begin to rebel, quit, or drop dead at their desks.

Symptoms include:

- Low employee morale
- Unusually high loss of personnel either through attrition, layoffs, firings, or outsourcing
- Degradation in employee performance, such as lateness, low productivity, insubordination, dishonesty, theft, and backstabbing
- Overall drop in the organization's effectiveness

Vignette

Consider the following fictitious, but all too plausible scenario in Amphibian Enterprises, a $10 billion, multinational electronics and software systems engineering firm. For the past three years, revenues have spiraled downward. The reasons why are unimportant. However, in response to the situation, Amphibian's executive management has subjected the company to a series of cost-saving measures, including, business unit consolidation, salary and hiring freezes, and staff reductions through attrition, layoffs, and outsourcing of many functions. Through each tribulation (read: increase in water temperature), the beleaguered but brave employees have held their collective breath and adjusted. But an outside consultant immediately recognized signs of trouble, including increased employee absenteeism, complaints of harassment, disciplinary infractions, and resignations of key employees. When the situation was brought to the attention of senior management, they were surprised. "We thought everyone was coping really well," they said; "We didn't realize it was so bad."

But the Boiling Frog phenomenon does not have to cut across the entire company — it can be localized to a single project. For example, within Amphibian Enterprises, one software engineering group was assigned a large systems integration project for an important client that was scheduled to be completed in six months. Three months into the project, with all proceeding according to schedule, the customer proposes changes that set back the project three months. Six months into the project, the team's top engineer quits. There will be no authorization for a replacement for budgetary reasons and the schedule cannot be slipped. Seven months into the project, it is discovered that a major design assumption is flawed. It will require some redesign of the system and 30 percent recoding of completed code. This results in a further two-month schedule slip. After each setback, the software engineering group meets to discuss the problem and comes up with a workaround. "We'll get by," everyone agrees. But eight months into the project, the group manager has a nervous breakdown. The stress was just too much for him.

Explanation

This antipattern derives its name from the alleged fact that if you place a frog in a pot of boiling water, it will instantly jump out. On the other hand, if you place the frog in a pot of tepid water and slowly raise the temperature, the frog, being unable to sense the gradual increases in the water temperature, will happily stay put until it boils to death.

Why would people accept a string of setbacks, takeaways, insults, etc.? The answer is that most people want to succeed. It is the nature of intelligent, motivated individuals to accept increasing demands on their time, good nature, and physical stamina, to adjust to them, and then convince themselves that everything is OK. Then they prepare for the next demand and resultant increase in water temperature. Finally, in the heat of battle, negative environmental changes are not always easy to detect. So, the Frogs do not know they are boiling.

Band Aid

Enjoy the warm bath (do not sweat it). Remember that is why they call it work — otherwise, it would be called fun. "Bye dear. I'm off to fun," you would say as you jauntily skip out to the car every morning!

Self-Repair

Managers: it is always good to have an outsider, whether it is a spouse, friend, confidante, or even (God forbid) a consultant to help you get a perspective from the outside. This outsider will help you avoid creating a Boiling Frog environment.

Refactoring

The only way for a frog or frog manager to recognize the situation is to have someone else point out the situation to them (if they could do it themselves, they are not a boiled frog because they would have just jumped out). This outside person can be a consultant, a spouse, friend, another frog manager — anyone who is not in the same hot water.

The solution to the problem is generally for the frog to leave the water because it is rarely possible for the frog or even a frog manager to change the temperature. Even if the water temperature can be changed through organizational improvements and best management practices, the changes probably cannot be implemented fast enough to save the frogs already in the hot water.

So, generally speaking, to refactor the boiling frog:

1. *Ask another frog.* That is, someone who understands the situation. This will help calibrate the water. However, if the frog is in the same water (i.e., is a close colleague), he might tell you that the water is OK when it is not.
2. *Ask a cook.* Another can tell if the water is too hot. So the manager of the software group at Amphibian Enterprises might ask a management colleague to assess the situation. Likewise, a team member of the software group might approach another manager to confirm that the water is too hot.

3. *Change the water.* This is very difficult to do. The same thermal inertia that led to the Boiling Frog situation can only be changed slowly. There are no quick fixes.
4. *Change the cook(s).* Sometimes, the only way to change the situation is to bring on a new manager.
5. *Change the frog.* Any frog that detects that he is in boiling water possibly needs to get out, which means asking for a transfer or leaving the company. Too often, employees think they can change the temperature of the water themselves by complaining or otherwise. This can rarely be done. If a manager detects that a frog is boiling, then he or she should take the initiative to remove the frog.

Observations

Improvements in a work environment that occur gradually can undergo a kind of Boiling Frog effect. That is, things get better but too subtly for employees to notice. This is an unfortunate situation that should be addressed in using appropriate refactorings from the negative Boiling Frog situation.

Identification

The following identification instrument can help you determine if your organization tends to be suffering from Boiling Frog Syndrome. Please respond to the following statements with a "Yes" or "No."

	Yes	No
■ My friends and family keep asking me, "Why do you work there?"	—	—
■ People keep leaving my project/team/company for no "good" reason.	—	—
■ For some reason, I find it harder and harder to drag myself to work. I just cannot put my finger on the reason.	—	—
■ I am suffering some of the physical signs of stress (e.g., high blood pressure, crankiness, weight gain, mood changes, depression, anxiety).*	—	—
■ I am praying that our company will go out of business.	—	—

* In which case, please see a physician immediately!

If you responded "Yes" to one or more of these statements, your organization is suffering from Boiling Frog Syndrome.

Name: Burning Bag of Dung[2]

Central Concept

An outgoing manager leaves a situation that is so bad that there is no way to resolve it without getting dirty or burned. Certain environments are conducive to such a practice.

Dysfunction

This antipattern has already been described in humorous metaphor. In the real sense, it describes any negative work environment left by one or more fleeing managers. In fact, often a sequence involves passing the "bag of dung" from one manager to another — talk about a "hot potato"! The situation fits precisely when every obvious remedy to the negative situation involves some sort of traumatic suffering, for example, layoffs.

Vignette

In the software world, the flaming doggy bag can appear in many forms. It can comprise software development practices (or lack thereof), which are so thoroughly embedded in the company that retraining would be futile (e.g., an "agile" shop where every malpractice is explained away as part of the Agile Manifesto). It can also appear as a culture of project management involving the misuse of metrics that leads to paranoia — you cannot suggest that metrics not be used, but neither can you get folks to use them properly.

Explanation

Many of us can remember the terrible prank that kids used to play on unsuspecting neighbors. They would set a paper bag full of — well, you know what it was full of — on fire on the front porch and then ring the doorbell. The poor neighbor would stamp out the fire but ruin his shoes in the process.

A "Burning Bag of Dung" situation is often created when transitional managers (often career climbers) focus on short-term gain at the expense of long-term pain in an effort to enhance their resumes and move on. Senior managers must be aware of this "scorched earth" mentality when hiring, and make sure that the motivations and plans of management candidates are well understood.

Bad managers can leave a similar situation for their successors. They depart, leaving a situation akin to the burning bag of doggie dung — there is no way to resolve the negative situation without getting messed up. The only possible refactoring is for the brave manager to prepare himself for the dirty business.

Band Aid

It is "fun" to sit back and watch the manager dance his way out of the problem. Or, you can try to throw some cold water on the problem — that is, depending on the situation, try a quick and dirty fix.

Self-Repair

Managers: do not leave Burning Bags of Dung. Resolve all problems before moving on. Your reputation will be enhanced.

Refactoring

In most cases, the fire alarm must be sounded; that is, the rest of the organization must help out. This is a plausible solution strategy because it may be that the previous manager was left to deal with the Burning Bag of Dung alone because he was disliked. In the situations described previously, for example, repairing the abuse of agile practices can only be done by proselytizing the correct application of agile methods. While this takes great courage, if the conditions are right, there can be collective reform. If you are a senior manager, you can force retraining, or restructure your team through hiring and firing. The same kind of refactoring might work for an environment where metrics are being accidentally or maliciously misused.

Other refactoring strategies include:

- Demand accountability — this makes it more difficult to leave problems behind.
- Document any new situation that you discover — this helps memorialize the situation in time and protects you from future culpability.

▼

Wise Alec!

There is a story about an outgoing manager who was giving advice to his successor. He said, "I left three envelopes in your top desk drawer marked 'end of year 1,' 'end of year 2,' 'end of year 3.' At the end of each year, I want you to open the appropriate envelope and do what it says." The first year went badly for the new manager. Uncertain of what to do when it was time for his annual evaluation, he remembered the envelopes left by his predecessor. He opened the first envelope. It read "blame your predecessor." And so, he did, and it got him off the hook. The same thing happened the second year. It was an awful year for the manager. But he remembered the second envelope just before his annual review and he opened it. It read "blame the system." And so he did, and he bought himself another year. By the end of the third year, things were still going badly. But he remembered the third envelope. Knowing it held the key to his salvation, he reached for it opened it and read it. It read "prepare three envelopes...."

▲

Observations

Sometimes, the Bags of Dung are left maliciously for the next manager, particularly if he or she is an unwanted successor. This situation is sometimes referred to as a "turd in the bed," as once the new manager gets snug in his new situation, surprise, a problem is discovered.

Identification

The following identification instrument can help determine if your organization tends to create Burning Bags of Dung. Please respond to the following statements with a "Yes" or "No."

	Yes	**No**
▪ The managers around me all seem to blame one another all the time.	___	___
▪ I am afraid to take a new position in my company for fear of what I might discover.	___	___
▪ My predecessor seems very willing to let me take over a set of seemingly trivial problems.	___	___
▪ When I took my current position, I soon needed a new pair of shoes.	___	___

If you responded "Yes" to one or more of these statements, your organization has a tendency to create Burning Bags of Dung.

Name: Buzzword Mania

Central Concept

Organizations become obsessed with buzzwords that most in the organization probably do not really understand.

> Pointy-Haired Manager: We should go with SQL Server.
>
> Dilbert: What color?
>
> Pointy-Haired Manager: Mauve, it has more RAM.

> **—From one of Scott Adam's "Dilbert" cartoons**

Dysfunction

Name dropping and hanging one's hopes on things one does not really understand (see Worshiping the Golden Calf) is really counterproductive as it gives an organization a false sense of security and understanding.

Vignette

We once watched a candidate for a faculty position in our department painfully try to describe something about which he clearly knew nothing. He knew the buzzword for sure, but as he dug himself deeper, we could see the poor soul recognizing that everyone knew that he did not know what he was talking about. So be careful of using buzzwords indiscriminately.

There have been a number of automated, random buzzword generators over the years (just for fun, of course). And if you "google" on "buzzword generator," you will get a number of links to them. Running one of them (http://orion.it.luc.edu/~ahill1/buzzword.html) generated the following, real-looking but nonsensical buzzword sequences:

- Phased upward-trending budgetary management
- Realigned motivating executive solution
- Ameliorated empowering framework
- Future-proofed hybrid matrix
- Open-architected coherent middleware

Explanation

The origin of the name is quite obvious. Too many people like to do technical "namedropping" without knowing what they are talking about.

Every company has its own jargon that is used to help communicate within the company. But the shameless overuse of jargon can create an oppressive culture. Such a culture may seem uninviting to outsiders, new employees, and customers.

A variation of Buzzword Mania is shameless namedropping of important or famous people who one actually does not know, or who you have had only the most superficial of relationships. The acid test to determine if you are namedropping is to ask yourself, "For each person that I reference in conversation as an acquaintance, would they actually know who I am if asked?"

Band Aid

Go along with the game. Smile sweetly and laugh to yourself.

Self-Repair

Stop using buzzwords you do not understand. Ask yourself, "Do I really know what that means or am I just trying to impress?"

Refactoring

The following approaches can be used to deal with a situation of wanton Buzzword Mania:

- Call out the abusers of buzzwords. Ask them, "What does that mean?" or "Please tell me more."
- Education: identify areas where clusters of buzzwords are overused and develop training or educational programs targeted to that area.
- Act dumb; say things like, "Help me understand what that is."

Observations

Buzzword Mania is slightly different from Brown et al.'s Blowhard Jamboree. In Blowhard Jamboree, the dysfunction is too many consultants meeting too many buzzwords in an unproductive contest of who can name the most obscure methodology.

Identification

The following identification instrument can help determine if your organization tends to suffer from Buzzword Mania. Please respond to the following statements with a "Yes" or "No."

	Yes	No
■ There are acronyms used in my organization that no one can correctly identify.	—	—
■ In casual conversation, buzzwords are used at least in every other sentence.	—	—
■ When visitors come to my workplace, they frequently have to interrupt conversations to ask, "What does that mean?"	—	—
■ I use buzzwords in conversation that I really do not understand; I only know where and when to drop them.	—	—

If you responded "Yes" to one or more of these statements, your organization probably suffers from Buzzword Mania.

Name: Deflated Balloon

Central Concept

A once-mighty but now-crippled company reluctant to accept the inevitable. Sales are down, existing staff and computing equipment are underutilized, and many cubicles are empty. This company is failing fast.

Dysfunction

The company is suffering but no one wants to acknowledge it. Budget cutting is difficult to do, and it does tend to lower customers' and vendors' confidence in your company. But if the necessary cutbacks are not made, the staff sees this and it leads to increasing demoralization. Ultimately, a bloated infrastructure will destroy the company.

Vignette

HighFlying Enterprises is a multifaceted computer training and consulting company. One of its business units, the DB group (Deflated Balloon), exists within the confines of HighFlying Enterprises. Now, HighFlying Enterprises enjoyed ten straight years of revenue growth and profitability, much of it due to the astounding success of the DB group, which provides hands-on skills training in networking, Java and C++, database packages, etc. During the dot.com era, the DB group grew fantastically. But as its contribution to the bottom line increased, it demanded more and more resources — personnel, space, the best equipment, special privileges. At the time, it seemed wise to fuel the growth of the DB group.

Over the past three years, the market has changed, and the products that the DB group provides are very limited in demand. True, there may be some future demand for these products or future variants of them, but not now. The senior management of HighFlying Enterprises is unwilling, however, to scale back the DB group proportionate to its decline (some cutbacks were made, but these were mostly superficial). Unfortunately, the drag that DB places on the financial health of HighFlying Enterprises is so great that HighFlying Enterprises is in a great deal of trouble.

Explanation

Imagine a large balloon filled with hot air; now deflate the balloon. The flabby, empty container of a company is a mere shell of its former self.

This situation often arises from Orange Stand Economics or from a Spineless Executive, but there are many other causes — the Atlas Shrug or relying on a product that was once marketable but is no longer (how many buggy whip manufacturers are there?), increased pressure from competition, friction created by new government regulations or taxes, the discovery that your product is dangerous or unhealthy, a looming or recently lost lawsuit — any of these can weaken a company to near death.

The Deflated Balloon can also exist as a flagging business unit within the context of a successful company. In some cases, the Deflated Balloon is well hidden from upper management by the unit's head. In other cases, the Deflated Balloon is allowed to exist because of some sentimental value; for example, if the failing business unit is part of the brand identity of the company or if its manager is favorite of the CEO.

Deflated Balloons abounded during and especially after the end of the dot.com era. These Balloons were largely the product of a false economic model and spending excesses.

Band Aid

Enjoy the ample parking and pick of offices and computer equipment until you do not have a job anymore.

Self-Repair

Do not allow yourself to get into this situation in the first place. But if you are in it, you must make the tough choices now, and not put them off for later when they will be more difficult to make.

Refactoring

The main approach to refactoring this situation is to use commonsense management. Unfortunately, this is not easy to do, even in the good times, but is that much more complicated when once highly successful companies are reduced to a shell of their former existence. Then hubris takes over and there is a reluctance to make the decisions that finally recognize that the company is ill. While downsizing is considered a dirty word to many, when gangrene sets in on a diseased limb, the only recourse is to amputate, so get out your scalpel and cut away.

- If you are a mid-level or senior manager, make the hard decisions such as downsizing staff, breaking the lease, or rightsizing the physical plant.
- Point out worst-case scenarios to management.
- Use a game-theoretic approach or financial analysis to point out the situation.
- Encourage the use of metrics and other cost reduction approaches, such as Six Sigma methodologies, to "clinically" deal with the problem.

Identification

The following identification instrument can help determine if your organization has too much infrastructure. Please respond to the following statements with a "Yes" or "No."

	Yes	No
■ Every other cubicle in my office pod is empty.	___	___
■ I do not leave early for work, hoping to get a good parking space.	___	___
■ Some of my colleagues are wandering around looking for something to do.	___	___
■ I rush to the bank to cash my paycheck before the utility checks are cashed.	___	___
■ The Friday staff pizza parties are attended only by the maintenance guy and me.	___	___

If you responded "Yes" to one or more of these statements, then your company is a Deflated Balloon.

Name: Divergent Goals

Central Concept

Everyone must pull in the same direction. There is no room for individual or hidden agendas that do not align with those of the business.

Dysfunction

There are several direct and indirect problems with Divergent Goals:

- Hidden and personal agendas divergent to the mission of an organization starve resources from strategically important tasks.
- Organizations become fractured as cliques form to promote their own self-interests.
- Decisions are second-guessed and subject to "review by the replay official" as staff members try to decipher genuine motives for edicts and changes.
- Strategic goals are difficult enough to attain when everyone is working toward them; without complete support, they become impossible and introduce risk to the organization.

Vignette

Everyone in an organization must understand the top-level objectives and priorities. It is the reason behind mission statements on coffee mugs and business cards, for example. The organization has tried to condense its strategic goals into concise, evangelical snippets of wisdom so that every employee understands the objectives of the company and, therefore, themselves. Unfortunately, the reality seldom meets the lofty ambition. Most employees look upon mission statements with cynicism because they usually seem like trite clichés in the face of real adversity.

At one aerospace company, we saw a mission statement on everyone's ID badge that included: "No post-delivery failure; Always on time" — as if the mission would be to deliver faulty products late! At the same organization, we witnessed the reality of Divergent Goals within a single plant.

In conversations with the Director of Manufacturing, the changing business world for post-Cold-War defense contractors was explained. The days of cost-plus contracts were over and they now had to compete for commercial and government contracts with fixed-price tenders. This change had to be reflected in the priorities in production. In the days of cost-plus, where the customer (government) paid whatever it cost the contractor to develop and deliver a system or product, plus some predetermined percentage, the government contracts always came first, no matter the cost (because those costs and more would all be recovered). Nowadays a government contract was viewed just the same as a commercial contract and so was prioritized in the same way...the most valuable contracts came first and so on.

Unfortunately, this culture had not been disseminated sufficiently throughout the plant. In talking to the Delivery Manager responsible for packaging and shipping products, the priorities were very different. He still set his priorities as if the Cold War was still going strong and this was clear for all to see. As in most departments at this plant, a whiteboard hung on the wall with the list of job priorities clearly displayed. At the top were AOFG and SIFP, followed by a list of other acronyms. These top two were "Aircraft on Foreign Ground" and "Ship In Foreign Port." This was a clear indication that he still considered the military contracts to be the most important, regardless of the business impact. When questioned about this, he made his position crystal clear. He was from a time when the company was ostensibly a military contractor, he was previously military himself, and he did not care what the "company line" was, he would always put military shipments at the top of the list even if it meant that commercial products with deadlines and delay penalties must wait.

Explanation

In every significant endeavor, we can expect contrary viewpoints and opposing beliefs. These differences of opinion are natural and healthy as they stimulate innovation and risk-taking that are central to success. There is a point, however, where the strategic goals must be set and everyone must be on the same page in trying to attain them. This requires that the goals are meaningful — not mutually exclusive — and, most importantly, fully understood by everyone. Problems arise when these goals are not widely understood or communicated, or if individuals or groups unilaterally decide to work toward alternative goals.

Band Aid

There is no band aid for Divergent Goals...a quick-and-dirty fix cannot effect cultural change. The only short-term fix is therefore micromanagement. Take control of all decisions so that those promoting a different path are removed from the loop. This will be the beginning of a bumpy road, however, leading to Institutional Mistrust and Ant Colonies!

Self-Repair

It is under your control if you are currently not working toward the organizational goals. You really have three options:

1. Get in line.
2. If you feel the company line is wrong, get involved and be a legitimate agent of change.
3. Leave.

Refactoring

Because Divergent Goals can arise accidentally or intentionally, there are two sets of refactorings.

Dealing with the first problem of comprehension and communication involves explaining the impact of day-to-day decisions on larger objectives. This was the case with the shipping priorities at the aerospace company described in the vignette. The manager did not understand the "bigger picture." This is more than providing a coffee mug with the mission statement printed on it, however. Remember that the misunderstanding is not because staff members are not aware of the mission or goals; organizations are generally very good at disseminating them. It is that they do not understand that their decisions have any impact on those goals. They have a very narrow perspective on the organization and that must be broadened.

The second problem of intentionally charting an opposing course is far more insidious, however, and requires considerable intervention and oversight. The starting point is to recognize the disconnect between their personal goals and those of the organization. Why do they feel that the stated goals are incorrect? If the motives really are personal, that they feel their personal success cannot come with success of the organization, radical changes are needed. Otherwise, the best recourse is to get them to buy into the organizational goals. This is most easily achieved if every stakeholder is represented in the definition and dissemination of the core mission and goals, and subsequently kept informed, updated, and represented.

Identification

The following identification instrument can help determine if your company is in a Divergent Goal situation. Please respond to the following statements with a "Yes" or "No."

	Yes	No
■ I find myself arguing a lot with colleagues about things that should be obvious.	___	___
■ My colleagues and I spend a great deal of effort undoing and redoing each other's work.	___	___
■ I feel like some of my colleagues are working for a different company — they just do not seem to get what we are all about.	___	___
■ In our office, there appear to be two or more cliques that cannot seem to work together.	___	___

If you responded "Yes" to one or more of these statements, your company may be facing Divergent Goals.

Name: Dogmatic about Dysfunction

Central Concept

Obsession with an incorrect, or inefficient, technique or process.

Dysfunction

Using the wrong techniques or even the right techniques wrongly does not imply failure, but it does impact time, budget, and quality needlessly.

Vignette

Software engineering is still a maturing discipline, and new techniques arise every day that claim improvements in the gathering and modeling of requirements, the analyzing of systems, and the designing of solutions. In the race for competitive advantage, groups adopt these new techniques before they are fully understood and before the staff knows how best to apply them. Very quickly, a standard approach is defined for applying these new techniques as local "experts" evangelize their use and soon the whole company is indoctrinated. This is a situation we deal with often when we teach practicing professionals techniques they might already be using in work.

In one case, the student was a business analyst at a medical informatics company with responsibility for writing customer requirements as use cases — a form of requirements document that records user input and outcomes as a scenario of interaction between the user and the system. During a lecture on the proper approach to writing these use cases, he kept interrupting to point out how this was not how they did it at work. With each interruption it became obvious that his company's approach was wrong. They were structuring and organizing the use cases incorrectly, specifying the wrong information, and omitting other critical aspects. Each time this was explained to the student, he became more animated in his defense of his company's approach until he eventually resorted to pointing out how profitable the company was, so how could they be doing it wrong? This was also the last resort of another student that decried the approach to software architecture that was being taught. "Our architect founded the company from nothing and it now has $50 million in annual revenue, so his architecture can't be wrong," he announced one evening. "Perhaps if the architecture was correct, the revenues would be higher, or at least the profit from those revenues would be greater," was his answer.

The point was that incorrectly applying a technique, using it at the wrong time or for the wrong purpose, will rarely cause a catastrophe, but it just would not be as efficient as possible. But because these students had not seen the possible efficiencies of doing it right, they assumed that they already were and defended it vigorously...even in the face of compelling evidence to the contrary. Eventually, after completing the course and applying the techniques correctly, the business analyst realized the problems at his company; the architecture student still has a ways to go.

Explanation

We can all become obsessed with a particular technique and then convince ourselves that, because it seems to work, we must be performing it correctly. A great example is swimming. When Colin was in college, a friend challenged him to a swimming race one evening; that friend was the captain of the women's swim team at Swansea University. Colin can swim, and he actually considers himself quite fast, in a thrashing energetic kind of way. Now he protests that he always knew he would not win the race, as, after all, she was the captain of the swim team and he was a basketball player, but he thought he would at least compete. As it turns out, before he had reached three quarters of the first length, she had completed both lengths to win easily. Colin could not believe it. She was so fast and beat him with seemingly little effort even though he was stronger and just as fit (or perhaps almost as fit). It was obvious that while he could swim and succeed in reaching the end (he could, after all, swim two lengths of a pool!), he was not nearly as efficient or effective as she was. It turns out, to no one's surprise, that while Colin's technique worked, it was not optimal, as demonstrated by his challenger's comfortable win.

The odd aspect to this story, and to this antipattern, is that almost everyone accepts that he or she has an acceptable swimming technique, but that it is not nearly as good as a competitive swimmer. Those same people, however, often refuse to accept that the techniques they employ in work could be improved or optimized, or that they in fact are not applying them properly.

Band Aid

The short-term fix is not particularly short term. As an individual in a dogmatic organization, you can probably only change the way you do work. Your success with improved techniques can then allow you to evangelize a little. You can also use any of the strategies for dealing with Bulldozer types to deal with such a person on a temporary basis.

Self-Repair

It is hard to know when you are being dogmatic, but the best way is to listen to what others have to say. They might tell you directly or indirectly about your dysfunction. Once you know you are being perceived as being dogmatic, you need to enlighten yourself.

Refactoring

Dogma is never good and should be discouraged at all turns. It assumes that we have nothing to learn and that we cannot all improve, and this is a very dangerous assumption to make. Instead, foster an atmosphere of inquiry and advancement. Encourage staff to explore new techniques, set up training in their current techniques and ensure that the evangelists in your organization are themselves open to self-improvement.

It is also important to challenge dogma with logic. Whenever someone dismisses a new idea or a new way or working merely because "we have always done it this way," they should be challenged to show how the changes would have a negative impact, just as it is incumbent on the proposer to show how their suggestions will have a positive impact.

Identification

The following identification instrument can help determine if Fred (who might be a manager or other colleague) is Dogmatic about Dysfunction. Please respond to the following statements with a "Yes" or "No."

	Yes	**No**
■ Even in the face of incontrovertible evidence, Fred is never convinced that he is wrong.	___	___
■ No one agrees with Fred on this theory or that — he seems to be out on his own.	___	___
■ If Fred ever realizes that he is wrong, you would not know it because he admits it to no one else.	___	___
■ Fred will only miss "Star Trek" reruns to attend "methodomatic" conferences.	___	___

If you responded "Yes" to one or more of these statements, then Fred is probably Dogmatic about Dysfunction.

Name: Dunkirk Spirit

Central Concept

Despite terrible planning and awful decision making, valiant efforts by good people, usually "on the front lines," get the job done.

Dysfunction

While success against great odds should be lauded, success despite woeful management and ineffective leadership should not. The danger is that when this is performed regularly, the poor planning and decision making is not identified and allowed to continue...success is achieved despite the worst efforts of the administration, and the administration thinks it is because of them! Workers are not given the credit they deserve, and they see their superiors getting credit that they do not. This can only cause disharmony and discord.

Vignette

It seems that Dunkirk Spirit is called upon in every software development project these days. Ed Yourdon called them "Death March" projects [Yourdon] and suggested that they are the norm rather than the exception. Software project managers have failed for a long time to accurately estimate the time, effort, and cost of development projects. Either that or they consistently disregard empirical evidence and intentionally create overly optimistic schedules.

Since 1995, the consulting firm The Standish Group has published a semi-annual assessment of the state of the software industry, called the *Chaos Report*. This widely cited report generally portrays the software industry as being in, what else, chaos with many projects ending unacceptably. These so-called "challenged" projects experienced such problems as cancellation, late delivery, scaled-down functionality, and high defect rates. For example, in 2004, 82 percent of all software projects suffered delivery time overruns [Standish].

So, what do you think is happening in these "challenged" projects? Developers, analysts, and architects are not resting on their laurels as time ticks by and costs ratchet up; they are working around the clock trying to get back on track. This is not because the task is too difficult or the technologies too unreliable; it happens too often for that to be the case. Responsibility—blame—rests with the managers and their superiors who refuse to accept the realities of large-scale software development.

As is so often the case, this is not solely the domain of software engineers, however. A fellow plane passenger on a recent business trip related a similar experience. Harry was a project manager for a construction company that specialized in commercial office buildings. His company usually acted as a subcontractor working on the steel substructure, so their schedule was largely dictated by the master schedule created by the primary contractor for the project. He could not remember the last time that schedule was remotely attainable. Now, this was not purely the fault of the primary contractors. The steelwork contracts were won on tenders submitted by Harry's bosses and these included work breakdowns and schedules that were knowingly unattainable (optimistic was how they characterized them), just so they could win. Harry was then stuck trying to make them work while under the "screw" of the primary contractor, and it was left to him to turn that screw on his subcontractors and laborers.

Toward the end of every contract, Harry's weekends were spent on-site fighting the inevitable fires as deliveries arrived late, materials arrived out of specification, laborers were absent, etc. He was clearly very frustrated with the situation and felt that his own reputation and character were on the line when deadlines were missed or quality was compromised.

To compound his issues, he was also working under a Spineless Executive who refused to attend subcontractor meetings with the primary contractor and would send Harry to face their wrath instead. Harry was gutting it out because he was approaching retirement, but he had to fill in for so many younger managers who had quit under the conditions. His laborers were also growing sick of the constant time pressures, and it was becoming increasingly difficult to find good workers willing to subject themselves to such compressed schedules without additional pay. If you are reading this Harry, we feel your pain and hope that you enjoyed San Diego.

Explanation

The "Dunkirk Miracle" is remembered by many for the bravery and valiant efforts of the merchant navy, local fishermen, and every other type of seafarer with as much as a harbor dingy crossing the English Channel in rescue of the tragically outnumbered and out-armored troops of the British Expeditionary Force (BEF) that had been driven back across France and were now trapped in the small port town of Dunkirk.

The BEF was a respected fighting unit and was deployed across Europe in the early days of World War II to halt the advance of the Nazi war machine as it marched across Western Europe. The rescue mission, Operation Dynamo, saved the lives of over 300,000 Allied troops and is remembered with great pride in Britain. We forget, conveniently, about the horrendous planning and pitiful intelligence that led to such a catastrophic situation in the first place.

Allied commanders, as they appeared wont to do, drastically underestimated the size, power, and strategy of the Nazi forces that would oppose them. The blitzkrieg that rained down upon the BEF and the remainder of the French Army devastated their lines and pushed them all the way back from the Franco-Belgian border to Dunkirk. Now desperate, the British Admiralty called upon the "Little Ships of Dunkirk" (a motley collection of hundreds of hastily recruited fishing vessels and pleasure craft) to save their beleaguered brethren. It was a testament to the British never-say-die attitude in the face of incredible odds without doubt, even despite the fact that they had to leave over 40,000 French troops and most of the equipment (estimated at over 50,000 vehicles) behind.

Band Aid

You cannot always get the credit you deserve. Take solace in the success of the organization. Eventually, the real heroes will be found.

Self-Repair

Managers that allow "Dunkirks" to occur ought to be on the front lines themselves. Do not allow a Dunkirk to happen; but when it does, roll up your sleeves and get in there with the troops to resolve the crisis. Your leadership will inspire these heroes and make them feel appreciated.

Refactoring

Yourdon's preferred solution to Death March projects is to resign. That might be the most efficient choice, but it is not a particularly practical one in the current economy. Instead, one must deal with the significant drivers that create the need for Dunkirk Spirit. Kent Beck realized this and in eXtreme Programming he introduced the notion of sustainable pace. That the 40-hour week should be respected and if overtime was required for consecutive weeks, the plan should be revised. He was not so naïve to think that this one change to the prevailing wisdom would be sufficient, so he included practices that promote teamwork and cooperation over competition and negotiation, including collective code ownership (no one person "owns" any particular aspect of the project) and on-site customers that facilitate communication and collaboration between stakeholders.

Even if these measures seem extreme (well they would, would they not?), the principles they represent should be respected. Using time-to-market pressures as an excuse for ridiculous schedules really just masks the real reasons that managers overwork staff: political capital, one-upmanship, disrespect, or hubris.

Identification

The following identification instrument can help determine if your organization is getting by on Dunkirk Spirit. Please respond to the following statements with a "Yes" or "No."

	Yes	No
■ A few of us always seem to "save the day" at the end, but we rarely get credit for it.	——	——
■ I am always wondering what kind of disaster our management is going to cook up for us next.	——	——
■ I refer to work in terms similar to some kind of battle (e.g., "back to the trenches").	——	——
■ Every day I feel like I am fighting and not making any progress.	——	——

If you responded "Yes" to one or more of these statements, your organization is surviving on the Dunkirk Spirit of a few.

References

[Standish]   The Standish Group International, *Chaos Report*, 2004.
[Yourdon]   E. Yourdon, *Death March*, 2nd ed., Prentice Hall, 2003.

Name: The Emperor's New Clothes³

Central Concept

The classic situation of no one wanting to point out the obvious, embarrassing truth about a situation or person.

> "But the Emperor has nothing on at all," cried a little child.

—The Emperor's New Clothes,
Hans Christian Andersen

Dysfunction

The fundamental problem in such a situation is that the organization is not one in which honesty is valued. If anyone can get away with some kind of charade and everyone is willing to let it go, even a seemingly innocuous one, then what other half-truths are being told? What other essential information is being brushed aside?

Vignette

For this example we must thank Colin's father, who is a contract manager for a fenestration engineering company (we will let you look that up). On this occasion, the company was a subcontractor on a multi-million pound (Colin is from the United Kingdom, remember) construction project and, as was often the case, the project was running late and the general contractor was getting pretty steamed about it.

As time slipped away, the general contractor decided that a rallying speech was in order so he called all the subcontractors to a meeting. "We need to get this finished," he began. "No more excuses, no more mistakes." (Yes, not particularly peppy, but what do you expect from a British building contractor?) He then spent the next ten minutes detailing how the project was to progress from then on and encouraged everyone to pull out all the stops to get the project finished on time. He closed by asking if anyone knew of any reason why they could not accomplish this goal. Everyone fervently agreed and promised to come through, although they all knew it was impossible...no one wanted to point out to the boss how out of touch with reality he was, in fear of suffering the consequences — well, everyone except Colin's father. He had seen this all too many times before to think that a 20-minute pep talk was going to change things; they were still months behind schedule, there were still many problems to overcome, and the budget was already shrinking. He suffered the wrath of the boss for his candor, but he was right in the end.

Explanation

The Emperor's New Clothes is a short story written by Hans Christian Andersen in 1837. It tells the story of an emperor so consumed with his appearance and vanity that he seeks out increasingly elaborate clothing until he hears of a new suit made from the finest, most magnificent cloth. So magnificent is this cloth that it is invisible to the foolish and unworthy. He sends out two of his most trusted lieutenants to check on the cloth; and although they cannot see it, they do not wish to admit to being foolish and unworthy so they both praise it. When the emperor then parades in front of his subjects in the new suit, they too praise its color and magnificence, too afraid to admit they see nothing, until a small child, unencumbered by fear, observes, "But he has nothing on at all!"

Now, it is very rare that management chooses to deliberately fool everyone with a false technology except when the situation is a case of a One-Eyed King or Worshiping the Golden Calf. As in the fairy tale, someone has sold management on this flawed technology; we will call it "methodomatic." We have mentioned the humorous term "methodomatic" previously. Credit should be given to Steve McConnell for coining this term in his classic book, *Code Complete* [McConnell].

Band Aid

Go along with the charade. It is the easiest thing to do and you can always chuckle quietly to yourself.

Self-Repair

You might not know that you are a naked emperor. The only way to find out is to be told. So, listen to those around you. If you know you are deliberately playing the charade, you really should stop — you are not getting real respect from those around you.

Refactoring

You need to call out the situation. Even when the situation is discovered, obvious or not, it does take some courage, however, to speak the truth, much like the courage shown by Toto when unmasking the humbug in *The Wizard of Oz*.

Observations

This situation is somewhat different from the Potemkin Village, in that the deception is not masked by some elaborate façade. In fact, the deception is quite obvious — it is simply the case that no one wants to point out the obvious truth of the situation for some political or financial reason, or out of fear of the backlash.

Identification

The following identification instrument can help determine if your organization tends to fall for naked emperors. Please respond to the following statements with a "Yes" or "No."

	Yes	No
■ I really do not understand why my boss is hanging his hat on this new technology/vendor/process. No one seems to know.	—	—
■ We all know that the technology/vendor/process does not work, but no one has the courage to tell the boss.	—	—
■ There are moans and groans whenever "methodomatic" is mentioned.	—	—

If you responded "Yes" to one or more of these statements, then someone in your organization is probably an emperor in false duds.

Reference

[McConnell]   Steve McConnell, *Code Complete*, Microsoft Press, 1993.

Name: Fairness Doctrine

Central Concept

One can use blind obsession with fairness and uniformity in management as an excuse to avoid dealing directly with problematic people.

Dysfunction

We have repeatedly touched upon on the falsity in the assumption that treating everyone the same way in an organization is the key to success. When the identical treatment of everyone in all situations is institutionalized, this leads to the antipattern: a team is as slow as its slowest worker, and a chain is as weak as its weakest link. The Fairness Doctrine is the failure to identify, remediate, and, if necessary, remove those who act as distractions in the organization or who do not pull their own weight.

Vignette

Colin's favorite example of the Fairness Doctrine is the "No Child Left Behind" program currently in vogue in America. In fact, he prefers to call it "No Child Allowed to Progress." Phil is less critical and prefers to recall when he worked for a chief executive whose practice it was at ribbon cuttings, kickoff events, and celebrations to congratulate everyone in the room, name by name, for their role in the success. This was an effort to be inclusive, of course, and to not accidentally fail to acknowledge someone deservedly. But this was a small organization, and the CEO should have known who participated and who did not. In some cases, he congratulated and praised people for their role in an effort that was concluded before they had even joined the organization. This ridiculous pandering and trying to be fair was so transparent as to embarrass both those who actually participated in the project and those who knew they did not.

Explanation

Fairness is a good thing. Who does not want fairness? But when the quest for fairness comes at the deliberate overlooking of failure and inadequacy and reluctance to reward excellence, it becomes doctrinal. And that is not fair to those who are doing their fair share or more.

The Fairness Doctrine can lead to Mediocracy, as it demoralizes those who wish to be excellent and rewards those who wish to be sub-par. Some managers and executives prefer to make across-the-board decisions that affect everyone equally, regardless of the hard work and ingenuity of the best and despite the poor performance of the worst. This approach can anger and discourage the very people most important to the organization's success, those doing all the work, and fails to punish or rehabilitate those weighing the organization down.

Band Aid

Take advantage of the situation, knowing that the Fairness Doctrine can get you out of any jam.

Self-Repair

True fairness comes when you hold people accountable for their failures and weaknesses as well as their successes. Not everyone should be treated equally unless their contributions are precisely equal. Recognition and reward should be rewarded commensurate with performance. To do otherwise is not fair.

Refactoring

Sometimes people fail, under-perform, or are downright evil. They must be dealt with directly. Indirectly attacking individual problems with broad strokes leads to resentment. Point this out to your manager. Let them know that the situation is not escaping the attention of others. At other times, people perform excellently and go beyond what is required of them. This must also be recognized.

On a shameless, personal level, you can fight the Fairness Doctrine by demanding personal recognition and promoting yourself.

Observations

The Fairness Doctrine can lead to a project sequence that is probably posted on some Wise Alec's door where you work:

> The Six Steps in a Project:
> 1. Enthusiasm
> 2. Disillusionment
> 3. Panic
> 4. Search for the guilty
> 5. Blame for the innocent
> 6. Rewards for the uninvolved

In an environment where there is true accountability and the price for equity is not tolerance of incompetence, the above sequence could never happen.

Identification

The following identification instrument can help determine if your organization may be living under a Fairness Doctrine. Please respond to the following statements with a "Yes" or "No."

Yes **No**

- When we celebrate successes, the laundry list of everyone who "contributed to the success" includes some who were not involved in the project.   ___   ___
- I do not feel like I am being properly recognized when I perform work that is "beyond the call of duty."   ___   ___
- I do not feel that those who are shirking their duties or performing poorly are being properly called out.   ___   ___
- Salary increases are the same for everyone on a percentage basis, regardless of performance.   ___   ___

If you responded "Yes" to one or more of these statements, you may be living under a Fairness Doctrine.

Name: Fools Rush In

Central Concept

A rush to use a new methodology, tool, or platform. Generally, any organization where rash behavior is permitted.

Dysfunction

The IT and software development world is an ever-changing one; and new ideas, technologies, methodologies, and practices arise all the time. It is often not wise to be one of the earliest adopters. Usually, the "latest and greatest" is based more on hype than trusted evidence — more sizzle than steak.

Vignette

The almost meteoric rise in popularity of agile software development methodologies, and eXtreme Programming in particular, is a great case in point. That is not to say that these approaches are actually guilty of more show than substance. Rather, the hype surrounding them, like many technical advances, lures people before they fully understand the requirements and constraints needed to use them, or the effects they will have on current work practices or the organization.

Agile development, for those who have avoided the passing bandwagon, is a general approach to software development that eschews the comprehensive (read voluminous) documentation, planning, and general ceremony that accompanies most engineering efforts. The intent is that without these encumbrances, the engineers can focus on the real task of building useful software systems that meet the expectations and needs of the customer, even as those needs change over time.

Early adopters should be careful, however, because there is a certain cultural inertia in all organizations and the move to agile development constitutes a cultural shift that many software producers may find difficult to implement, and therefore difficult to succeed with; they experience Process Clash.

There are other issues that must be considered — issues that go beyond the cultural difficulties in changing processes. The promise of agile development is built upon some pretty important assumptions, and it is important that any implementers understand them. To go into great detail of these issues merely to make the point would be gratuitous; but for interested readers, we hint that you might want to look at the economic models of requirements change as a starting point.

Explanation

Alexander Pope said that "fools rush in where angels fear to tread...fools are reckless in situations that the wise avoid" [Pope]. Although we are all intuitively aware of this sentiment, even if we have not read Pope, it seems that the allure of new technologies or techniques is too much to resist. In the 1990s, Western automotive manufacturers were seduced by the successes of their Japanese counterparts who had instigated a new type of customized manufacturing known as Just In Time. Here, an integrated supply chain and a highly adaptive manufacturing plant allowed for an almost build-to-order approach. This was in stark contrast to the build-to-stock, large inventory system at work in the West. In response, the Western automakers attempted to adopt this mass-customization approach and the practices associated with it. Except for a few examples, the auto industry is still struggling with this transition. You cannot just replicate the evolutionary processes that allowed the Japanese manufacturing industry to mobilize so efficiently. To adopt their processes, you must realize what culture sustains it and what infrastructure supports it.

Band Aid

Try to keep up with the rush while trying to slow down things for everyone by asking questions and trying to focus attention on the theory (if there is any) behind the bold initiative.

Self-Repair

Be deliberate. Think and study before adopting any new-fad technology. Be skeptical.

Refactoring

We have emphasized the importance of planning throughout this book, and we will keep emphasizing it. Rushing into anything without planning is foolish.

If you must be an early adopter hoping to be the first to catch a wave to success, your business sense must be well tuned to the odor of vaporware.

Other techniques that can help include:

- Ask a lot of questions to slow things down.
- Provide the group and management with papers and research that help put the new technology in perspective and highlight the pros and cons.

Identification

The following identification instrument can help determine if your organization rushes to use the latest fad. Please respond to the following statements with a "Yes" or "No."

	Yes	No
■ My organization is so "agile" that we change technologies on a dime.	___	___
■ My organization is not one in which reading technical literature is valued.	___	___
■ I wonder what the "technology du jour" will be when the senior management team gets back from the conference.	___	___
■ My company does not have a long-range technology plan.	___	___

If you responded "Yes" to one or more of these statements, then your organization may be one of Fools Rushing In.

References

[Neill]   Colin Neill, The Extreme Programming Bandwagon: Revolution or Just Revolting?, *IT Professional*, 5(5), 62–64, September–October 2003.
[Pope]   Alexander Pope, *An Essay on Criticism*, Lewis, London, 1711.

Name: Founderitis[4]

Central Concept

The founder of a company has difficulty letting go when the company grows beyond his skills. The founder still wants to control everything as he did in the days when it was a one-person shop and he had to wear all the hats.

Dysfunction

The condition and its name used here are well known. While this anti-pattern is attributable to a single individual (or small group of founders), the effects are so profound and so tightly woven into the fabric of the company that it is environmentally transforming. The effects are pervasive micromanagement from the founder on down and a stifling climate.

Vignette

We have seen many organizations from a few million to billions of dollars in revenues suffering from Founderitis. For example, we know of two $100+ million software companies, each with more than 200 employees, where the founder still codes and personally approves the code changes made by anyone else.

Colin met with a vice president of a medium-sized financial services solution provider to discuss a radical change in software development strategy, including considerable outsourcing and the introduction of practices and policies to support and enforce agility. During the discussion, it came out that a consistent fly in the ointment in recent history has been the frequent "tinkering" of the underlying processing engine by the CEO.

The company was created from the guy's garage, à la Hewlett-Packard, and this engine was something he had personally built in those halcyon days. Unfortunately, he could not then detach himself from his "baby" and would modify and recode aspects of the stable codebase whenever he felt necessary, despite the company now being a several-hundred developer organization and the fact that the CEO was no longer party to the development, planning, and system architecture decisions. In essence, he now "broke" the system on a regular basis, causing considerable rework and repair for his staff, but his stature and position in the company prohibited anybody from broaching the topic.

At the end of the day, creative people find it very difficult to relinquish control or influence over the fruits of their labor, even when they are no longer best placed or informed to provide that oversight. Their role has changed and they cannot devote the time or energy to keep abreast of a constantly changing and evolving technology or discipline.

Explanation

The origin of "Founderitis" is unknown. Phil learned of it from a person specializing in raising capital for nonprofit organizations. Founderitis is especially widespread in nonprofit institutions. But we have seen $2-billion companies, small companies, and many colleges and universities suffering from Founderitis.

Founders of nonprofits manage to retain control of the organizations they founded because they are often the main source of financing. The same is true in many for-profit ventures.

Most experienced venture capitalists are aware of Founderitis and will seek to remove the founder of even a successful start-up once it reaches a certain level of revenue (e.g., $5 million). The reason why Founderitis and its effects are so evil is that the skills needed to start a company from scratch to a successful small level are very different from what it takes to run even a medium-sized and certainly a public company. Because many software companies started as basement operations, when they grow, they often suffer from Founderitis.

For an excellent treatment of two companies that suffered from Founderitis, including one in which the influences of the founder were mostly positive, read *The Emperors of Chocolate* by Joël Glenn Brenner [Brenner].

Band Aid

Say "yes sir" and do not worry for the founder — for he will worry enough himself.

Self-Repair

If you are a founder of a company, you must encourage diversity of thought, have a succession plan, and listen to outsiders. And please take a vacation sometime!

Refactoring

A trusted lieutenant must reign control from the founder somehow, and occasionally this might have to be somewhat subversive to succeed. In the case of the financial services solution provider, perhaps a change in the configuration management system — that would leave a version of the engine available to the CEO, but that is not linked into to the sold solutions (unknown to him, of course) — would avoid the consequences although not cure the "disease."

Other refactorings include:

- Developing a succession plan that everyone knows about
- Getting a third party respected by the founder (e.g., board members) to talk with the founder about the negative culture
- Learning to accept the situation
- Keeping the founder involved (if you have their buy-in, anything is possible)
- Leaving the company (this is most likely — often even the sons of founders leave because they cannot survive in an environment suffering from Founderitis)

Observations

Unfortunately, when founders leave progeny, they can extend the case of Founderitis to a long legacy.

Identification

The following identification instrument can help determine if your organization suffers from Founderitis. Please respond to the following statements with a "Yes" or "No."

	Yes	No
■ No one in this company is empowered to make real decisions except the founder.	___	___
■ The board of directors of this company is stacked with relatives and close friends of the founder.	___	___
■ The founder of this company arrives before and leaves after everyone else.	___	___
■ The founder refers to this organization as "his baby."	___	___
■ Everyone in this company wonders what will happen to the company if the founder dies.	___	___

If you responded "Yes" to one or more of these statements, your organization suffers from Founderitis.

References

[Brenner]   Joël Glenn Brenner, *The Emperors of Chocolate*, Broadway, 2000.

Name: French Waiter Syndrome[5]

Central Concept

An environment where rudeness prevails and interpersonal dynamics are bad. In general, an uncivil environment.

Dysfunction

Managers, staff, or both are surly, and interpersonal dynamics are bad all around. Vendors and customers are also treated poorly. Business declines.

Vignette

Interestingly, Colin and his wife suffered at the hands of a surly waiter on their first wedding anniversary. They were vacationing in Florida and decided to spend the evening of their anniversary at one of the highest acclaimed steak houses in America. While the food was very good (over-priced, but good), the experience of ordering their wine soured everything. The $30 bottle of red wine they selected to complement their steaks was immediately ridiculed by the waiter. "That's not a good wine, Sir," he told them. "The only cheap wine I could recommend is this one," he continued, pointing to the $90 bottle on the list. It seems waiters in Florida make a very good living to consider $90-wine cheap. His derogatory attitude did not help that good living, however, not that time at least.

In the general sense, many of the interactions depicted for the seven difficult personality types are symptomatic of an environment that tolerates such behaviors. In particular, take a look at the Exploder confrontation between Tom and Sue.

Explanation

Think of the stereotypical snooty French restaurant where waiters are rude and incompetent. Why are we picking on French waiters? We thought about French garbage men. No, really, nothing against the French (after all, Phil's ancestors were happy to live there up until about 1675) or waiters (most of our experiences with them have been excellent). It is just that there is an image of condescension, rudeness, and resentful service that comes to mind when we think of a snooty, fake-French accent waiter in an uppity restaurant.

Rudeness creates an environment where people do not feel valued. Moreover, if you treat your employees rudely, they are likely to treat customers rudely, and that is not good business.

It is possible that the French Waiter Syndrome situation could be a function of Managerial Cloning, where nasty senior management hires those in their own image and so on down the organizational hierarchy.

Band Aid

Use the coping strategies discussed for dealing with difficult people to handle each French Waiter on a case-by-case basis.

Self-Repair

Be kind to people. Be respectful and caring. The Golden Rule really does make good business sense (see Chapter 7).

Refactoring

Set the tone of the culture from the top. Top managers need to create an environment that aligns with the mission of the organization, and then hire staff members who are likely to succeed and be happy in such an environment. If you are not at the top of the "food chain," you can still help foster a transformation by setting a positive example — we talk about the Golden Rule as an appropriate general refactoring — this is a great situation to use that principle. Techniques useful here include:

- Retraining to improve the group dynamics can help. When necessary, misfits and troublemakers should be removed.
- Outside audits can help reveal the severity of the negative situation.
- Establish codes of civility.

Observations

A frequently used solution to deal with a bad waiter is to promote him in an effort to get him away from customers. However, he is apt to treat his staff poorly and they, in turn, will treat more colleagues and customers badly. This can only lead to Mediocracy.

Sometimes, when an organization is failing — in part because of poor treatment of customers and staff — management will misidentify the problem as a human resource shortage. Then the organization goes on to hire more "French Waiters," thus amplifying the problem. This illustrates a classic principle in management — one good person is better than two bad ones.

Sidebar 6.1 The Fly in the Soup Joke

This is such a classic joke we cannot help ourselves from repeating our ten favorite punch lines to it, most of which we think we invented.

Customer: Waiter, what is this fly doing in my soup?

Waiter: [Here are his top ten possible answers]

10: The backstroke, no... the butterfly.
9: There's a fly in your soup? We have to charge extra for that.
8: That is impossible, we serve only cockroaches in our soups.
7: Oh my God, he's drowning. Quick, throw him a Cheerio.
6: I think he is wretching.
5: He's actually a member of our quality control team and he is taking soup samples for analysis.
4: Oh, I'm sorry. You don't like soup with your fly?
3: Just a moment, I'll scoop him out with my hand as soon as I finish picking my nose.
2: Well, take your pants out of the soup then!
1: Saving the spider.

Why not retrain the bad waiters? We are not fans of retraining to remedy personality issues. If someone is in a customer service role and their attitude stinks, then fire them. If any amount of retraining, therapy, electro-shock, or whatever could possibly adjust their attitude, it would cost too much anyway.

Identification

The following identification instrument can help determine if your organization has a culture of rudeness and disrespect. Please respond to the following statements with a "Yes" or "No."

	Yes	No
■ I do not believe that anyone has been disciplined about rude or abusive language or treatment of colleagues and customers, although this behavior is pervasive.	—	—
■ Leading managers in my company are well known to be rude and sharp-tongued.	—	—
■ Sarcasm, derision, and humiliation are regular techniques used in my organization for identifying mistakes.	—	—
■ I have seen people brought to tears because of the way they have been treated or spoken to.	—	—

If you responded "Yes" to one or more of these statements, your organization probably suffers from the French Waiter Syndrome.

Name: Geek Hazing[6]

Central Concept

Novice software engineers are assigned mundane tasks rather than more challenging tasks from which they can learn. Geek hazing can occur in any setting, however, where some form of initiation or rite of passage involving doing onerous work precedes any real job assignment.

Dysfunction

This strategy works to a degree if the mundane tasks really are mundane, although it is somewhat petty. While rookies on sports teams are assigned menial tasks by the veterans during their off-time or at practice, a great player, whether a rookie or a seasoned veteran, will be given the ball and is expected to "make plays" right from the get-go. Not allowing talent to shine will forego that talent.

Vignette

Phil's first job (in 1982) was working for an aerospace company working on very high-profile navigation systems for various aircraft and the Space

Shuttle. He thought he would be preparing code for some of these projects. But his first few months were spent flow-charting (that is, reverse-engineering the documentation) for Fortran code as well as instruction counting assembly language for the purposes of performance analysis. Later, he was given the task of maintaining code that had been written ten years before — and it was bad code at that. He learned to look for "code smells" (indicators of possibly bad design) based on the identity of the author of the code, but he hated it and eventually moved on.

Explanation

We use the term "Geek Hazing" rather than Phil Brainerd's IO Divorce because the new name reflects the kind of "bullying" that geeks can inflict. It is probably the only time in their lives when the geeks wield power. The IO Divorce relates to the fact that the "mundane" is often anything but; maintenance in software development is one of the toughest tasks; it is not desirable, however, because the creative work has been done already.

Geek Hazing tasks can be varied and diabolical. Post documentation of the code of another is a favorite one because the excuse can be given that "this is the best way to learn the system" (maybe it is, when there is no other documentation — but shame on the organization that allows this to happen). Other mundane and possibly useless tasks include adding comments to code, beautifying code, reading procedures manuals, reading programming language books, and building useless tools. One of our reviewers reported having to search through a large code base (several hundred thousand lines of C code) to remove "#if" and "#define" compiler statements for a platform type that was no longer supported as one of his first jobs out of school. You can probably think of dozens of other busy works.

We know of several organizations, however, where a form of Geek Hazing is used while new hires await security clearances, which can often take months to process. This would not qualify necessarily as Geek Hazing because there is a legitimate reason why the new guys cannot be given certain work. But knowing that this is the situation ahead of time means that there should be in place a number of meaningful but unclassified tasks for these new hires to perform.

Band Aid

Go along with the hazing but make the most out of it. Even a very mundane job has some value to it if you look carefully. Perhaps there are lessons to learn from the inadequacies of the project you have been assigned to. Maybe it provides you with an opportunity to connect with an important person involved with the project. Whatever the case may be, look for some value in the "valueless" and mundane jobs.

The other possibility is to find yourself meaningful work so long as it does not interfere with your busy work.

Self-Repair

Do not haze the newcomers. Understand that while there is some learning to be done by mundane tasks, more is learned when new members of the team are mentored properly.

Refactoring

In his famous *Mythical Man Month*, Fred Brooks talks about the "second system effect" — the over-engineering and carryover of bad design decisions in second versions of systems. He notes that this problem is often due to the fact that the maintainers of legacy systems are very junior engineers who are afraid to challenge the design decisions of the "masters." He suggests that the solution is to involve junior engineers in new systems designs (together with experienced engineers) and put the experienced engineers on the legacy systems. From our anecdotal observations, this rarely happens in practice. Therefore, re-education and attitude adjustment are the two main refactorings.

Education involves:

- Correcting the mistaken notion that the generation of reports is the province of beginners alone
- Providing training alternatives for beginners involves a rethinking of the problem that occurs in all disciplines; the idea that some tasks are beneath the status of the experienced.

In general, you should be careful not to let great talent get disheartened, disenfranchised, or resentful; and do not confuse experience with proficiency or excellence. Assign tasks based on ability, not age, experience, etc.

Identification

The following identification instrument can help determine if your organization tends to haze "geeks." Please respond to the following statements with a "Yes" or "No."

	Yes	**No**

- Every new member of our team has to go through some sort of "initiation," that is, they have to do menial work before we give them choice projects. ___ ___
- Senior members of our organization never do menial work, even when it involves important projects. ___ ___
- I do not think I learned anything on the first few projects that I worked on in this organization. ___ ___
- I like giving menial tasks to the "fresh-outs" (a derogatory term referring to someone having just graduated from college). ___ ___

If you responded "Yes" to one or more of these statements, your organization engages in Geek Hazing.

References

[Brooks]   Frederick Brooks, *The Mythical Man Month*, second edition, Addison-Wesley, 1995.

Name: Institutional Mistrust

Central Concept

In many organizations, there is a general lack of trust in the abilities and motives of every job function, business unit, and person; this is human nature, but sometimes it pervades the culture so much that it is effectively institutional.

Dysfunction

Without trust, very little can be achieved. As a result,

- Tasks are duplicated because the results from one group are not trusted by another group.
- Responsibilities are constantly on the move as senior management struggles to find the truth among the lies.
- Organizational structure is lost as business units or departments are dismantled, restructured, or neutered.
- Energy is lost by pointing fingers.
- Morale declines and the good staff members leave.

Vignette

In the IT and software development industry, it is well known, and often the punch line to dry jokes, that:

- Developers do not trust that the customers know what they want or need.

- Architects do not trust the decision-making abilities of the coders — they over-specify aspects of a design that should really be left to the coders themselves.
- Coders do not trust that the test groups have the skills to find and repair errors without causing more damage than they fix.

The same situation occurs everywhere of course, and can be just banter, but we have seen it almost destroy companies. In one high-tech business unit of a large traditional engineering firm, the downturn in the economy following the dot.com bust put considerable pressure on all the workers as they tried to meet revenue targets. It is at these times when trust, teamwork, and fellowship are most important, but also most elusive, and this was the case here.

A number of factors played into their downward spiral, including Headless Chicken Managers, Divergent Goals, a Fairness Doctrine, and a liberal distribution of Golden Children, among others. In fact, it was a very sick organization when we were called in and it exhibited all the dysfunctions listed above. The organizational structure could only be called chaotic. Sales and marketing were separated and not on speaking terms. Each product family was in a separate department, and each had sales staff that did not report to either the central sales unit or the central marketing unit. Each department defined its own processes in isolation and went to great lengths to point out the flaws in each other.

The lack of coordination and cooperation was so bad that two departments even produced competing products. No one trusted anyone — not their motives, their ability, their ethics, or their effort. This meant that everything was done six times because no one trusted anyone else to do it; and when margins are tight, that type of ridiculous inefficiency cannot be tolerated. It was not long before the company headquarters started to receive a constant stream of complaints, accusations, and charges leading to a vote of no confidence in the CEO, who was finally replaced. Hopefully, the unit will survive, although it went beyond Mediocracy and into Idiocracy before change came. The economy is on the upturn, so that will help; but the company must realize that the economy was not the problem; it was just the heat that was applied to the pressure that they could not handle. The worst of times can bring out the best in people — or their worst.

Explanation

Unfortunately, Western culture seems to promote competition and prejudice cooperation. So often, people in one job function or unit decry and distrust everyone else. Perhaps this is because they do not understand the work of others, or because they feel the need to self-promote at the expense of others (perhaps the result of an incentive-based compensation policy) or even just through arrogance that no job is beyond them. Regardless of the root of the problem, the situation cannot continue.

At the heart of the problem it is the inability of the organization, or its senior staff, to move from independence to interdependence [Covey]. In such dysfunctional organizations, individuals are fixated with personal achievement above group success so much so that they are convinced that their own success is at risk if they trust others. They see life as a zero-sum game, where their success must come at the hands of another's defeat. In that sense, even if they get through the first three of Covey's seven habits, they cannot accept the fourth: think win/win. Their development ends there and so does their efficacy.

Band Aid

Take personal responsibility for your own work, and do not worry about everyone else's performance. Assume the best in people, but do not fret when some let you down.

Self-Repair

Be trustworthy yourself. Set and meet expectations effectively. Then help everyone else do the same.

Refactoring

Assuming that Institutional Mistrust is not simply the result of an organization or team moving through Tuckman's Forming Phase (in which case, simply wait), the only way to succeed is to be accountable for your own duties and expectations and to accept that everyone else will do the same...there is too much work to be done for a few individuals to start taking on the roles and responsibilities of everyone else. Interestingly, this is the definition of cohesion in software systems — distribute the responsibilities evenly across the set of resources, placing the responsibilities in the right place under the general principle that "he who has the knowledge does the work." The best starting point we can think of is to disseminate Covey's book and for the senior staff to embody it. They set the moral and ethical compass for an organization, so they should work to be interdependent, empathetic, and synergistic; others will then follow suit.

Identification

The following identification instrument can help determine if your organization is suffering from a case of Institutional Mistrust. Please respond to the following statements with a "Yes" or "No."

	Yes	No
■ There is a lot of backroom chatter and intrigue in my organization.	——	——
■ Whenever an announcement of some kind is made, we wonder "what does it *really* mean?"	——	——
■ There are some people in my organization who I do not trust.	——	——
■ I know there are some people in my organization who do not trust me.	——	——

If you responded "Yes" to one or more of these statements, your organization is probably suffering from Institutional Mistrust.

References

[Covey]   S.R. Covey, *The 7 Habits of Highly Effective People*, Free Press, 1990.

Name: Kiosk City

Central Concept

Organizational memory is not shared but, rather, exists scattered among various individuals (kiosks).

Dysfunction

An organization should never allow itself to be in a position of hostage to one or more individuals' experience, expertise, or business relationships. This is particularly true when that experience or expertise is related to the core business or products of the organization. This is what CMMI and related process management frameworks are meant to address because they insist on documentation and warehousing of such organizational memory and knowledge.

Vignette

Consider a company or business unit in which many individuals have a significant amount of domain or business information in their heads that is not readily available elsewhere. Each individual is a "kiosk" of abundant information; but because this information is not published anywhere, there is no easy way to know which kiosk to visit. Go talk to Bill about a problem and he might say, "Talk to Sally; I think she might know the answer." But she says, "Oh, I used to ask Tom about that, but now that he is not here anymore, you will need to chat with Greg."

IT in general, and software engineering in particular, has long suffered from isolated islands of knowledge and expertise that could answer questions about proprietary and legacy languages, compilers, operating systems, etc. The organization's success can become tied to these individuals who retain the knowledge and competency. Such dependence is unhealthy because it is not scaleable, it is location confined, and it is high risk. It is even more problematic when these experts get cranky and irritated by business strategies, some Rising Upstart, or technology innovations...their "kiosk" is soon always closed — perhaps it becomes a Knowledge Closet.

Explanation

Think of a mall where there are numerous kiosks or pushcarts selling only very specific items (e.g., watches, or glassware, or scarves). If you want to do comprehensive shopping, you have to go all over the mall to collect what you need. Now envision an entire city where there are no one-stop-shopping places such as supermarkets and department stores, much the way shopping used to be done a couple of generations ago — the bakery for bread, butcher for meat, cheese shop, greengrocers, etc.

Modern technology is both part of the problem and the solution to the emergence of a Kiosk City. More on it as a solution later. But as a causal mechanism, heavy reliance on automated archiving, storage, and connectivity of information can make the human part of the loop complacent, even arrogant. Therefore, never assume that the existing communications structure is efficient enough.

In the real sense, this kind of situation is often found in long-lived organizations where many "old timers" have been working in the same job role "forever."

---- ▼ ----

Wise Alec!

Phil: On the first day of my first job as a warehouseman, I was asked to retrieve a "left-handed dollywog." I roamed throughout the plant looking for one. There were some right-handed ones I was told, but I always seemed to be a few steps behind the left-handed one. "Bob just had it," or, "Dave just returned it to the tool bin in the west warehouse" I would hear. I never did track down that tool.

Colin: There is no such thing as a dollywog.

Phil: Oh.

━━━━━━━━━━━━━━━━━▲━━━━━━━━━━━━━━━

Band Aid

Run around and try to connect the knowledge brokers (connect the dots).

Self-Repair

Do not hoard information. Document what you know and do it as often as possible.

Refactoring

The refactoring for this situation is to extract the information from the kiosks (through a business process reengineering exercise, for example) and then publish it to a central repository. That is, the individual knowledge should be collected, codified, and indexed. Generally speaking, a concerted effort should be undertaken to merge the distributed information into an organizational "data warehouse." Other refactorings include:

- Ask a lot of questions. This will force information to the surface.
- Push CMM, ISO 9000, Six Sigma — any quality initiative that empowers and requires the sharing of knowledge.
- Using technology to prevent a Kiosk City from forming or to break one. E-mail trails, automated configuration management tools, sales support tools, etc. can all be used to recover missing information. Today's more powerful archiving tools are especially helpful. But do not be careless or complacent in doing so.
- Set up a Lessons Learned repository — this is the latest trend in institutionalizing knowledge.

Observations

Japanese-style Theory Z management would avoid the building of a kiosk-based culture because no one would spend a long enough time in one job role to accumulate that kind of information. Moreover, sharing is essential to the learning of each job role.

Identification

The following identification instrument can help determine if your organization tends to be suffering from a Kiosk City. Please respond to the following statements with a "Yes" or "No."

	Yes	No
■ When I need information to do my job, I do shop around for the answer rather than go straight to the "obvious" owner of the information (e.g., chief architect, test manager, etc.).	___	___
■ Information sharing in my organization is spotty at best.	___	___
■ There is some necessary information in my organization that seems to have been lost in history.	___	___
■ There are acronyms that we use that no one can identify accurately.	___	___

If you responded "Yes" to one or more of these statements, your organization tends to be a Kiosk City.

Name: Mediocracy

Central Concept

An organization that has persistently settled for mediocrity in its workforce, processes, and products. The early stages of Idiocracy.

Dysfunction

Clearly striving for mediocrity is not going to expand an organization's business, leverage its core competency to fight off competition, or operate at any level of efficiency that would produce productivity gains. Indeed, the best way to advance in a Mediocracy is to be self-interested and competitive to the point where finding the flaws in colleagues is more profitable than highlighting your own strengths. This is unproductive. Actually, it is counterproductive.

Vignette

There is certainly no truth to the premise that the best person doing a task is the best candidate for the management of that task. That fails to recognize the skill, talent, and training in management and leadership. However, that does not mean that the worst at a task is the best manager either!

Sidebar 6.2 Idiocracy in *The Office*

Phil: How do you define "Idiocracy"?

Colin: An organization of idiots led by idiots. Have you ever seen the British sitcom, *The Office?*

Phil: No, but it won a Golden Globe didn't it?

Colin: Yes. It's about a paper merchant run by a complete incompetent, David Brent, who is blissfully unaware of his utter failure at motivation, leadership, management, and general interpersonal skills. Instead, he thinks he's the funniest, coolest, most beloved and inspirational manager his staff has ever known or could ever imagine. When he is eventually confronted with the reality of a genuinely charismatic leader, he becomes ridiculously competitive and divisive. It's hilarious.

"This is the accounts department, the number bods. Do not be fooled by their job descriptions, they are absolutely mad, all of 'em. Especially that one, he's mental. Not literally of course, that wouldn't work." David Brent, Series 1, *The Office,* BBC Television.

Our favorite example of this was discovered at a European aerospace company. The company was undergoing the early stages of requirements discovery ahead of the transition to an enterprisewide computing system. These requirements elicitation and gathering efforts typically include numerous focus groups and workshops that pull together subsets of the stakeholders that will be using the new system.

On this occasion, the focus of the session was production planning and master scheduling. The session brought together all available production planners, their supervisor, Director of Manufacturing, Director of Engineering, production engineering staff and assorted other personnel, as well as the IT staff and representatives from the enterprise solution provider, one of which was the facilitator leading the meeting. As the meeting turned to the production planning aspects, the facilitator sought input from the planners on how they currently accomplished the task, including the tools used, the data and where it came from, and the general strategy applied to ensure due dates were met and the shop floor operated efficiently.

Unfortunately, as soon as any one of the planners started to describe their approach (and each used a different approach), they were interrupted abruptly by their supervisor. He was a very abrasive character with a dominating tone and demeanor who was quick to dismiss his subordinates' approaches with colorful language and public derision. As you would expect, they soon stopped offering their suggestions and sat back silently

Sidebar 6.3   A Hidden Mediocracy

Even organizations where mediocrity, at least publicly, is scorned include practices that support it. For example, in IT and software development, the commentators and luminaries have long prescribed an approach that pursues excellence and the application of best practices. In recent years, however, we have seen an increase in the idea that best is the enemy of good enough. Perhaps we misconstrue the true sentiment, but to suggest that we provide or offer anything but our best in any situation seems alien to us. We would accept "best, time permitting" as a compromise, but never that the best is the enemy of "good enough," or that our goal is to be merely "good enough."

as this supervisor detailed the "right way" to schedule production. Sitting there watching this was quite an experience, particularly as none of the directors present, or the facilitator, had the courage to confront this Sherman Tank, even when his descriptions were obviously flawed. Not only was the session almost completely wasted following his outbursts, but the entire integration effort was now considered pointless and subversive by the planning staff, and soon most other workers on the shop floor.

They had been deserted by their senior management when the middle manager, who had long demonstrated that his talents in that area were severely lacking, had publicly humiliated them. It was clear after further discussions that he had really been promoted out of respect for his longevity and because he was behind the times with respect to current practices — in other words, he had been there a long time and was no longer very good at his job! If there is any consolation here, it is that the deli-line career strategy still works.

Explanation

Page-Jones discussed the phenomenon of the Mediocracy as a dysfunctional organizational situation in his book [Page-Jones]. The situation can arise for many reasons, including poor HR-related management, a lack of leadership, ill-founded strategy, the Fairness Doctrine (that fails to punish under-performers or reward over-performers), and promotion of the incompetent, a practice humorously captured in the refrain "rise to the level of your incompetence" but unfortunately true of many organizations as they try to fill middle-management positions with those who provide the least value in their current positions.

Page-Jones identified the causes and effects of the Mediocracy as shown in Figure 6.1. At the heart of the problem is the Western culture of

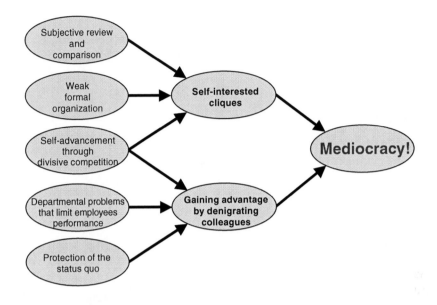

Figure 6.1 Cause-effect diagram [Page-Jones].

individualism and win at all costs that focus energy on trampling over people to reach the top, rather than everyone working together to get everyone to the top. In Covey's terms, the focus in a Mediocracy is on independence (taking care of ourselves) rather than interdependence (cooperating to achieve more than can be achieved individually) [Covey].

To make matters worse, the Mediocracy is self-perpetuating. Managers who have risen within it are loathe to hire anything but mediocre candidates for fear of being usurped, and competent employees soon leave when they realize the futility of their efforts. What is left is the "bland leading the bland."

Band Aid

Unfortunately, the best way to survive in a Mediocracy is to limit your own contributions. The better your own work, the more productive you are, and the more of a target you become for the ruthless mediocrats. The best tactic other than resignation is to "eight and skate." Put in your time going through the motions of work, but producing nothing of consequence that might draw the ire of your colleagues, and then go home.

Self-Repair

If you fall into the trap of mediocrity, whether a manager or not, you are perpetuating Mediocracy. You must fight this temptation and strive for excellence. If you feel you cannot do this, then leave.

Refactoring

As the band aid suggests, overcoming and reversing a Mediocracy is very difficult; and as an individual, your success is contingent upon your position in the organization:

- Those at the lowest levels of the organization who are trying to climb the ladder jumping ship is the best solution.
- Middle managers who have been born-again, or have sneaked into the malaise unnoticed, have more opportunity, especially if the situation has not reached full Idiocracy. They can start a personal crusade to promote interdependence and cooperation by offering to help others. They will need to build trust in a trustless society, but charismatic leaders have that capacity. Motivational workshops for the staff, such as FISH, are great for this.
- Senior managers and executives are obviously in the best position to effect change, and they must do so by focusing on the two primary drivers of the Mediocracy: self-interest and competition. To do this, they must:
  - Outlaw politicking, and abandon it themselves
  - Foster a cooperative atmosphere and raise team spirit
  - Encourage everyone to identify and recognize the good in one another, not the flaws

Identification

The following identification instrument can help determine if your organization is a Mediocracy. Please respond to the following statements with a "Yes" or "No."

Sidebar 6.4   FISH Philosophy

Phil: What's the FISH philosophy?

Colin: The FISH philosophy originated from the Pike's Place Fish Market in Seattle, famous for the positive attitudes and playful nature of the employees. The philosophy is:

- *Play* — treat work as play
- *Choose your attitude* — you have the power to choose your state of mind
- *Make their day* — make personal encounters memorable (in a good way)
- *Be there* — for your colleagues

	Yes	No
■ I worry that when I do something good that I will be criticized for making my colleagues look bad by contrast.	—	—
■ I do not even care anymore if I am doing things well — no one else cares.	—	—
■ The word "excellence" cannot be applied to my organization in any way.	—	—
■ Everyone is rewarded for an achievement, regardless of whether or not they actually contributed to it.	—	—

If you responded "Yes" to one or more of these statements, your organization may be a Mediocracy.

References

[Covey]   S.R. Covey, *The 7 Habits of Highly Effective People*, Free Press, 1990.

[Page-Jones]   M. Page-Jones, *Practical Project Management: Restoring Quality to DP Projects and Systems,* Dorset House, 1985.

Name: One-Eyed King

Central Concept

An organization in which the leader or head technical guru is just someone with a tiny bit more knowledge or ability than everyone else (and perhaps a whole lot more moxie).

Dysfunction

The main problem here is that any organization led by a One-Eyed King performs at a sub-par level and is not able to adapt and learn. The king (manager or senior executive) perpetuates the situation by only hiring those who he perceives know less than he and running out of the organization anyone who challenges him or shows the potential to challenge him in any way.

Vignette

One of our students recounted the tale of a company he worked for in which the flagship product was a software tool that was written in a proprietary language invented by the founder of the company. Now at the time that the software product was originally developed (ten years prior), it might have been appropriate to base the product on this custom language. But over time, advancements in modern programming languages and software engineering obviated any advantages of this language and the software production environment.

New hires to the company were required to learn this unconventional programming language. Of course, no one ever could master the programming language like the founder of the company, a fact that he used to retain his domination even when most of the new people he hired were far better educated in software engineering than he was. The founder maintained his "one-eyed" dominance by blinding those who came to the company (in a sense, they came in blind).

The upshot is that the company failed to retain better software engineers and was unable to use modern software engineering practices and tools. This myopic dependence on a proprietary language allowed the competition to win and eventually put the company out of business.

We also see the One-Eyed King effect in academic institutions. Professors who have been rejected from good universities because of failed scholarship might be dominant at inferior institutions with only meager accomplishments. Sports analogies abound too; for example, a has-been major league player can be a superstar in the minor leagues.

Explanation

As the saying goes: "In the land of the blind, the one-eyed man is king."

The One-Eyed King is often responsible for a Fools Rush In environment because mindshare is too weak to make educated decisions and they are usually Dogmatic About Dysfunction because there is no one competent enough to challenge their false claims.

One-Eyed King situations do not occur because the rest of the organization is "dumb." They often occur because the King is the founder of the company (or a close relative or friend) or a significant financial backer.

Band Aid

Like Emperor's New Clothes and Potemkin Village, you can try to expose the situation. This may earn you scorn of or punishment from the king.

Self-Repair

You may not know if you are a One-Eyed King. But if your practice is to avoid hiring anyone you think is "smarter" than you are because you do not want them to make you look bad, think again. The best thing you can do is hire good people — they will make you look good too.

Refactoring

The main challenge in refactoring the One-Eyed King antipattern without a simple exposé is that organizational awareness and commitment are needed to overcome whatever blindness is present. These can be achieved through:

- Organization-wide skills or technology training
- Hosting relevant technical programs (invited speakers) and distribution of meaningful technical literature
- Seeking input from an outsider, such as a confidante to the king or a consultant

The problem with all of these refactorings, however, is that they likely require the concurrence of the One-Eyed King, which means that he must acknowledge the situation. Therefore, your best approach is to continue to try to educate the One-Eyed King until he recognizes the dysfunction.

Observations

This antipattern is different from a "myopic" manager who has such focus on one thing that all others are neglected (see Leader Not Manager).

Identification

The following identification instrument can help determine if you are being led by a cyclops. Please respond to the following statements with a "Yes" or "No."

	Yes	**No**
■ In any other place that I have been, my boss would have little of the authority and respect that he seems to command here.	——	——
■ Even in the face of indisputable evidence to the contrary, my boss refuses to acknowledge that he is wrong on a major technical or business issue.	——	——
■ My boss likes saying "It's my way or the highway" whenever anyone disagrees with him.	——	——
■ Few people seek out my boss for technical or managerial advice.	——	——

If you responded "Yes" to one or more of these statements, your company needs to expand its vision.

Name: Orange Stand Economics

Central Concept

Failure to understand the cost structure leads to operating losses and, eventually, a death spiral.

Dysfunction

A business cannot survive when it does not truly understand its cost structure. But many senior managers deceive themselves and investors, leading the company into financial decline. When the situation is finally uncovered, it is often too late.

The problem is that understanding the true cost structure of all but the most simplistic products is difficult. For software, it is very difficult. If you do not believe this fact, consider how difficult it is to do accurate schedule and cost estimation for even a modest software product. And for software products, the more customers you have, the more support you have to provide — this eats into new product development time. Then think about the ongoing costs of supporting that product. And do not forget about the hidden costs of operating your business — they can be very significant.

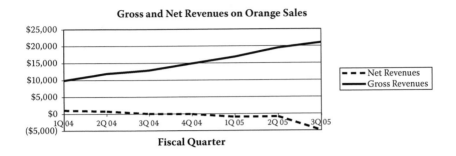

Figure 6.2 Heading down the "Orange River" without a paddle.

Vignette

Table 6.1 shows the cost of a crate of oranges, the number of such crates sold in a particular quarter, and the retail price of one crate. Over several quarters, the cost of purchasing one crate of oranges rises. So does the retail price — but not enough to keep up with costs.

By the fourth quarter of 2004, the company is losing money on every crate sold (Figure 6.2). While the danger of this situation seems obvious, if the true cost of the oranges is hidden somehow, then the retail price cannot be properly adjusted.

Now imagine that a crate of oranges is a unit of software. Here, it is easier to imagine that the cost of each unit is more difficult to determine. Now as you sell more software, the company loses more money.

Explanation

The name of this antipattern comes from an old joke about two hobos who are buying oranges for a dollar a crate, and selling them for 99 cents a crate. When a young business consultant asked them how they could survive this way, they said, we are "making it up on the volume."

If you do not think that this kind of flawed economic model can exist in a mature business environment, remember the dot.com era crash-and-burn stories of companies flush with cash from an IPO or venture capital blowing money on office parties, corporate perks, and outrageous advertising. Everyone took it for granted that these kinds of practices were going to lead to increased corporate value and eventual recovery of costs.

Table 6.1 Simple Financial Report for Orange Stand Industries

	1Q 04	2Q 04	3Q 04	4Q 04	1Q 05	2Q 05	3Q 05
Cost of 1 crate of oranges	$0.89	$0.93	$0.99	$1.00	$1.05	$1.10	$1.30
Number of crates of oranges sold	10,000	12,000	13,000	15,000	17,000	18,500	20,000
Retail price of one crate of oranges	$0.99	$0.99	$0.99	$0.99	$0.99	$1.05	$1.05
Gross revenue	$9,900.00	$11,880.00	$12,870.00	$14,850.00	$16,830.00	$19,425.00	$21,000.00
Net revenue	$1,000.00	$720.00	$0.00	($150.00)	($1,020.00)	($925.00)	($5,000.00)

Note: Pretend that "crate of oranges" is a unit of software product X and the cost is in tens of thousands.

The truth was that no one understood the economic model; and at the end of the day, there was no new economic model and companies that persisted in the above practices died.

While it seems obvious that one should not sell a $10 item for $9, the problem arises when the true costs, including overhead and hidden expenses, are not accurately known. For example, how easy is it for a customer to identify the true all-in cost of a software package that your firm is selling for $20,000 per seat? How easy is it for your company to accurately estimate its costs of production and, hence, price the software appropriately? Too often, companies set price points based on the cost of competing products without taking into account the true cost of production.

Furthermore, if the sale price is not adjusted properly over time as the price of production increases, then what once was a profitable product is no longer profitable. Hence, the more you sell, the more you lose.

Band Aid

None, unless you like plunging slowly to your death.

Self-Repair

You probably are not qualified to truly understand the cost structure of whatever product you produce unless you have good financial training. So listen to the people who do know cost accounting and help them understand what you do know about the application domain.

Refactoring

The main refactoring to Orange Stand Economics is to get a handle on the true cost structure of the product in question. This is not always easy, especially for software. The following techniques can be used, however:

- Correctly understand the cost structure by performing an appropriate cost-based analysis (not just an analysis of the cost of competing products).
- Evangelize the situation.
- Be honest about using real data.
- Stop increasing output until the costs are brought under control.

Identification

The following identification instrument can help determine if your company espouses Orange Stand Economics. Please respond to the following statements with a "Yes" or "No."

	Yes	No
■ No one can tell us the true cost of a unit of what we sell (or no one believes the proclaimed cost).	___	___
■ It seems that the more we sell of our product, the harder we have to work and the less we have to show for it.	___	___
■ Our product seems to be priced far too low in comparison to our competitor's equivalent product.	___	___
■ When we ask our management why we do not raise the price of our product, we are told that "we are trying to be competitive."*	___	___

*Low price can be an effective competitive strategy — but only if you understand your true cost structure.

If you responded "Yes" to one or more of these statements, your company practices Orange Stand Economics.

Name: Pitcairn Island

Central Concept

A "society" is created that functions, at least partially if not particularly efficiently, with such strange work practices, interactions, and norms that outsiders can either not penetrate or survive when they do.

Dysfunction

Just as in Dogmatic About Dysfunction, the goal of an organization is to run at peak efficiency, and a Pitcairn Island usually does not. There is also distinct danger of Kiosk City when such an insular and incestuous team or group takes root.

Vignette

Project teams or even organizations develop a unique but workable culture that, while effective, does not scale up and is not robust enough to survive when faced with serious challenges. One of our reviewers described her own project team in which over the last seven years only two people

Sidebar 6.5   Uncle Dad

> **Colin:** You know that recently some very bad things were discovered to have happened on that island.
>
> **Phil:** What do you mean?
>
> **Colin:** Let's just say that there were some inappropriate family structures.
>
> **Phil:** I still don't understand.
>
> **Colin:** Remember you told me the story about someone you heard of whose widowed father eventually married his wife's widowed aunt.
>
> **Phil:** Yes, and that made the guy's father both his father and uncle at the same time. There's nothing wrong with that, though.
>
> **Colin:** Pitcairn Island went a little farther than that.
>
> **Phil:** Oh, that goes to show you that these kinds of situations don't turn out well in the long run.

have been able to join (many have tried) and no others have left. While successful, they do it despite themselves, often covering up the shortcomings of more than one quirky team member.

Explanation

The mutinous survivors of the HMS Bounty marooned themselves on Pitcairn Island to avoid the detection and punishment of the Royal Navy. Over time, their isolation and fear of detection led them to evolve into a highly insular (and incestuous) society.

Groups that go through Tuckman's formation phases and eventually become Performing do not always end up looking like other high-performing teams. Because of a unique industry, composition or members, or environmental conditions, each high-performing team can "look" and act differently than one would expect. And such an "odd"-performing team might be difficult for outsiders to break into or even understand.

Band Aid

When in Rome, as they say.... Learn to live on Pitcairn Island by adapting to its unique culture. It may be that you are right for that environment.

Self-Repair

Managers: diversity is a good thing. Find ways to diversify your team in thought, ethnicity, social background, education, work experience, etc. This will help prevent a stagnated intellectual gene pool.

Refactoring

The unique culture of the Pitcairn Island must first be recognized, and then it must be transformed into a traditional, scalable, fault-tolerant culture. Identification of the situation often requires the observations of someone outside the group and the transformation usually takes a great deal of time.

Transformation of the situation is usually driven by outside forces such as higher management, process auditors, and the competition. Internal inertia is usually such that an internally generated transformation is impossible.

Identification

The following identification instrument can help determine if your organization tends toward being a Pitcairn Island. Please respond to the following statements with a "Yes" or "No."

	Yes	No
▪ When we interview prospective employees, they always seem to be so out of touch with the way we do things.	___	___
▪ My team/group/organization seems to have a core of "old timers" who have been here forever, and everybody else seems to only last a few months.	___	___
▪ People who have left my organization often return after a few months because they cannot seem to make it elsewhere.	___	___

If you responded "Yes" to one or more of these statements, your organization is a Pitcairn Island.

Name: Potemkin Village[7]

Central Concept

Any situation in which a fancy but superficial façade hides substantial defects or shortcomings. The perpetration of a management fraud based on trumped-up capabilities.

Dysfunction

The main dysfunction is one of dishonesty to customers, employees, creditors, and the public interest. Organizations that encourage the building of Potemkin Villages may experience short-term gain, but also suffer long-term loss of integrity and, eventually, corporate viability.

As well, delivering software with an impressive interface quickly, but where the interface hides severely flawed or functionally deficient back-end processing, is not good for business or morale because customers assume the application is almost ready to ship, when in fact that is some time away.

Symptoms of a Potemkin Village mentality include:

- Reaching for the solution before the problem is even fully described
- Reluctance to let the customer "look under the hood"
- Highly staged demos and presentations
- An abundance of liars

The undesirable effects are a distrustful organization, poor customer relations, and, eventually, legal problems.

Vignette

Consider one form of organizational Potemkin Village at the Ill Eagle Software Company. (Phil actually knows of a real company that was named Ill Eagle Manufacturing.) Here, the Software Quality Assurance (SQA) group is just set up as a shell. This way, customers can be introduced to the "SQA Group" with all kinds of exaggerated claims of what the group actually does. This scam helps Ill Eagle win contracts, but no software QA is actually done.

Another kind of Potemkin Village can be found in individual software applications where a prototype or demo is based on an off-the-shelf architecture, such as Jakarta Struts. Struts provides a framework in which you can throw together an application in no time based on the model-view-controller architecture, without a real understanding of how the framework works.

Unfortunately, many toolsets, frameworks, and off-the-shelf products allow for the quick manufacture of very sophisticated-looking solutions but do not promote robust designs and belie proper testing throughout the life cycle. We are not decrying the use of model view separation or any other framework. The uninformed use of such frameworks, however, can mask the fact that significant functionality is missing behind the façade.

Explanation

Prince Grigori Aleksandrovich Potemkin (1731–1791) was an army officer, politician, and a paramour of Catherine the Great, Empress of Russia. After he helped Catherine seize power in 1762, she installed him as administrator for the Ukraine and Crimea. All went well for Potemkin until around 1772. According to legend, rumors of poverty, disease, and misery in his protectorate led to Potemkin falling out of favor with Catherine. To confirm her suspicions, she contrived a surprise visit to his domain. But spies leaked word of the trip, and in preparation, Potemkin had elaborate façades constructed in front of dilapidated villages. He also had a few villagers cleaned up and strategically positioned around the towns. These shills happily waved at Catherine as her coach passed by from a distance and, of course, she never dismounted from her carriage for a closer look.

Potemkin executed the scam to perfection, saving his own skin. This possibly specious story has caused the addition of "Potemkin Village" to the English lexicon. According to one dictionary, a Potemkin village is "something that appears elaborate and impressive but in actual fact lacks substance."[8] The software analogies for the Potemkin Village are ripe for exploration.

A true mismatch between demo and delivered versions of software is a type of deception, but most customers would not tolerate a bait and switch. A more likely Potemkin Village situation arises when the delivered software incorporates an elaborate user interface with a flimsy back end. Unfortunately, less-sophisticated customers are easily distracted by the GUI's allure; they do not discover the software's fragility until it is too late.

▼

Our friend, Will Robinson, offers this variation on the Potemkin Village theme. It relates to automated car washes and the point where "Hot Wax Now Being Applied" is flashing in blue lights to indicate the "extra service" you are receiving amid the deluge of recycled dirty water. The customer is to believe that a protective wax was now being applied to the car — because the lights were in fact flashing. But no apparent proof of such wax being applied existed (yes, some fluid seemed to be sprayed, but was it wax?). In fact, there is every reason to believe that you have paid an extra dollar to have the blue lights flash only. This form of misdirected deception can and is sometimes used in organizations — e.g., pronouncements that "things are getting better" when no tangible evidence of such improvement exists.

▲

Band Aid

Go along with the charade.

Self-Repair

Managers: do not let Potemkin Villages be built. Do the right thing the first time.

Refactoring

When faced with a Potemkin Village, it must be exposed immediately. This is not so easy to do when the shortcoming is well masked with a high-quality GUI front end. Detection of the situation, however, can be done through design reviews, and code inspections, reviews, or walk-throughs. Therefore, these should be required by managers who are overseeing software projects, and by customers who are buying custom software. Testing can sometimes uncover the situation, but it may be too late at this point. Test-driven design, on the other hand, can help prevent a Potemkin Village.

What is the best way to confront the issue? It depends on the situation, of course. When the relationship between the customer-vendor or software project manager-development team is good, informality is appropriate. For example, having the customer on site can help avoid the problem or perception of this problem or lead to its early resolution. If the relationship is somewhat tense or distant, then the situation calls for the use of formal memoranda outlining the concerns.

If the problem is discovered during some kind of review, it should be called out immediately if the situation is justifiably demonstrated. Be sure that you have your facts straight before making unfounded accusations, as doing so can damage professional relationships. Discuss the situation and the resolution, and then memorialize it with an e-mail or memo. Follow up with appropriate review mechanisms to ensure that the issue has been resolved.

In the case of suspected deliberate deception or gross negligence, unfortunately, legal counsel should be sought. But whatever the case, do not let the situation go unaddressed:

- Work diligently to uncover the Potemkin Village and embarrass the builders to correct it.
- If the Potemkin Village is software, spend more time on the software architecture and design.

Observations

Apparently, the story of the Potemkin Village may not be true after all, or is, at worst, an exaggeration. Some historians assert that Potemkin was an able administrator and apparently both Crimea and the Ukraine fared well under his stewardship. It may have been that in preparation for Catherine's tour, an aggressive clean-up campaign was undertaken, which would have been appropriate. But jealous rivals of Potemkin or a few disgruntled citizens may have trumped up this simple beautification effort as a masking of fundamental infrastructure problems.

The scenario of unwarranted fraud allegations raises the question of how politics play a role in our perception of the truth, even with respect to software deliverables. For example, what is alleged to be "Potemkin

Village" software by a customer unwilling to pay may be, in fact, the robust, industrial-strength solution that they requested. Deciding the truth of the matter, however, falls into the purview of lawyers, judges, arbitrators, and mediators, particularly when the software requirements and contractual statements of work are inadequate. But dealing with or preventing that situation is another story.

This antipattern is closely related to Brown et al.'s Smoke and Mirrors, which describes software with a fancy front end but little back-end processing. The difference is that the Potemkin Village is more general and can apply to organizations as well as software.

Identification

The following identification instrument can help determine if your organization tends to build Potemkin Villages. Please respond to the following statements with a "Yes" or "No."

	Yes	No
■ My organization tends to select the software architecture before even knowing much about the application.	___	___
■ My organization spends more time on demos than on testing.	___	___
■ My organization could not withstand a process quality audit.	___	___
■ My organization does not reward good design; it rewards fancy interfaces.	___	___

If you responded "Yes" to one or more of these statements, your organization has a tendency to build Potemkin Villages.

The following identification instrument can help determine if a particular application might be a Potemkin Village. Please respond to the following statements with a "Yes" or "No."

	Yes	No
■ The software architecture for this application is a "secret."	___	___
■ There are numerous undocumented features in this application.	___	___
■ There are many cautions about using certain functions in the documentation.	___	___
■ The documentation describes many functions that do not exist or work.	___	___

If you responded "Yes" to one or more of these statements, then the software application in question is likely a Potemkin Village.

References

[Laplante]   Phillip A. Laplante, The Potemkin Village and Other Myths of Deception, *IT Professional*, Jan./Feb. 2005, pp. 62–65.

Name: Process Clash

Central Concept

The friction that can arise when advocates of different processes must work together without a proven hybrid process being defined.

Dysfunction

When organizations have two or more well-intended but non-complementary processes, a great deal of discomfort can be created for the employees. Symptoms of this antipattern include poor communications, and even hostility, high turnover, and low productivity.

Vignette

Consider the well-publicized "process wars" in the software profession pitting those who favor "agile" processes such as eXtreme Programming (XP) and more prescriptive processes such as the Rational Unified Process (RUP). Both of these process models have key advantages, and it is not unreasonable for an organization as a whole or groups within organizations to want to use both. In one case, the Pragmatic Software Company had a development group of agile practitioners and an analysis group that were used to analysis involving Use Case specification and domain modeling.

The analysis group expected to turn over its artifacts to the development group for implementation. But the implementation team, having adopted agile practices, eschewed the use of documentation as a development driver. The development group took exception to the detailed domain models as they were too prescriptive in defining internal attribute types, how the associations were to be implemented, and they used modeling constructs that were not easy to implement in code. They also found the large Use Cases too cumbersome so they started to develop their own User Stories — which were promptly rejected by the analysis group because they were incomplete and unnecessary in any case.

The overall disconnect further led to a lack of traceability from the requirements and analysis models into the design and code. Clearly, this clash of processes was inevitable, given the different viewpoints that the two groups took.

As an aside, Colin and Phil encountered the occasional Process Clash while writing this book. Colin prefers to focus on one relatively narrow idea (e.g., one antipattern) and write it to near-completion. Phil likes to multitask by writing several related or unrelated things simultaneously. Both techniques work, but our Process Clash led to some creative tension. How did we resolve it? See the refactoring section.

Explanation

The conflict between two well-intended but consonant dissident processes leads to the poetic naming of this antipattern. The name is also reminiscent of the 1981 movie entitled *Clash of the Titans*.

Most software professionals are well educated, experienced, and knowledgeable. They are also often opinionated and egotistical. The processes used on a project tend to solicit the most emotionally charged opinions. The process wars have been widely analyzed within industry trade journals. Each side has well-respected leaders who champion their process and critique the other side. The recent trend toward globally distributed agile development has intensified the need to overcome Process Clashes, however.

Band Aid

You have two choices:

1. Try to reconcile the "warring parties." However, this can become a full-time job amounting to putting out small brush fires of disagreement but never really resolving the fundamental process conflicts.
2. Select between one approach and the other.

Self-Repair

If you are involved in a Process Clash, you will need to be proactive in reaching out to the "other side" to try to hybridize the processes or resolve the differences at the processes' interface.

Refactoring

Develop a hybridized approach, one that resolves the differences at the processes' interfaces. For example, in the Pragmatic Software Company, an interface mechanism could have been defined between the analysts and developers to establish how the artifacts should look and how they should be used. For example, a new Use Case and Domain Model templates could be developed jointly by the two groups.

Retraining and cross-training could also be used. For example, by training the analysis group in XP and the development group in RUP, better understanding can be achieved.

Depart to a third process that resolves the conflict. For example, Domain Driven Modeling might have been used instead of RUP. Domain Driven Modeling can be used in conjunction with agile methodologies with no conflicts.

In the case of our own Process Clash, we handled it by recognizing that such a clash existed and communicating frequently when our preferred methodologies seemed to trip up one or the other. In each case, we worked through whatever difficulties our Process Clash caused (for example, by rereading each other's work frequently or by Colin contributing to Phil's incomplete thoughts and Phil "decorating" Colin's more cerebral prose). Neither of us required the other to change his process. We simply worked through the boundaries when our processes converged — Phil kept the master version of all the files because he would work on many at a time. Colin could work on one at a time with focus and then check them back to Phil. By accepting the differences in our approach and joining forces, the complementary styles actually led to a more lively narrative (we think).

Identification

The following identification instrument can help determine if your organization is experiencing a Process Clash. Please respond to the following statements with a "Yes" or "No."

	Yes	No
■ When I try to do my job, I sometimes worry that what I have to do is going to conflict with what someone else has to do or be undone later.	___	___
■ We have roadmaps showing where processes and procedures contradict.	___	___
■ I find that I often have to subvert certain processes that are in place because these processes can cause conflict.	___	___
■ When it comes to ways of doing things, we seem to have more than one incompatible philosophy.	___	___

If you responded "Yes" to one or more of these statements, your organization is probably experiencing a Process Clash.

Name: Rubik's Cube

Central Concept

Confused organization structure resulting from a multidimensional matrix management strategy.

Dysfunction

Adoption of a matrix management approach can lead to confusion, loss of focus, conflicting directions, and political intrigue. Note that matrix management is not necessarily a bad thing, and the creation of such a structure is not the dysfunction. The dysfunction arises when there are one or more of the following:

- Conflicting project goals
- A mismatch between manager personality and company management philosophy
- An improper rollout of new management methodology
- Poor communication of project goals

In any case, the effects include inefficient execution of company goals and employee stress created by trying to serve two masters.

Vignette

This example occurs in a large aerospace company. A former co-worker, Jen, had mixed feelings when her boss, Mike, was promoted to VP of the entire software development division. Although she was happy for him, she feared that the open-door policy, which he encouraged, would end for her and the others in the group. He assured her that anyone could always stop by and chat about work, or non-work, at any time. Although her fears were somewhat alleviated, her concerns were quickly refreshed when she learned about his replacement — Steve, a Theory X manager, who was very much into a strict chain of command.

As time went on, Jen found herself working as one of the main analysts on a division-wide project trying to get the division's several software products to interface with each other. The project was a highly visible one because the company's customers were having problems trying to get the products to work together. In addition to getting to learn the different products, Jen was happy to be working more closely with Mike. Prior to her moving to the other building, Steve made it clear to her that she was to get their product working with the main system as soon as possible and to return back to her other projects.

Shortly thereafter, while Mike and Jen were chatting, she mentioned that her focus was to get her product interfacing with the system prior to getting the other ones working together. Mike corrected her and explained why it was better, both from a financial view and from a customer service view, to integrate other products first. Jen related what Steve had told her about getting her product integrated first, but Mike dismissed it and said that he would talk to Steve about it.

After meeting with Mike, Steve felt betrayed by Jen and believed that she had gone behind his back to de-emphasize his product's integration. After the project was over, Jen returned to her original position, but Steve still resented her perceived betrayal. Over the next several months, Steve was overly critical of Jen's work and she eventually transferred to a different group.

The situation boils down to a company adopting a matrix management philosophy without doing a constructive judgment on the skills of the affected employees or adequately considering how the new philosophy should affect current performance evaluation criteria. Different people flourish in different situations, and there was little planning on the company's side to ensure that everyone was on board. Steve felt justified in expecting his employees to represent his group in these situations. He was rated based on how well his product goals were achieved in relation to the resources that he had been given. By having Jen work on tasks not related to his product, Steve's evaluation may suffer. To accomplish a beneficial matrix management situation, all involved employees must understand their roles and the criteria on which they will be rated.

Explanation

Named after the Rubik's cube, a three-dimensional puzzle toy consisting of an array with shifting rows and columns. The cube was the invention of Erno Rubik, a Hungarian who first conceived of it in the mid-1970s. It became a cult toy in Europe, the United States, and many other countries in the late 1970s and early 1980s, and can still be bought today.

A matrix-structured organization is one in which an individual can have two or more reporting lines. For example, a software engineer could report to a manager of software engineering and also report to the project manager of a specific program on which he works. If he works on multiple programs, then he would report also to the other program managers. He might also be part of a quality assurance team led by a quality assurance manager. There are many possible embodiments of a matrix-structured organization.

Band Aid

You can use the matrix organization to your advantage playing the "he said/she said" game with each manager.

Self-Repair

Matrix organizations can be effective but they must be configured properly. If you are manager of a matrix-managed organization, you need to work within the structure and be a team player. See the section on General Wisdom in dealing with antipatterns for various techniques that promote success in a matrix organization.

Refactoring

The key to the refactoring is to help align the goals of the matrix organization, and the processes in each row/column appropriately. Steps that can help in this regard include:

- Review all aspects of the work environment when making major changes.
- Conduct a measured rollout of any new management paradigm.
- Clearly document and publicize project goals.

Observations

This antipattern could also be called "Matrix Madness."

While the traditional matrix management framework is two-dimensional (line manager and project manager), some organizations use three or more dimensions in the hypercube (e.g., we know of companies that have four or more "matrix managers," including line manager, project manager, and multiple customer/managers).

Identification

The following identification instrument can help you determine if your organization has a failing matrix management structure. Please respond to the following statements with a "Yes" or "No."

	Yes	No
■ Although I work in a matrix structured organization, my colleagues and I talk about how it is not working.	—	—
■ I report to two or more managers; and much of the time, they disagree.	—	—
■ I often ask myself, "Which manager should I ask for permission?" because I know that they will not always give the same answer.	—	—
■ My boss regularly tells me, "Don't worry about what Dave (my other boss) told you to do."	—	—
■ I do not know if I am in a matrix organization or not.	—	—

If you responded "Yes" to one or more of these statements, your organization needs to realign its matrix.

Name: Shoeless Children[9]

Central Concept

When a company deprives itself of sufficient resources, sometimes even its own product, because of financial difficulties or managerial incompetence.

Dysfunction

The dysfunction is clearly in the deprivation of tools necessary to do the job right, but usually in the guise of conservation.

Vignette

We see this antipattern any time a company denies itself equipment, even its own products, because it is so busy going around fixing everyone else's problems or is financially strapped.

We heard the following story of shoeless children recounted by one of our students. The anecdote concerned a Fortune 500 integrated electronics and computer systems company, famous for its state-of-the-art software and software engineering practices. However, the company had a time and attendance system based on old mainframe technology. Moreover, it was a user-hostile application that required the use of function keys to navigate, and relied on user IDs that are a combination of eight randomly assigned alphanumeric characters. Other business-critical systems at this company are also antiquated.

Explanation

This antipattern is related to the story of the Shoemaker's Children who have no shoes because their shoemaker father is too busy scratching out a living and there are no shoes to spare.

In the extreme, a software company might be depriving itself of sufficient software and hardware resources, although it is selling "state-of-the-art" software solutions to others. Of course, there are times when it might be necessary to function in this way. The antipattern arises when the company continues to deprive itself of needed resources even after mitigating the financial situation.

The genesis of this antipattern could be other than economics, however. For example, a Theory X manager might view requests for necessary resources as simply an excuse for the staff's incompetence or laziness. This antipattern can also coexist with Founderitis, where the penny-pinching and controlling owner/founder recalls the days of running the business on a shoestring — and thinks this is the way business should always run (which might be the case, but is not always necessarily so).

Band Aid

Make do. And take responsibility for your own immediate needs.

Self-Repair

You have to feed yourself before you can feed others.

Refactoring

Call out the situation.

In some cases, the situation may be related to Founderitis, suggesting the appropriate refactorings. In other cases, the antipattern may arise from poor management that leads to bad cash flow and necessary deprivation of internal resources. In this case, the solution is strategic budget cutting that excludes essential infrastructure, which is never fun or easy.

Observations

Phil's grandfather actually was a shoemaker and he never made his children's shoes. Although the children grew up during the Great Depression, they did not go barefoot. His grandfather specialized in making custom shoes for people with disabilities. Because his grandfather was paid a premium for his special skills, it made better economic sense for him to buy his own children's generic shoes at local department stores. Of course, Grandpa would repair his children's shoes as necessary.

The point is that there are instances where it makes economic sense for a company to "deprive" itself somehow. An auto manufacturer would not give a top-of-the-line car to every employee. A restaurant would go out of business feeding all of its employees the most expensive food on the menu, and a software company would not have its best engineers troubleshooting the computer on the president's desk.

Identification

The following identification instrument can help determine if your organization is depriving itself of sufficient resources. Please respond to the following statements with a "Yes" or "No."

	Yes	No
■ Sometimes we have to cannibalize our internal hardware or software infrastructure to deliver product.	—	—
■ I remember when we had to cut back on [fill in your favorite essential infrastructure item(s)] when times were tough; but we have turned around the company now, and we still have not been authorized to buy it/them.	—	—
■ Our company is in good financial shape and I am still using five-year-old technology.	—	—
■ I am using five-year-old technology and I do not know what kind of financial shape my company is in.*	—	—

*It could be that your company is in good financial shape but you should know this. If not, ask.

If you responded "Yes" to one or more of these statements, your organization may be suffering from the Shoeless Children antipattern.

Name: Worshiping the Golden Calf[10]

Central Concept

In any environment where there is poor vision or leadership, it is often convenient to lay one's hopes on a technology or a methodology about which little is known, thereby providing a plausible hope for some miracle.

Dysfunction

Because no one really understands the technology, methodology, or practice, it is difficult to dismiss. This is an environmental antipattern because it is based on a collective suspicion of disbelief and greed, which could not be sustained by one or a few individuals embracing the ridiculous.

Vignette

A collective belief that changing the base programming language or development environment will cure problems that are related to a bad software architecture or management culture, is an example of praying to the gilded veal.

To a certain extent, the dot.com business model was a Golden Calf. Some failing businesses (and even non-failing ones) quickly switched to this model in the hopes of company salvation or quick rewards. Phil once met an MD/MBA combined degree student from an excellent Ivy League institution who was several weeks away from graduation. He left for the lure of a dot.com start-up, which crashed soon afterward. It is unknown what happened to the student except that he is not an MD/MBA grad.

Explanation

From the story in Exodus about the sin of idolatry:

> Now when the people saw that Moses delayed to come down from the mountain, the people assembled about Aaron and said to him, "Come, make us a god who will go before us; as for this Moses, the man who brought us up from the land of Egypt, we do not know what has become of him."[2] Aaron answered them, "Take off the gold earrings that your wives, your sons and your daughters are wearing, and bring them to me."[3] So all the people took off their earrings and brought them to Aaron.[4] He took what they handed him and made it into an idol cast in the shape of a calf, fashioning it with a tool. Then they said, "These are your gods, O Israel, who brought you up out of Egypt."

> **—Exodus 32:1 (New American Standard Bible)**

The Worshiping the Golden Calf antipattern is also related to the "hockey stick" revenue projection after recording many months of declining profits, with some hand-waving justification, the analyst projects a sudden, dramatic upward trend, which resembles a hockey stick. Everyone wants to believe such a miracle is possible.

This antipattern is somewhat related to Buzzword Mania. The main difference is that Buzzword Mania is a propensity to use sales speak and buzzwords although the company's fate might be tied to legitimate technology. In Worshiping the Golden Calf, everyone is closing their eyes, holding their breath, and jumping.

Band Aid

Keep worshiping the calf. Go along with the crowd and pretend nothing is wrong.

Self-Repair

Do not push golden calves. If you are pegging your hopes on a new technology or methodology, research it and make sure it really works, and that you are not just following other mesmerized worshipers.

Refactoring

The refactoring for a Golden Calf environment is to expose the calf for what it is. This will require significant courage and effort on the part of the exposers, as those who believe will cling to any thin hope even in the face of incontrovertible evidence to the contrary.

Another refactoring is to promote alternate technologies that really work (we call this "true religion").

Recall the famous cartoon with two professors at the blackboard with "and then a miracle occurs" written between two equations. The skeptical professor says, "I think you have to be more explicit in step two." Likening the current Golden Calf to previous exposed ones can also be helpful.

Identification

The following identification instrument can help determine if your organization tends to Worship Golden Calves. Please respond to the following statements with a "Yes" or "No."

	Yes	No
■ No one in the organization understands the "GildedVeal" technology but everyone talks about it.	___	___
■ No one can produce a well-documented case of success using the "GildedVeal" technology (although there are claims that such cases exist).	___	___
■ I see tee-shirts, coffee mugs, pens, whizzy things, and all kinds of conference junk with the "GildedVeal" technology logo on it.	___	___
■ The vendor of "GildedVeal" keeps pushing back the delivery dates.	___	___
■ A few non-believers (usually old timers) insist that the "GildedVeal" technology is just the old "BrownBull" technology with a fancier interface.	___	___

If you responded "Yes" to one or more of these statements, your organization has a tendency to Worship Golden Calves.

Notes

1. This antipattern first appeared in: Phillip A. Laplante, "Staying Clear of Boiling Frog Syndrome," *IT Professional*, March/April, 2004, pp. 56–58. It is excerpted from that source with permission.

2. This antipattern is based on an earlier work entitled "The Burning Bag of Dung: And Other Environmental Antipatterns," by Phillip Laplante, ©ACM, 2004, *Queue*, 2(7), 78–80, October 2004, http://doi.acm.org/10.1145/1035594. 1035617.

3. A version of this antipattern appeared in Phillip A. Laplante, "The Potemkin Village and the Art of Deception," *IT Professional*, January/February, 2005, pp. 62–64. Most of this is excerpted from that source with permission.

4. This antipattern is based on an earlier work entitled "The Burning Bag of Dung: And Other Environmental Antipatterns," by Phillip Laplante, ©ACM, 2004, *Queue*, 2(7), 78–80, October 2004, http://doi.acm.org/10.1145/1035594. 1035617.

5. A version of this antipattern first appeared 12/15/03, with our permission, on the Web site for the Harris Kern Enterprise Computing Institute, www. harriskern.com.

6. This antipattern first appeared in "The I/O Divorce," Phil Brainerd, Byte.com, December 2004, http://byte.com/feature/2004/, last accessed January 30, 2005. Phil was our graduate student here at Penn State University.

7. A version of this antipattern appeared in Phillip A. Laplante, "The Potemkin Village and the Art of Deception," *IT Professional*, January/February 2005, pp. 62–64. Much of this antipattern is excerpted from that source with permission.

8. *The American Heritage Dictionary of the English Language,* 4th ed., 2000.

9. This antipattern is based on an earlier work entitled "The Burning Bag of Dung: And Other Environmental Antipatterns," by Phillip Laplante, ©ACM, 2004, *Queue*, 2(7), 78–80, October 2004, http://doi.acm.org/10.1145/1035594. 1035617.

10. This antipattern is based on an earlier work entitled "The Burning Bag of Dung: And Other Environmental Antipatterns," by Phillip Laplante, ©ACM, 2004, *Queue*, 2(7), 78–80, October, 2004, http://doi.acm.org/10.1145/1035594. 1035617.

Chapter 7

General Advice in Dealing with Antipatterns

We would like to leave you with a collection of tools that can be used in conjunction with the refactoring strategies already described. None of these tools are profound — they are largely based on well-known management principles and just down-home good advice. Surprisingly, one can handle most situations with some simple strategies that involve honesty, hard work, kindness, and humor. But you probably already knew that. It is just that it is not always easy to respond this way in the face of very negative situations.

It might seem that many of the antipatterns and refactorings are common sense — good old, "cracker-barrel wisdom." That is probably true. But then again, we find much of the theoretical and even practical management mantras to be just that. Much of good management is based on how you treat people, how you treat yourself, how you view the world, and your basic philosophy of life. If you are going to be a corncob, people are going to treat you that way in response. On the other hand, if you take the time to get to know people, understand their needs, and understand the underlying organizational culture in which you function, you will probably do OK.

In any case, one can use the following recommendations as general refactorings in many situations. Moreover, these are good principles to live by in any relationship — work, social, and family. We offer these in no particular order.

7.1 Be Kind

Using kindness is one of the best ways we know to get what you want, effect change, and win support for your initiatives. Many of the problems in the software and IT world illustrated by the antipatterns involve capturing deliverables from reluctant providers. A lesson about dealing with such resistance, and about the value of persistent kindness, can be learned from the Amish people who live in various parts of Pennsylvania, Delaware, Ohio, Wisconsin, and elsewhere. The Amish are well known for their farm products and fine finished goods, but they are also remarkable for their kindness, honesty, industry, and ingenuity. The Amish do not rely on lawyers or collection agencies to collect debts. They rely on polite persistence. The apocryphal story in Sidebar 7.1 epitomizes their approach to debt collection.

Polite persistence is a helpful approach in dealing with virtually all of the antipatterns, both management and environmental. Kindness would be particularly helpful, for example, in dealing with a Three-Headed Knight, Rising Upstart, Headless Chicken, and even a Doppelganger if used with caution.

Sidebar 7.1   A Lesson in Persistence

A non-Amish retailer owed a large sum of money to an Amish businessman who provided fine woodworking products. Each week, the businessman would appear at the office of the retailer, provide him with a home-baked cake or pie, and genuinely engaged him in conversation about family. At the end of the conversation, the craftsman mentioned to the retailer that he would very much appreciate collecting the overdue funds. This occurred for some time until finally, overwhelmed by his persistence and kindness, the retailer paid his debt.

The lesson is to use kindness and persistence to refactor difficult situations.

7.2 Do Not Blame Other People

Many dysfunctional organizations are often characterized by a culture of blame. This is probably because it is easy to transfer responsibility for one's own fault to another. Another manifestation involves Spineless Executives who find their way out of a bad situation by blaming their poor leadership on something else (e.g., it is the economy, it is the other guy, it is the system, etc.). Think of Divergent Goals, where one faction accuses the other of ignorance or incompetence, or even Dunkirk Spirit, where it might be convenient for the heroes to blame management for the situation in which they find themselves.

> In a famous cartoon that appeared in the late 19th century, "Who Stole the People's Money," a circle of shoddy characters are shown pointing to each other to pass on the blame for the corruption in New York City. This cartoon and other scathing cartoons by Thomas Nast started a chain reaction of blame, mistrust, and defections that eventually brought down powerful Tammany Hall boss William Tweed.

But one of the problems with the Blame Game is that once someone starts using it, everyone else does too, as a defensive response. Therefore, the only way out is for someone with leadership quality (the actual team leader or a member of the team) to step up and break the chain of blame.

Breaking the chain, however, takes a great deal of courage, as it is not without risk. But we reemphasize that inspirational leaders relish such challenges.

7.3 Learn to Deliver Bad News

With respect to truthfulness and courage, sometimes a manager has to deliver bad news to the team, or a team member has to deliver bad news to the leader. We will talk about the inherent dangers to whistleblowers shortly. But for the team leader, it can often be difficult to deliver bad news, especially when it involves organizational change of any kind.

We have found that the best way to deliver bad news is to be direct, polite, and, if possible, to soften the situation by preceding the message with some kind of humor.[1] What we mean is that sometimes a story can be used to send the message in a nonthreatening way. Consider this scenario of an IT manager who had to reassign a staff member from a choice, high-profile position to a much less desirable position because his skills were severely lacking. This person was well liked by his junior teammates, however, and the manager was in no position to inform the teammates of the details of the incompetence of their beloved colleague. Therefore, they were angry over the reassignment. The manager was in a dilemma — he could not directly bad-mouth the reassigned person by disclosing the details of his poor performance. Instead, he told a story that highlighted the dangers of "ignorant infatuation" (see Sidebar 7.2).

Sidebar 7.2   The Chinese Restaurant Story

As told by a manager to a subordinate concerning the firing of a beloved teammate. "When I was young, our family liked to dine at a Chinese restaurant in town. It was the only one nearby, but it had excellent food. So every Friday night we faithfully dined there. This went on for several years. One Friday night we were surprised and angry to find that the restaurant had been closed down by the department of public health. We were angry, indignant — how could they close our favorite restaurant? Eventually, we found out why — the restaurant had been serving, shall we say, off-the-menu meat products, instead of the advertised chicken, beef, and pork. Later in life, my family and I all ate at many different Chinese restaurants, all of them better than the one we originally loved. But because it was the only Chinese restaurant we had tried at the time, we did not have anything to compare it to. It was literally the best Chinese food we ever had because it was the only Chinese food we ever had. Now we know better."

The idea, of course, was that the junior teammates were so infatuated with the charming, but incompetent senior colleague that they did not have enough experience to recognize his incompetence. The story tried to convey that message. Of course, the manager could conclude his message by stating the theme directly.

So, try to deliver bad news preceded by a joke that has a related moral to it. Refactoring such antipatterns as the Potemkin Village, Emperor's New Clothes, One-Eyed King, and others requires a great deal of courage. This book contains a number of stories that can often be used to deal indirectly with such difficult situations.

7.4 Do Not Worry for Other People

Many of the antipatterns described can create problems that do not directly affect you or for which the solution is really out of your hands (e.g., Founderitis). But many of us like to worry — about everyone and everything. This can be a very destructive habit. Sidebar 7.3 provides an apocryphal story that illustrates the concept.

Yet it is the nature of many good people to take the weight of other people's troubles onto their shoulders and grin and bear adversity. This can lead to a Boiling Frog situation and requires Dunkirk Spirit to succeed.

Sidebar 7.3 Do Not Worry for Other People

A husband is anxiously pacing the floor of the bedroom late one evening. His wife asks what is troubling him. "Well," he says, "you know that we are overdue on our mortgage payment and we are not sure if we can pay it this month. And with Bob being our neighbor and banker at the same time, it is so embarrassing, I do not know what to do." His wife reassures him, tells him to go back to bed, then steps out to make a phone call. When she returns she tells him, "Now go back to bed, I just called Bob and told him we are going to be paying the mortgage late. Now it is his problem to worry about."

Therefore, do not accept other people's problems. Only worry about the things you really need to worry about. Put another way, "Don't sweat the small stuff."

7.5 Do Not Shoot the Messenger

A good general principle to operate by as a team leader or member is never to shoot the messenger. When people bring you bad news, even if they are the cause of the problem, it is not in your best interest to take it out on them there and then (see Sidebar 7.4).

Sidebar 7.4 A Very Unwise Manager

Phil used to work for a manager whose policy was, ostensibly, "I will not bring you surprises, you do not bring me surprises." This statement was taken as an invitation to bring both bad news and good news as it occurred to the manager. However, the first time the manager was informed of a negative situation, he exploded and chewed out the messenger.

Because the manager would harass those who brought him bad news (even if they were not the cause of the problem), a game-theoretic strategy was to withhold information from the manager. Why? Because although there would be a chance that the manager would learn about the bad news from someone else, the only way not to get shot was to not bring bad news. Moreover, others had learned the same lesson and thus the likelihood of anyone bringing the manager bad news diminished — he essentially isolated himself from information.

So, if you find yourself as the recipient of one of the refactorings contained herein (e.g., if you are a Spineless Executive), do not take it out on those who are trying to help you see that reality. And if you have to deal with someone who is Dogmatic About Dysfunction, do not shoot them if you disagree.

7.6 Let People Learn from Their Mistakes

As a manager, it is often easy and tempting to blast someone when they mess up. We have already seen that this aggressive course of action is likely to cut off your sources of information (see "Don't Shoot the Messenger"). In addition, you have to let people learn from their mistakes; after all, you would expect the same for yourself (see Sidebar 7.5).

Sidebar 7.5   A Very Costly Mistake

Thomas Watson, Sr., who helped build IBM into the giant it became, was well known as a demanding boss. But he had wisdom too as the following apocryphal story illustrates. A young executive appears before the intimidating Watson, believing that he is about to be fired for a multimillion-dollar failed project. After going through all the errors made in the execution of the project, the junior executive sat stunned awaiting the bad news. In the uncomfortable silence, he finally summoned the courage to ask, "Aren't you going to fire me?" "Hell no," said Watson, "we just spent $3 million teaching you a lesson and we cannot afford to fire you now."

Even as a subordinate, you have to allow your boss to make mistakes without bad-mouthing him or complaining directly. For example, with a Spineless Executive, Three-Headed Knight, or Headless Chicken, you might need to sit back and let the manager work his way through the problem. Even with your help, he is going to make mistakes and you have to let him do that without resenting it.

7.7 Just Get It Done

How much energy is wasted procrastinating, complaining, asking meaningless questions, jumping through Fruitless Hoops, etc.? For some people, this is a deliberately obstructive strategy. For others, it is a form of timidity — if they keep asking questions, they do not actually have to make a decision or act. For others still, they just do not want to act before they have all the facts. There comes a point, however, when people just need to buckle down and get it done. It is what military leaders look for in their people. So, it is no coincidence that this sentiment will help you with Dunkirk Spirit. But it can also come in handy in many other antipattern situations, such as Boiling Frog Syndrome, Deflated Balloon, and most of the management antipatterns.

▼

Getting it Done on Happy Days

Garry Marshall, creator of the long-lived television program "Happy Days," told a story about how he got around the network's moratorium on Fonzie wearing leather clothes. Early in the show's existence, the network, apparently, thought that having him wear "leathers" would make him look like a punk, so they forbid it. Marshall protested and was able to negotiate a "compromise." The Fonz could wear leathers only when he was riding his motorcycle. Marshall promptly instructed his writers to make sure that the Fonz was always on his motorcycle! That is why you will see him in the soda shop on a motorcycle most of the time.

▲

The best leaders and team members need to instinctively know when the time for asking questions, awaiting instructions, or looking for meaning in it all has passed. Sometimes you just have to do what you have to do and just get it done!

7.8 Remember the Law of Unintended Consequences

We all know that the things we do as managers, team members, and in life can have unintended consequences. But sometimes we forget to consider that even small actions or passing words can have great consequences because of unforeseen amplifying effects of a hastily constructed e-mail or a few passing words said in anger (see Sidebar 7.6 for a related story). Consider the unintended and possibly profound consequences of small actions such as task assignment or teaming up of two people. Also consider examining the source of an event before reacting to its effects.

Sidebar 7.6 Unintended Consequences

Thanks to our friend Tom Costello, CEO of Upstreme, Inc. (www.upstreme.com), for sharing this story with us.

The following legend, which is recounted in many Native American Indian cultures, illustrates how small actions can have great consequences.

The legend involves a tribe located near a small stream. The village is periodically and unpredictably flooded by the stream. So, the chief of the tribe asks each of his braves to go out and find a site for a new village.

One curious brave decides to go upstream to discover why the river floods. He continues until he finds a huge waterfall. When he climbs to the top of the falls, he finds a vast, smooth lake. On the far side of the lake, there is a steep incline with boulders at the bottom, smaller stones in the middle, and small pebbles at the very top.

When a pebble begins to roll down the hill, it strikes the bigger stones, which then begin to fall down the hill. They, in turn, strike the boulders that crash into the lake. The resulting ripples cascade across the lake and cause a huge rush of water to pour over the falls... and flood out the valley.

So the brave swept away the pebbles!

7.9 Listen

Effective speaking is usually taught in high school and even college, but not effective listening. That is unfortunate because effective, empathic listening is really the key to problem resolution, team building, and good interpersonal relations. By empathic listening we mean that it must be sincere and not superficial. This is not the place for a crash course in listening skills, but it is worth mentioning some very simple guidelines that can really help the way you listen.

First, posture plays a role. There are many subtle messages conveyed by body position, facial expressions, hand gestures, etc. Most of these are obvious — a very relaxed posture might indicate that you are not too serious about the matter. Leaning forward, placing your hand on your chin, reflects thoughtfulness, etc. Of course, looking around and being distracted by the phone, clock, or e-mail suggests that you really are not very interested in what the person has to say. So, when you are listening to someone, be deliberately aware of your body language and make sure that it fits the situation.

Other empathic listening techniques include:

- *Playback.* Repeat what has been said to you. "OK, so what you are saying is that the system crashed because there were too many users trying to load the diagnostic program at the same time. Is that right?"
- *Do not interpret, probe, or use self-analogies.* For example, after hearing a complaint, you would not say, "Well, that's very nice but let me tell you about the time I was lost in the Antarctic. Now that was real trouble...."
- *Do not formulate your responses while listening.* Too often, we are thinking about what we want to say before the other person has had his say. And that is distracting to you. Stephen Covey says: "Seek first to understand, then to be understood" [Covey2].
- *Agree that one cannot proceed without confirmation from the other.* "OK, do you think I understand the problem...? Good, now let me tell you what I think you can do about it."
- And of course, never interrupt someone when they are speaking.

When the listening has concluded and it is time for you to speak, be very careful to focus on the issue at hand and not to attack people. Focus, instead, on your or others' feelings about the situation. Make sure that you listen to all sides of the story when arbitrating a dispute. It is often said that there are three sides to an issue— the sides of the two opponents and the truth, which is somewhere in between.

7.10 Negotiate

We briefly explored win-win negotiating in Chapter 4 relating to Theory W. The point to be made here is that you negotiate all the time, whether or not you are aware of it. So, it is worthwhile to practice your negotiating everywhere you go. And you can do this without being obnoxious. The trick is to just ask.

So, when you are in a hotel or getting on a plane, ask for an upgrade. They can only say "no." If they ask you "why," then you can wind up your negotiating pitch.

Never take the first offer on anything. Always propose more. Again, the worst you can get is "no" and, as described before, there is something more satisfying to your negotiating counterpart when they feel that they have satisfied some need that you have (think win-win). If you give in too easily, they might even feel that you are hiding something. Monty Python aficionados will recall Eric Idle's market haggler in *The Life of Brian*: "Four? For this gourd? Four?! Look at it. It's worth ten if it's worth a shekel."

For example, if someone is asking $10,000 for a used car and you offer him $5000 for it and he accepts immediately, you think that he is hiding some defect in the car, or, he was deliberately trying to gouge you from the outset. On the other hand, if he pushes back, and insists on $8000 and you settle at $7500, then you and he both feel satisfied.

In any case, it is very advantageous to be a great negotiator when coping with difficult people and dealing with certain antipatterns — the Cage Match Negotiator most obviously.

7.11 Never Give Up

Persistence in the face of all annoyances, even catastrophic failures, is often the only recourse a beleaguered individual has, but it works. That is what the Dunkirk Spirit is all about, but do not let the heroics go on forever or you will end up in the Boiling Frog Syndrome. Sidebar 7.7 further illustrates the spirit of persistence.

Sidebar 7.7 Never Give Up

We recall (probably with some editorial license) a vignette from the 1950s comic "Duck Tales," featuring Donald Duck's Uncle Scrooge McDuck, the "richest duck in the world." Scrooge McDuck was famous for his parsimony, but also for his wisdom and hard-nosed belief that persistence can overcome all manner of adversity. In one cartoon, Scrooge's three precocious nephews, Huey, Dewie, and Louie, decide to play one of their many pranks on him. They fake a newspaper with the headline like "Money Declared Worthless, New Currency To Be Fish."

Suddenly, Scrooge's fortune is worthless. But is Scrooge a broken man? No, for the rest of the cartoon, he sets out for a job on the fisherman's wharf, where he begins working for fish. By the end of the day, miraculously, he has parlayed his meager fishy earnings into an amount of fish equal to his old fortune.

7.12 Never Attribute to Malice What Stupidity Can Explain

"Never attribute to malice that which is adequately explained by stupidity." What a great sentiment. Really, most people do not want to fail. Most people do not set out to disappoint you or to be a jerk. Indeed, most jerks do not know that they are jerks. Most of the time, people's failings are due to their own stupidity, naiveté, lack of information, etc. Remember that there is always more than meets the eye. Take the time to know what is truly behind people's actions and behaviors.

When you view things from this perspective, suddenly you may even have sympathy for that jerk, slacker, or whatever. So, it is worth the time to try to shift your perspective for the moment and consider if the behavior of an individual is not motivated by malice or greed, but rather simple ignorance. Then you should try to educate that person, if possible.

7.13 Remember that Luck Can Play a Role

An old saying says: "No amount of planning can replace dumb luck." Think about how many times this has proven true in your lifetime, both in the workplace and in your personal life. This notion has proven true in our lives too.

Sometimes, bad situations work themselves out. Bad managers get fired or leave on their own. The external environment can change for the better (e.g., the economy could improve, a new owner might arrive at the company, a new contract can change a company's fortune and relieve tense situations). The point is that sometimes it is good to bide one's time, be optimistic, and wait. So for many of these antipatterns, simply hunkering down and waiting can work. In the Deflated Balloon, for example, new financing, new management, or an upturn in the economy can resolve the situation. Similarly, any of the negative management antipatterns can be relieved if the manager simply gets a new job or is fired — the same is not true of environmental antipatterns, of course.

Finally, we talk about courage, for example, in confronting various negative personality types such as exploders, bulldozers, and snipers; or in refactoring such situations as the Potemkin Village, One-Eyed King, and Emperor's New Clothes. But confronting these situations incurs a certain degree of risk — there is no guarantee that you will succeed, and there is some possibility that you will incur the wrath of others. However, if you follow our advice, the likelihood of success is very high and therefore, worth the risk involved.

7.14 Remember that No Good Deed Goes Unpunished

Clare Booth Luce once observed that "no good deed goes unpunished." Of course, this rather sobering thought is worse than a tribute to the unappreciated — it is a warning that good deeds can sometimes backfire. Why might that be?

In stagnant institutions and those where antipatterns have taken hold, there are strong forces that defend the status quo. Thus, when one is inspired to do something good, or to try to change things, there are always those behind the scenes who will work against you. Sometimes they do this by deliberately misinterpreting your intentions. Other times they sow the seeds of doubt and misunderstanding. In some cases, there is just a genuine misunderstanding of what you are doing — in an environment of fear and doubt, good deeds are often taken with skepticism and optimists are derided as fools. But take this advice as a warning when refactoring any of the antipatterns that require the courage to speak up, such as the One-Eyed King or Emperor's New Clothes, or when refactoring a Spineless Executive. You might reap the whirlwind for your good intentions by becoming a convenient distraction and scapegoat for the real situation.

Before you let this possibility get you down, however, it is worthwhile remembering that forewarned is forearmed. Knowing that our good deeds can be misinterpreted empowers us to head off any of the "punishments" for our good doings, or at least prepare ourselves for the coming onslaught. Take heart that, over time, the cumulative effects of positive energy will displace the negative energy and the negativists.

7.15 Remember that People Despise in Others What They Hate in Themselves

The book *Conflict Management* [Mayer] is subtitled "The Courage to Confront." And clearly, courage is needed to implement most of the refactorings we have discussed. In addition to discussing various conflict management techniques, Mayer stresses the need for self-understanding. He describes an exercise in which you list the characteristics of a person who is giving you difficulty. Then you put your name on top of that list. You should see that you share many of the characteristics of the person who is bothering you. We tend to dislike in others that which we dislike in ourselves. This fact can sometimes help you when dealing with difficult situations and people. In short, perhaps sometimes the problem is you.

Why does this principle matter? Because your response to the antipattern may be simply a reflection of your dissatisfaction with the personality flaws that you see in those around you, which may be a sign of your own need to improve those same attributes. For example, when confronting a Cage Match Negotiator, consider if this is the way he sees you. Or, when you resent a Spineless Excecutive, are you really the spineless one — expecting your manager to show courage where you cannot? Honestly assess yourself first before assuming the existence of an antipattern.

7.16 Use Golden Rule Management

The first step in the refactoring of any antipattern described herein is to remember to treat people the way you want to be treated. We briefly described Principle Centered Leadership and how, by behaving with integrity and morality, you will eventually reap the same from others. Occasionally, however, leaders will need to remove those from the organization who do not have a set of behavioral principles consistent or compatible with the rest of the team.

The Golden Rule is obviously a great principle to use in all aspects of human interaction, but it really can help in mitigating antipatterns, for example, with French Waiter Syndrome, and for dealing with most negative management types, such as a Cage Match Negotiator.

7.17 Never Mess with Space, Title, or Salary

Most managers know that there are three "sacred cows" that, if meddled with, will upset an employee. That is, when you change their space (office or cubicle), their title, or their salary, only bad things can happen. Remember this if you are, or become, a manager.

Obviously, with respect to salary we mean any kind of monetary takeaway. This could be a salary reduction but also an increase in an employee's work hours or responsibilities without increasing salary. Decreasing benefits or requiring an increase in employee contribution to benefits is another takeaway.

Messing with an employee's title is another no-no. Much of an employee's identity is invested in their title. Any downgrading (or perceived downgrading) of title is likely to cause trouble. Again, aside from punitive action, it is unlikely that a manager is going to downgrade someone's title. But there are indirect ways that downgrading can happen.

For example, if a prized employee holds the title "Staff Engineer" and a new title is created for an incoming "superstar" called "Principal Staff Engineer," then a downgrading of title has occurred, and a potential point of contention created. Sometimes, the effect can be even more subtle. Someone who is a "Sales Representative" might be considered inferior to an "Account Manager" even if the responsibilities and pay are the same. A "Sales Engineer" might be considered inferior to "Engineer," for example.

Changing office space — for example moving someone to a smaller office — is surely considered a rebuke. But sometimes, even a positive measure might be considered a negative. For example, moving someone to a much larger office, but one that does not have a cherished window view, might be considered a negative. Most people take their office space very personally; and any intrusion, no matter how well intended, can have devastating consequences to morale.

Conversely, you can appease or reward an employee by upgrading any of the three pressure points. The key is perception — the employees' perceptions, not the manager's. Therefore, before any changes in pay, title, or facilities are made, a sincere effort should be made to understand the public and hidden ramifications of such a change. Informal discussions with staff are the best way to determine the potential effects of change.

Remember this principle when refactoring the Autonomous Collective or Ant Colony in particular.

7.18 Be a Mentor

A great deal of research shows that the best leaders exhibit a mentoring personality and serve as mentors for one or more people. Certainly, most of the great managers we know have a mentoring personality. Mentoring an individual actor in a negative situation, such as the Golden Child, Ultimate Weapon, or Rising Upstart, is an excellent solution strategy. But even in those environmental antipatterns where the problem is systemic (e.g., in the Autonomous Collective), mentoring individuals to resist the negative aspects of the system can have a far-reaching effect. "Think globally, act locally" is a buzzphrase indeed. But this adage is the premise of using pervasive mentoring to eventually transform a culture.

You can use mentoring even if you are not a boss. Mentors can serve at all levels in the organization and there need not be a formal mentoring program — you can take the initiative. You can also mentor your boss, although he does not have to know it, by setting an example and making valuable suggestions. We contend that mentoring is a useful sub-strategy in virtually all antipatterns.

7.19 Always Set and Meet Expectations

Throughout this book we have discussed situations that involve disappointments — of managers, peers, subordinates, customers, even society. Where do disappointments come from? Well, the word itself gives the clue — "dis" meaning different from and "appointment," something that was appointed or planned. Disappointments are failed expectations.

It is clear that being the kind of person who does not leave others feeling disappointed will help you in your personal and professional life. Even if you are not a team leader, being a faithful deliverer on expectations will help change the culture around you.

Finally, setting expectations helps avoid lawsuits. Particularly in software and IT, but really, in any other environment where there is contracted work, the way to avoid lawsuits is to clearly set expectations, in writing, up front. Only deviate from the expectations when there is a mutual, written understanding.

Here are some hints in helping to meet others' expectations:

- Set expectations early in the process.
- Make sure that everyone understands the expectations.
- Continue to monitor the expectations and refine them if necessary.
- Circumstances may change — change expectations around them.
- Never lie about, hide, or downplay critical issues.
- Your credibility is your main asset.

In summary, always work to set or clarify expectations. This helps promote honest communications, which can assist in dealing with any antipattern.

7.20 Remember that You Take the Same Person with You Wherever You Go

There is an apocryphal story about an army private in training who goes in to see his platoon sergeant to complain that "everyone else in the platoon is starting with the wrong foot first when marching. Why am I the only one who is getting it right?" Of course, you can imagine how the sergeant responded. Thus, sometimes people identify antipatterns that might not be present at all. If wherever you go, for example, you encounter the French Waiter Syndrome, perhaps it is not the environment. Maybe this is everyone's response to your bad behavior.

We wrote previously about despising those attributes in others that we hate in ourselves. So maybe you ought to look at yourself and your response to situations rather than worry about things that cannot be changed. Perhaps it is you who are the problem. An old proverb goes: "You take the same person with you wherever you go." So, be sure you are bringing the best person with you before you blame everyone else for your problems.

Note

1. By this we do not mean that you say, for example, the following: "Let me tell you the joke about the traveling salesman and the farmer's daughter...; oh, by the way, you're fired." But the joke about the drill sergeant breaking the news of a private's mother's death might be OK: "All those with a mother take one step forward... where the heck are you going, Johnson!"

References

[Brown]   W.J. Brown, R.C. Malveau, H.W. McCormick, and T.J. Mowbray, *Anti-Patterns: Refactoring Software, Architectures, and Projects in Crisis*, John Wiley & Sons, 1998.

[Covey1]   Stephen R. Covey, *Principle Centered Leadership*, Fireside Books, 1992.

[Covey2]   Stephen R. Covey, *The Seven Habits of Highly Effective People*, Fireside Books, 1989.

[Jones]   Capers Jones, *Patterns of Software Systems Failure and Success*, International Thomson Computer Press, Boston, MA, 1996.

[Laplante]   Phillip A. Laplante, Remember the Human Element in IT Project Management, *IT Professional*, Jan./Feb. 2003, pp. 46–50.

[Mayer]   Richard J. Mayer, *Conflict Management: The Courage to Confront*, Battelle Press, 1990.

Index

Chaos Report, 198
Characteristics, antipatterns, 8–9, *9–11,* 11
Chinese Restaurant Story, 276
Christian, Fletcher, 101
Churchill, Winston, Sr., 94
Clams, 32–34
Clash of the Titans, 259
Cobb, Mayer and, studies, 19
Cockburn, Alistair, 69
Coddington, Boyd, 99
Code Complete, 204
Cohen studies, 60
Colin (vignettes, sidebars, and examples),
    see also Neill, Colin
   dollywog, 232
   eyewitness accounts, 5
   idiocracy, 235
   process clash, 259–260
Collins and Porras studies, 167
Combination personalities, 38, *38*
Commodore, 166
Communication, *9–11, see also* Mushroom
   Management
Competence, *9–11*
Complacency, 166–167
Complainers, 32
Completeness, 11–12
Composers, 17–18, *18*
Conduits, *see* Ultimate Weapon
Cone of Silence, 69
Conflict, 4, *61,* 61–62, *see also* Dysfunctions
Conflict Management, 284
Confrontation, *see* Spineless Executive
Confusion, *see* Headless Chicken; Rubik's
   Cube
Consistency, antipatterns, 11–12
Consulting Psychologists Press, 14
Control, *see* Founderitis
Coping strategies, 21, 129, *see also* Band aids
Coping with Difficult People, 21
The Corncob, *6,* 20–21, 38
Costello, Tom, 280
Cost structure, *see* Orange Stand Economics
Counselors, 17–18, *18*
Courage, *9–11, see also* Spineless Executive
Covey, Steven, 54, 60, 228, 237
Coward, *see* Spineless Executive
CPM, *see* Critical Path Method (CPM)
Crafters, 17–18, *18*
Crippled companies, *see* Deflated Balloon
Critical Path Method (CPM), 139

Culture, *9–11*
Cunningham, Randall, 153

D

Data requests, *see* Fruitless Hoops
Dave (vignette character), 29, 31
Death by Planning, *6*
"Death March" projects, 198
Debbi (vignette character), 137–138
Decisions, *149, see also* Dunkirk Spirit
Deflated Balloon
   antipattern locators, *10*
   basics, 185–188
   getting it done, 279
   luck, 283
   Plate Spinning, 125
Dekkers and McQuaid studies, 110
Delivering bad news
   advice, 275–278, *276–277*
   Spineless Executives, 143
DeMarco, Tom, 111, 113
Dennis (vignette character), 170–171
Deprivation, *see* Shoeless Children
Despising others/self, 284–285
Difficult people, 20–22, *see also* Fairness
   Doctrine; The Corncob
Dilbert (vignette character), 182
The Discovery Channel, 99, 105
Disorganized type, Rising Upstart, 134
Divergent Goals
   antipattern locators, *10*
   basics, 189–192
   culture of blame, 274
   Fruitless Hoops, 82
   Golden Child, 86
   Institutional Mistrust, 227
   Three-Headed Knight, 149
Dogmatic about Dysfunction
   antipattern locators, *10*
   basics, 193–196
   One-Eyed King, 241
   Pitcairn Island, 249
Dolphins (Miami), 48
Domain Driven Modeling, 259–260
Donald Duck's uncle (Scrooge McDuck),
   282
Doppelganger, 78–81, 274
Downsizing, *see* Deflated Balloon
Dr. Jekyll/Mr. Hyde personality, *see*
   Doppelganger
Dual personality, *see* Doppelganger